THE

GARDEN

CHEF

THE

GARDEN

CHEF

My passion for produce was first ignited when I worked at David Kinch's Manresa in Los Gatos, California. The produce coming into the kitchen from Cynthia Sandberg's 22-acre (9-hectare) Love Apple Farms fuelled serious creativity among the chefs. Herbs, flowers, and vegetables would arrive in the kitchen, hours after being harvested at their absolute peak. And when you've seen first-hand the experience and patience that has gone into growing a plant, you don't want to waste a single bit of it. You want to highlight it; you don't want it to play just a supporting role on the plate. You really think about it.

We had all this produce and we wanted to use as much of it as we could: leaves, roots, trimmings. You wait all that time for things to grow, and the anticipation is like . . . it's like when you've made charcuterie. When you've made a terrine and pressed it, you can't wait to go in first thing the next day and unmold it and cut it. Multiply that by one hundred, by one hundred and fifty, when you're waiting for something to grow—the anticipation and excitement really builds. And then you might only have that ingredient for a week or two before it's gone. You are building that relationship for months while the plant is growing, and once you have it you don't want to waste it. You want to use every part of it to pay respect to it, this special thing you've grown and waited so long for.

By the time I opened Ubuntu in Napa Valley, we treated vegetables with the same kind of reverence we'd given meat in the nose-to-tail decade that had emerged in the years before. It was also about finding creative ways to celebrate the incredible ingredients that would be harvested daily in our kitchen garden. Say, for example, I had broccoli leaves. I wouldn't want them to disappear on the plate and for no one to know what they were. Instead, I'd be like, how do I create a dish where broccoli leaves are the star? And that's not really what chefs had been trained to do, or at least not when I was learning. It was something completely new. A whole different part of the brain was being exercised. We had to create a fresh approach. It was exciting.

In Los Angeles, where I now live (actually, not even just LA), you have the farmers' market, and the chefs who go to the farmers' market all get the same things, and so naturally every menu is going to have the same ingredients, and all the menus are going to be very similar. When you are growing ingredients yourself, you can grow things that aren't available at the market, and you gain a real connection to what you're cultivating. In the garden or on a farm, everything is growing, and there are bees and birds and worms, there's wind and sun, and everything is happening right there, and it definitely changes how you think. They say "what grows together, goes together," and this approach makes it easier to put together something that isn't "conceptual," to look at what's growing and decide what the dish will be and how your menu will take shape. As a chef with a kitchen garden, you're not shopping for ingredients; it's more like you are translating for the garden. It is a whole different story when you know exactly which row a vegetable was grown in, when you know who's planted it, who's maintained it, who's picked it, who's brought it to you, and you know every step of the way what has gone in to growing the ingredients you end up with. It puts a lot of responsibility on you as a chef. There's much more of a connection, like it's your family and it's your kid, and you want to make sure you do right by it.

In a way, it creates a story. If the restaurant is doing it properly, there's a ripple effect. All the excitement and anticipation felt by the gardeners, farmers, and chefs feeds through to the front of house team and the servers, too. Everyone becomes excited by, and has a personal connection to, the ingredients that have been grown. They know that we planted them in March, and that we picked them in October. I feel like all this energy—whether that's from the excitement in the kitchen, or the chef's passion for the ingredients, or all the months of hard work that went into growing the ingredients—is somehow transferred to the food, and people might not necessarily know why they're enjoying the food as much as they are, but that energy's part of it.

It's exciting and inspiring for me to read this book and see what all these different chefs from around the world are doing with the land, whether that's growing things that no one else has, trying out different cultivation techniques, or finding different ways to create something new.

Jeremy Fox

FROM PLANT TO PLATE

Over the past three decades the plot-to-plate movement has gone from niche endeavor to a global phenomenon, and chefs' gardens have helped restaurants to champion plants, putting vegetables front and center after many years of playing a supporting role with little or no fanfare. There were some early trailblazers, such as Michel Bras in Languiole in the Aveyron region of France. In 1980, he created his *gargouillou,* inspired by walking through the pastures of France, lush with flowers and herbs. The dish, made up of about sixty separately prepared vegetables, herbs, flowers, and shoots, is a snapshot of what is growing at any one time throughout the year. Today, those ingredients are gathered in the restaurant's kitchen garden, and seven chefs work for hours to create each day's *gargouillou.*

Chefs like Bras have led the way, waking us up to the mind-blowing potential, the depth of flavor and versatility of plants, and the joy of growing them. That passion is shared by all the chefs in this book, for whom the kitchen garden is the beating heart of their operations. It's where everything begins.

This reverence for vegetables didn't necessarily start off as a vegetarian movement, but it has converged with a big shift towards new approaches to food and the rise of more plant-based diets, whether for ethical, environmental, or health reasons. And the same factors have fuelled the popularity of more sustainable approaches to growing—organic, biodynamic, and permaculture methods among them—as well as new horticultural tech, such as aeroponics. It's made us change other processes, too. As well as using as much of a plant as possible, many professional kitchens have built slick recycling programmes so that any food waste can go back to the garden as compost, to refresh the soil and provide nutrients for future crops in a planet-friendly 360.

The chef's garden is now as diverse as gastronomy itself. There are sprawling country estates, like SingleThread Farm in California or Heckfield Place in Hampshire, England, which has the luxury of acres of land with regimented rows of biodynamically-grown vegetables and orchards abundant with seasonal fruit and nuts, as well as polytunnels of salads crops and glasshouses that can extend the growing season. Elsewhere, working gardens are created amid the eclectic remains of former ornamental gardens, such as at Mirazur, set into the hills overlooking the Côte d'Azur in the South of France, or they are carved into such seemingly inhospitable sites as Slippurinn on the volcanic Westman Islands in southern Iceland, where the garden is whipped by fierce off-shore winds. Necessity is the mother of invention, and nowhere is that more apparent than in the innovative inner-city locations where chefs are creating edible gardens on rooftops (Quintonil in Polanco, Mexico City), in backyards (Olmsted in New York), in shipping containers (Roberta's and Blanca, both in New York), or on hand-built tables crammed with recycled pots and repurposed boxes (The Dairy in London).

Such idiosyncratic environments set these gardens and their kitchens apart, conjuring a rich sense of place that is not only inspiring for chefs and their teams, but also evocative and transformative for the people that visit them and eat there. It's understandable that these edible gardens have now become as intriguing for diners as the restaurants themselves. Sometimes kitchen gardens are purposefully sited as close to the kitchen as possible; elsewhere they wrap around a dining room, and guests can start or finish their meal by having a drink or wandering among the beds where the food they've enjoyed was pulled from the ground just hours before.

Chefs' gardens have also been transformed into community spaces. In Napa Valley, Chris Kostow started his organic garden within a 10-acre (0.4-hectare) farm developed by the Saint Helena Montessori school, and his staff now provides lessons in growing for its pupils. Every few months the children, helped by restaurant staff, prepare a lunch for parents and the wider community. At Amass in Copenhagen, chef owner Matt Orlando launched the Amass Green Kids Program, a farm-to-table initiative for local school children. Alice Waters' Edible Schoolyard project began as a kitchen garden in one school in Berkeley, California, in 1995, teaching children how to grow; it now inspires children in thousands of programs around the world.

Waters was one of the pioneers of the plot-to-plate movement in California, advocating organic and sustainable produce when these ideas were in their infancy. She recalls starting out at Chez Panisse and asking farmers to grow certain crops. Before long, it was the farmers who would suggest things to Waters and her chefs. A dialogue began that has enriched gastronomy, forging close links between those who intimately understand their terroir and what to grow, and the cooks who take inspiration from the incomparable depth of flavor in vegetables that are plucked straight from the ground, or herbs that are cut and served on a plate within hours, sometimes minutes. Being truly seasonal—although that means very different things in different locales—has spurred a new inventiveness. In Sydney, Peter Gilmore is typical of so many chefs who now use plants at all the different stages of their life cycles, from early shoots to flowers to seedpods. In his "Lamborn peas, green miso, and lemon" dish, Gilmore uses pods, growing tips, and flowers from the pea plant.

This growing revolution has also sparked a return to pickling, preserving, and finding clever ways to store the bounty of the summer and fall (autumn) for the depths of winter using syrups, sauces, and other bottled and canned treasure. At Hell's Backbone Grill in the high mountain desert of Utah, where chef owners Jen Castle and Blake Spalding pickle, jam, freeze, and dehydrate produce for the lean months, they refer to this return to pioneer traditions as "true seasonal." It's a stark reminder that Mother Nature is in charge: losses through weather, pests, or crop failure as much as there can be gluts. For Nicolai Nørregaard, owner chef of Kadeau, on a tiny island off the coast of Denmark, preserving is an enormous part of the kitchen culture. "In the more abundant months, we pickle, cure, ferment, dry, and smoke like mad, as well as making spirits, syrups, oils, and vinegars," he says. "Winter is my favorite season because it's when I get to use this huge library of preserves the most."

Nørregaard and many chefs like him focus on a super local approach, too. If ingredients can't be foraged, grown, or sourced on their doorsteps, they will only buy them from their region or country, so that their cuisine becomes an absolute reflection of their own environment. For the same reason, chefs are growing super local heritage varieties, preserving a unique sense of place and history. For many it's part of their mission not only to grow these varieties that give more flavor, but also to ensure that these plants live on for future generations. In Russia, Ivan and Sergey Berezutskiy of Twins Garden are raising old and rare native breeds of potato, such as "Lorkh" or "Sineglazkha," and work closely with specialists to continue this endeavor.

It goes without saying that all of this is in no way the easy route; it's far more challenging, more expensive, and more unpredictable for chefs, but it's also more exciting, dynamic, and—as every chef in this book would probably argue—it results in far more interesting food on the plate. The rise of the kitchen garden has reconnected chefs to the earth and inspired them to be better cooks.

Gastón Acurio &
Juan David Ocampo

ASTRID Y GASTÓN
San Isidro, Lima, Peru

Set within the grounds of a seventeeth-century plantation house in
the financial district of Lima, Astrid y Gastón—owned by renowned
chef Gastón Acurio and his wife, Astrid—is at the forefront of the
innovative Peruvian restaurant scene. With greenhouses and a
circular kitchen garden, the tasting menu is in part based around
what can be grown on site: anything from wild patches of ají ama-
rillo chiles to Peruvian herbs.

I was born near Casa Moreyra, a seventeenth-century hacienda building in the heart of Lima's dynamic San Isidro district. I remember strolling around the neighborhood at weekends as a child. The shopping area, the Chinese restaurant, the pizzerias with their checked tablecloths, the skating rink, the cake shop, the burger joint, were all there. And right in the middle of it all, the huge Casa Moreyra, encircled by high walls: mysterious, forbidden, and solemnly silent for countless years. It filled us with fear, so we always hurried past.

Today, many years later—and five years after relocating Astrid y Gastón to Casa Moreyra—things have changed. Now, a low wall separates us from the outside world and on the inside, a large botanical garden of herbs and flowers has been returned to the city and its landscape. The house has become a state-declared historical monument; the garden is part of the main entrance to the restaurant and it is open to everyone.

San Isidro is the financial center of Lima and one of its most densely developed neighborhoods. Casa Moreyra was once the main house of Hacienda San Isidro, a large estate that functioned as a pantry to the city. The soil is made up of rocky outcrops, layers of gravel from the beds of the Rímac and Chillón rivers, as well as colluvial-eluvial gravel deposited at the foot of the slopes. Lima's climate is a very particular one: it combines an almost total absence of rain, a very high level of atmospheric humidity, and persistent cloud cover. It is a climate that is neither too hot nor too cold, with temperatures in summer varying between 70 and 86°F/21 and 30°C, and 53 and 66°F/12 and 19°C in winter. San Isidro is 357 feet (109 meters) above sea level.

The first thing customers see on arriving at the restaurant is the garden in the front courtyard, planted with edible flowers, common aromatics, and native herbs and chiles. We are able to appreciate what the garden has to offer, every day. Thanks to Lima's temperate climate, many of the plants are available all year round, such as mint and peppermint, nasturtium, fennel, sweet basil and purple basil, oregano, lemon verbena, salad burnet, and chincho (a type of French marigold, *Tagetes patula*). Others require more specific temperatures: chives, borage, pansies, and begonias in spring, and spinach, Peruvian black mint (*Tagetes minuta*), and lemon balm in winter. We also grow lemons, wormseed, and hot chiles (including ají panca, ají limo, and ají mochero chiles) in summer.

Our original idea was to have a botanical garden where we could reclaim certain native plant species and crops, but also to have an educational program for children, to allow them to learn about nature and help them to connect with the earth and the kitchen. The garden has been restored for neighboring school children to use,

in partnership with ANIA, a non-governmental organization working to promote environmental awareness among young people. We jointly welcome around 500 children into the garden every year. They learn about biodiversity, how to start their own vegetable garden, and how to care for the soil and what it produces. The garden is therefore a fruitful planting ground for teaching, as well as a great pantry available to our kitchen team.

With the restaurant and garden, our intention was to forge a link between the house and its past as a hacienda, as a place in harmony with nature and its produce. That is why we decided to plant the kitchen garden as a space that celebrates environmental sustainability. Initially, we planted the garden in a spiral with small furrows, attempting to make the most of the allocated space. Then we worked on plots, small areas of land and independent crops. Nowadays, we see the garden as a unique and connected space, which is why we manage it as a whole, with individual crops as well as companion planting. The garden, in its spiral form, was designed by Luis Alejandro Camacho, an agronomist who now supplies the restaurant with tomatoes from his own vegetable garden "Chisco Tomateros," outside of Lima.

We feed the garden using organic principles, based on manure and compost. It is tended by a visiting gardener as well as the chefs. In the morning, the first task for the gardener is to prune and weed and tend to any plants that need attention. Next, the plants are watered, as necessary. Finally, the chefs arrive to pick whatever is needed to meet the day's cooking requirements. Herbs such as Peruvian black mint, Andean mint (*Minthostachys mollis*), and wormseed represent our kitchen; they are our most-used plants. They always come from our garden along with chincho, lemon verbena, spearmint, chamomile, aniseed, and culantro (*Eryngium foetidum*). Also, flowers like borage, pimpernel, potato flowers, basil flowers, and cilantro (coriander). The garden provides us with shoots, plants, and herbs on a daily basis and is useful for trying out new things, but since we are a country of diverse microclimates and environments—many of them inimitable—we rely on produce from around Peru, such as Cusco mushrooms, Pachacamac vegetables, ayacucho tubers (*Oxalis tuberosa*), and quinoa from Puno. While it may not be the creative starting point for what we offer at the restaurant, even so, we always know what is available in the garden and its influence is undeniable.

The garden is a place to escape the daily routine. The kitchen and waiting staff, as well as the administrative team, use it as a space where they can breathe, meditate, and socialize. It is a refuge for the most diverse species. It is a peaceful place for everyone to enjoy.

BIODIVERSITY IN THE HEART OF THE CITY
Keeping a garden in the middle of a fast-paced city is no easy feat, but it is well worth the effort. It's incredible to see how much life a few square feet of garden can accommodate. Amid the concrete, buildings, cars, and the hustle and bustle, nature follows its own rhythm and that of the seasons.

The birds that flock here in search of refuge and food include west Peruvian doves (*Zenaida meloda*), croaking ground doves (*Columbina cruziana*), hum-mingbirds (Trochilidae), shiny cowbirds (*Molothrus bonariensis*), budgerigars (*Melopsittacus undulatus*), groove-billed anis (*Crotophaga sulcirostris*), tyrant flycatchers (*Phyllomyias*), blue-gray tanagers (*Thraupis episcopus*), scarlet flycatchers (*Pyrocephalus rubinus*), red-masked parakeets (*Psittacara erythrogenys*), and Harris's hawks (*Parabuteo unicinctus*). We also have plenty of ladybugs, ants, woodlice, bees, wasps, beetles, and the caterpillars that develop into butterflies.

1. POTATOES AND TUBERS OF A THOUSAND COLORS

SERVES 1
- 180 g native potatoes (including "Peruanita," "Sangre de Toro," "Huayro Rojo," "Amarilla Runtus," "Queccorani," and "Leona" varieties), unpeeled

OCAS, ULLUCUS, AND MASHUAS
- 100 g ocas (Oxalis tuberosa)
- 100 g ullucus (Ullucus tuberosus)
- 100 g mashuas (Tropaeolum tuberosus)
- 30 g butter
- 50 ml extra-virgin olive oil
- 5 g granulated sugar
- 5 g salt
- 40 g Peruvian black mint leaves
- 30 g cilantro (coriander) leaves
- 20 g chincho (culantrillo) leaves

ROCOTO HOT CHILE CONFIT
- 2 liters vegetable oil
- 1.7 kg rocoto hot chiles, stemmed, seeded, and cut into ½-inch/1-cm dice
- 1.5 kg red onions, cut into ½-inch/1-cm dice
- 30 g cloves garlic (left whole)
- 8 g salt

OLD-STYLE HUANCAÍNA SAUCE
- 800 g Rocoto Hot Chile Confit (see above)
- 150 g queso fresco (cow's milk)
- 50 ml evaporated milk
- 10 g salt

HOT YELLOW CHILE CONFIT
- 2 liters vegetable oil
- 1.5 kg hot yellow chiles, stemmed, seeded, and chopped

CREAMY HUANCAÍNA SAUCE
- 400 g Hot Yellow Chile Confit (see above)
- 250 g hot yellow chiles, stemmed and seeded
- 110 g mantecoso cheese
- 200 ml evaporated milk
- 4 saltine crackers or savory crackers
- 90 ml sunflower oil
- 15 g salt

TO SERVE
- 60 g Old-style Huancaína Sauce (see above)
- 60 g Creamy Huancaína Sauce (see above)
- 2 g Peruvian black mint (huacatay leaves)
- 2 g chincho leaves (culantrillo)
- 2 g Andean mint leaves
- 6 borage flowers
- 2 nasturtiums

Steam all the native potatoes until tender, and then fry only the "Peruanita," "Sangre de Toro," and "Huayro Rojo" varieties. Chop and serve the remaining ones: "Amarilla Runtus," "Queccorani," and "Leona."

OCAS, ULLUCUS, AND MASHUAS
Preheat the oven to 350°F/180°C.

Place the tubers on a baking sheet, add the remaining ingredients, and cover with aluminum foil. Roast in the oven for 50 minutes, then remove the foil, turn up the heat to 400°F/200°C, and roast for another 15 minutes. Remove from the oven and set aside.

ROCOTO HOT CHILE CONFIT
Heat the oil in a deep, heavy pan to 185°F/85°C, then add the vegetables and salt. Cook for about 45 minutes until soft, keeping the temperature constant throughout.

OLD-STYLE HUANCAÍNA SAUCE
Strain the rocoto hot chile confit, remove and finely chop the garlic. Add the chopped garlic and the cheese and mix carefully until well combined. Add the evaporated milk to loosen the sauce. Add a little salt, if needed.

HOT YELLOW CHILE CONFIT
Heat the oil in a deep, heavy pan to 176°F/80°C, then add the chopped hot yellow chiles and cook for about 45 minutes until soft, keeping the temperature constant throughout.

CREAMY HUANCAÍNA SAUCE
Blend the chiles, cheese, and milk in a blender. Gradually add the crackers and oil and continue to blend until you get the right consistency—it should be smooth and creamy. Add a little salt, if needed.

TO SERVE
Arrange the tubers (ocas, ullucus, and mashuas), the potatoes, half of each sauce, the leaves, and the flowers on a plate.

2. CHUCUITO SIAM TIRADITO

SERVES 1
CURED SEA BASS
- 300 g salt
- 40 g ají limo chile, chopped
- 15 g chopped cilantro (coriander)
- 40 g seaweed
- 110 g sea bass

SHELLFISH MAYONNAISE
- 10 Peruvian sea scallops, roe removed
- ice cube, as needed
- 700 ml vegetable oil
- 10 g blended garlic
- 135 ml lemon juice
- salt

CHUCUITO MILK
- 200 ml tiger milk
- 600 ml Shellfish Mayonnaise (see above)
- salt

COCONUT GEL
- 150 ml coconut milk
- 20 g superfine (caster) sugar
- 20 ml water
- 3 g Ultra-Sperse (modified food starch)
- 3 g salt
- 1 g grated lemon zest

CHESTNUT SLICES
- 300 g whole chestnuts

MANGO GARNISH
- 5 g mango, finely diced
- 5 g rocoto hot chile, finely diced
- 1 g cilantro (coriander), sliced very thinly to make a chiffonade
- 2 ml lemon juice
- salt

TO SERVE
- 70 g Chucuito Milk (see above)
- Mango Garnish (see above)
- 30 g Coconut Gel (see above)
- 110 g cured sea bass (11 slices)
- 8 g Chestnut Slices (15 slices) (see above)
- 5 g chili oil

CURED SEA BASS
Mix the salt with the chopped limo chile, cilantro (coriander), and seaweed. Form a layer in the bottom of a dish with a third of the mixture, place the sea bass fillet on top, and then cover with the remaining salt mixture. Refrigerate for 26 minutes, then shake the salt off and rinse the fillet with water. (You can use the mix once again immediately with another fillet if needed.)

SHELLFISH MAYONNAISE
Blend the sea scallops with 1 ice cube until smooth and slightly creamy.

Whisk the scallops and the oil together to create an emulsion, then add the garlic, and finally the lemon juice. Season to taste with salt and set aside.

CHUCUITO MILK
Mix the tiger milk and shellfish mayonnaise together until well blended. Season to taste and keep in the refrigerator until needed.

COCONUT GEL
Put the coconut milk, sugar, and water into a pan and heat until the sugar dissolves, stirring continuously. Transfer to a bowl set over an ice bain-marie to cool rapidly. Once the mix is cold, use a balloon whisk to gradually mix in the Ultra-Sperse, then add the salt and lemon zest. Adjust the seasoning to taste and transfer to a pastry (piping) bag.

CHESTNUT SLICES
Use a mandoline to slice the chestnuts as thinly as possible without breaking them. Roast the chestnuts on a grill or in a nonstick pan until lightly toasted. Remove from the heat and let cool, then store them in an airtight container.

MANGO GARNISH
Place the mango, rocoto hot chile, and cilantro (coriander) in a bowl and combine. Season with lemon juice and salt, then taste and adjust the seasoning as necessary and set aside.

TO SERVE
Spread the chucuito milk on a flat plate. Add the mango garnish and some dots of the coconut gel and the pieces of cured sea bass placing them all randomly on the plate. Finish with the chestnut slices and a few drops of chili oil.

1

Andoni Luis Aduriz

MUGARITZ
Errenteria, Basque Country, Spain

Occupying an old country house in the mountains above San Sebastián, Mugaritz epitomizes modern and innovative Basque cuisine. More than a sensory experience, the kitchen plays with conventional notions of food, with chef Andoni Luis Aduriz's creativity being driven by the extensive on-site herb and vegetable garden.

The Mugaritz project took its first steps 20 years ago, in a place where nature was not an option but a reality. At the edge of parkland amid other country houses, the project is located in a property with the long-established name of Mugaritz. Not dissimilar to a medical transplant, the Mugaritz project was forced to undergo an arduous process of adaptation to the Basque culinary context, while simultaneously suffering some degree of rejection by the host body. A complete absence of bookings provided us with the opportunity to explore our gardens, the forests, and meadows beyond. With the help of various botanists, we learned to identify useful herbs for the kitchen, such as water mint (*Mentha aquatica*), pignut (*Conopodium majus*), cuckoo flower (*Cardamine pratensis*), and ground ivy (*Glechoma hederacea*) in a place where we'd previously only seen what looked like grass.

Twenty years later, the garden at Mugaritz does not seem so much like an option but the only way in which the project could possibly have defined itself. After our early initiation, Nature became the cornerstone of our philosophy. Nowadays, it continues to be engaged in our vision and is inextricable from other components of our identity.

The garden is an extension of the places and landscapes we have visited on our many journeys over the years. Every time we return from a trip, we try to bring back a small piece of the culinary culture that we have visited, in the form of seeds or edible plants. We try to grow these new varieties and we trial them in a lab to see if we can cultivate them in the Basque Country: Mexican pepperleaf, Peruvian black mint (*Tagetes minuta*), Japanese ginger, papalo (an ancient Mexican herb similar to cilantro/coriander, *Porophyllum ruderale*), and so on.

The garden is around 3,750 square feet (350 square meters), with eight raised beds overlooked by the kitchen. It is open to our visitors who usually have a walk around it, either on their own or with our team who know all about the plants and where they come from. We used railway ties (sleepers) for the raised beds, which are evolving into the fabric of the garden, after 18 years of containment.

We prefer to follow organic principles, to be respectful toward nature and what it brings to us. We have a compost area; we avoid chemicals and we dry the seaweed that we use in the kitchen for fertilizing the land. We mainly sow seeds in two ways: by direct seeding or via seedbeds in the greenhouse, which is small and unheated. With the help of a small seedbed and other homemade gadgets, we cultivate about 80 varieties of plants each year, using any combination of leaves, flowers, stems, roots, fruits, or seeds for our dishes.

We keep one raised bed just for plants in which flowers play the only interesting role. It is usually the bed that most draws the eyes of visitors. This riotous area includes nasturtiums, cosmos, tricolor chrysanthemum, nigella, poppies, several marigolds, mallows, and dahlias. It is an orgy of color that only explodes in July, due to the weather and the latitudes in which we find ourselves. Seeds, for example, don't always germinate within our specific range of temperature, which is characterized by mild winters, moderate summers, and a lot of moisture. Air masses, moved around by the Cantabrian Sea, also have a big influence on our immediate environment. Our garden's main season usually runs from May to November or December, like that of Mugaritz itself. In December the garden enters into a state of latent calm, preceding the arrival of a new season in April.

The cuisine at Mugaritz is punctuated by the daily nuances and rhythms of the garden. It is a way of remaining anchored to the land, which we try to compound with our knowledge. The Mugaritz garden is open to the elements, unaided by artificial temperature and irrigation systems. It is an orchard with active and passive cycles, entirely respected by our team. There is an annual calendar of sowing and germination, but the development of the plants and their specific organoleptic definition are decided by Mother Nature. These cycles motivate the cuisine of Mugaritz; it is the kitchen that respects our garden, not the other way around. Depending on the weather of a particular year, along with other factors, the kitchen amalgamates whatever nature brings to us. This generates a sense of expectation, of how we will celebrate all the different plants in every year.

Every day a group of chefs led by the head gardener (who is also a cook) selects, collects, and cleans specific portions of plants and herbs. It is important to wash them with cold water so that they don't lose their texture. The secret is to drain them softly with rags or lay them out on dry paper. Arranged in special containers for this purpose, using humidified paper towels, they can wait for a couple of days in the refrigerator before jumping into a dish. Each day between 700 and 1,000 different portions can be prepared for different dishes.

A plant's idiosyncrasies are expressed in a dish; they play different roles in different dishes. We love spinach for its texture, the wild garlic leaf for its garlicky bite. We appreciate nasturtium for its bitter and sharp flavor, and the pleasantly fleshy marigold for its citrus aroma. A lack of olfactory terminology limits one's ability to describe such aromas and flavors. It is the moment when the story of a spinach that we brought from a trip to Southeast Asia has its deepest meaning; when the homage that we pay to the Japanese pepper tree, treated with more care every year because of its delicate health, makes the most sense. When the table is laden with aromatic geranium, rau ram (Vietnamese cilantro/coriander, *Persicaria odorata*), and anise hyssop (*Agastache foeniculum*), it is that instant when nature, the kitchen, and the diner converge...

PLANTS IN THE ALLIACEAE FAMILY
We love all members of the Liliaceae family for both their garlic flavor and their long story with us: they were one of the first plant species sown in our garden. We still use them today. The leaf of wild garlic (*Allium ursinum*), for instance, is the perfect tool to bring a bite to the mouth. Our idea is to have that onionish or garlicish flavor without the strong flavor of onion and garlic. And sometimes, as with the Chinese onion (*Allium chinense*), we serve the whole plant as the main product of the dish.

We grow many varieties of the Alliaceae family: wild garlic (ramsons/bear's garlic, *Allium ursinum*); nodding onion (*Allium cernuum*); pink, wild, and "tear of the Virgin Mary" garlic (*Allium triquetrum*); chives (*Allium schoenoprasum*); and the Egyptian onion (*Allium x proliferum*). One of our raised beds is devoted to these varieties, from which we use the whole plant: stems, flowers, and bulbs.

1. THE END OF HERBS

SERVES 4
FILM
– 0.25 g pullulan
– 0.75 g agar agar
– 100 ml water
– 1 packet food-safe silica gel
BUTTER
– 30 g salted butter
TO SERVE
– 12 g mix of 10 summer herbs from the garden,
  such as marigold, mallow, Peruvian black mint,
  nasturtium, garden orache, papalo, red orache,
  tree spinach, huauzontle (hairy amaranth blossom,
  Chenopodium nuttalliae), St. John's wort, and
  New Zealand spinach (*Tetragonia tetragonioides*)
– 4 units Film (see above)
– salt

FILM

Preheat a non-fan oven to 158°F/70°C.

Mix all the ingredients in a small pan and heat them to 200°F/95°C, removing the pan from the heat as soon as it reaches the correct temperature. Pour onto a tray lined with a Silpat mat and bake for 30–40 minutes. It should be soft and malleable but dry. Let cool, then cut into 3-inch/8-cm squares and store in a sealed container lined with food safe-silica gel.

BUTTER

Heat the butter in a pan over low heat until the solids separate from the fat and the fat becomes brown and smells nutty. Remove from the heat and strain through cheesecloth (muslin) to remove the solids.

TO SERVE

Dress the herbs with the strained melted butter and a few grains of salt and serve on top of the film.

2. A SEQUENCE OF WILD AND CULTIVATED HERBS ON A MIXTURE OF DRY CREAM, EGG, AND PICKLES

SERVES 10
MILK SKIN
– 1.5 liters locally produced milk
– 1 liter liquid cream
EGG YOLK
– 10 farm eggs
PICKLES
– 5 g pickled pearl onions, finely diced
– 5 g garlic pickles, finely diced
– 5 g pickled gherkins, finely diced
SCENTED BUTTER
– 400 g unsalted butter
CREAMY CORE
– Milk Skin (see above)
– Egg Yolk (see above)
– Pickles (see above)
– Scented Butter (see above)
HERBS AND SPROUTS
– fleshy leaves
– 1 handful seasonal herbs and sprouts such as yarrow,
  nasturtium, wild celery, shiso, and chickweed

MILK SKIN

The ideal way to create the milk skin is to start the day before it is served, so the fat has time to solidify on the surface, creating a consistent cream.

Mix the milk and cream in a pan. Bring to a boil, then pour it into a broad, deep metal tray (Gastronorm gn 1/1). Briskly beat the liquid in the tray with a pastry whisk, immediately after pouring it in, to homogenize the fat proportions over the entire surface layer once it is cooled. Refrigerate for 12 hours, uncovered.

EGG YOLK

Separate the egg yolks from the whites and reserve the whites for another use.

Preheat a water bath to 175°F/80°C. Cook the egg yolks in the water bath for 9 minutes. Drain the yolks and set aside in the refrigerator.

PICKLES

Mix the pickles in equal parts: 10 portions of 5 g chopped pickles.

SCENTED BUTTER

Heat the butter in a pan over low heat until the solids separate from the fat and the fat becomes light brown and smells nutty. Remove from the heat.

CREAMY CORE

Once the milk skin is ¼ inch/5 mm thick, cut it into ten 2¼-inch/6-cm squares. (If it is not thick enough, add more cream.)

Put a sheet of plastic wrap (clingfilm) on a wide tray. Spread one of the portions of chopped pickles on the plastic wrap. Pick up the milk skin with a slotted spoon. Dry it with a clean cloth and place it on the bed of pickles. Cover the skin and pickles with another layer of plastic wrap. Turn over the milk skin with pickles and gently remove the plastic wrap in contact with the pickles. Put an egg yolk in the center of the pickles on the skin and add a few drops of scented butter inside the ball. Fold the skin over the yolk with the help of the plastic wrap to form a ball. Repeat with the remaining milk skin, pickles, egg yolks, and scented butter.

HERBS AND SPROUTS

Keep the herbs covered in the refrigerator until needed.

TO SERVE

Serve the milk skin, egg yolk, and pickle balls on the center of a flat dish. Add fleshy leaves and seasonal herbs and sprouts, arranging them on the dish in a way that creates form and volume.

1

2

Eneko Atxa

AZURMENDI
Larrabetzu, Basque Country, Spain

A love of the long-standing traditions of Basque cuisine is the foundation of chef Eneko Atxa's restaurant Azurmendi. Rebuilt in 2012, the ultra-modern, bioclimatic restaurant showcases technological innovation, as well as the culinary excellence that has earned the chef three Michelin stars. A meal at Azurmendi takes guests on a culinary and physical journey. The dining experience begins in the restaurant's interior garden, where a picnic with different snacks is served. Guests then wend their way through the kitchen and greenhouse, before settling down to eat.

I am privileged to live close to the ocean, surrounded by mountains and countryside, and to have four absolutely different weather seasons providing me with a generous pantry of produce. Added to this, I come from a region with a deep gastronomic and culinary tradition. These are often my starting points. I am inspired by what nature tells me with every season; nature is the one in charge.

Our restaurant is built into the slope of a hill, surrounded by native vineyards. The climate is fairly damp and the thermoregulatory influence of the Atlantic protects us from extremes of temperature. We use the roof as a garden for growing aromatic plants and vegetables that are native to the Basque Country; these include violet onions from Zalla, dwarf chard from Derio, and tomatoes from Busturia. They are grown to the highest standard, with supervision from Neiker-Tecnalia (the Basque Institute for Agricultural Research and Development). Under the watchful eye of technicians, a member of the Azurmendi team takes great care in selecting and cultivating the best crops for the palate.

We have two areas of cultivation: a glass-covered greenhouse on the roof and an outdoor garden that stretches beyond the footprint of the restaurant onto the surrounding hillside. The 2,150-square-foot (200-square-meter) greenhouse contains a cultivation system of next-generation containers, developed and designed to achieve optimum vegetal production. We have developed new methods for irrigation and drainage collection, selecting different substrates. An important focus is in creating compost that is rich in natural nutrients, with the aim of producing a greater density of crops in a smaller space. We practice crop rotation and use edible flowers such as borage for companion plants, as well as herbs that include lemon verbena, rosemary, and chives. This is a way of deterring pests, helping the resistance of plants from their roots upward.

At the entrance to the greenhouse there is a germplasm bank, granted to us by Neiker-Tecnalia. It contains more than 400 types of seeds from the varieties of vegetables that were traditionally cultivated by local farmhouses. It demonstrates the importance of preserving the genetic diversity that enriches us and helps to mitigate the loss of native phytogenetic resources. The seed bank preserves the genetic potential of plants that are native to the region.

All vegetables are produced under the strict rules of integrated production. This involves the use of biological control against pests (such as ladybugs, to prey on aphids) and plant extracts that combat crop diseases, while remaining harmless to humans. Next to the greenhouse, outside, we have a larger cultivation area for produce such as brassicas, onions, and chard that require more space and are winter hardy. A covered rainwater tank provides 100 percent of our annual irrigation needs, both for the outdoor production garden and the greenhouse. It also functions as a water tank for fire protection.

Guests are invited to visit the gardens. It has never been our intention to become self-sufficient; we want the gardens to function like a mirror for visitors, reflecting the work that our small producers do for us but in a beautiful horticultural space. We are committing to the surrounding environment and its people by continuing to buy from small producers, and we want our guests to understand their work.

Ours is not a vegetable-only kitchen. I love all fresh produce: meat, fish, and dairy. Red mullet, for instance, appears in three separate dishes, as fritters with caviar, flame roasted, and as tempura with red bell peppers roasted on charcoal. Identity is central to our cuisine; cultural roots and traditional Basque recipes are the foundation for every one of our dishes. Many of these feature fruit and vegetables, in jelly, sorbet, cornbread, and so on. Sometimes our fresh garden produce is visible in recipes; other times it is in the background, but it is always there.

TEARDROP PEAS (*GUISANTE LÁGRIMA*)
There is a very special vegetable that we adore: the tear, or teardrop pea. It is special because it is a pea that we only find here. Its character is defined by its flavor and texture, reminiscent of fish roe to the touch. When the pod is broken, its vegetable flavor has sweet nuances. Each pea explodes in the mouth. Each explosion brings with it an authentic vegetable hit, tinged with extraordinary sweetness.

Teardrop peas are expensive; their season is very limited. With only a few days for harvesting them in spring, growers and chefs have the highly meticulous task of handling each pod without breaking the delicate pea.

More than the variety, the secret to teardrop peas lies in the way they are collected: they are gathered in the morning before the sun rises. It is essential that they are picked very early for tenderness, when they only have sugars and have not begun to produce starch.

1. LIQUEFIED VEGETABLES, FATTY FISH, GREEN PEA SORBET, AND APPLE

SERVES 4
GREEN PEA, APPLE, AND ARUGULA SORBET
- 150 g green peas in the pod
- 150 g Granny Smith apple
- 25 g arugula (rocket)
- 0.5 g ascorbic acid
- 5 g dextrose
- 1.5 g Añana's salt
- 6 g maltodextrin powder
- 1 g xanthan gum
- 25 g Prosorbet (Sosa)
- 4 g glycerin
GREEN PEA JELLY
- 25 g green peas in the pod
- 20 g arugula (rocket)
- 30 g green apple, cored and skin left on
- ⅓ golden gelatin leaf sheet
- 2 g Añana's salt
SPICY TOMATO EMULSION
- 300 g ripe Busturia tomatoes, stalks removed
- 50 ml extra-virgin olive oil
- 2 g Añana's salt
- 0.03 g hot smoked paprika
- 25 g cornstarch (cornflour)
VEGETABLES AND FLOWERS
- 2 *Kalanchoe blossfeldiana*
- 2 autumn buttercup flowers
- 2 common verbena flowers
- 2 Swiss chard sprouts
- 2 Antzuola yellow tomatoes
- extra-virgin olive oil, for drizzling
- pinch of Añana's salt
- 1 green pea pod, tips removed
PICKLED APPLE
- 150 ml apple cider vinegar
- 2 bay leaves
- 50 g superfine (caster) sugar
- 20 g Añana's salt
- 0.13 g black peppercorns
- 300 ml Txakoli Gorka Izagirre
- 1 Granny Smith apple
FATTY FISH
- 1 anchovy
- 1 horse mackerel
- 1 sardine
- Añana's salt, to cover
- 100 g Txakoli vine shoots
- 3 g tsuyu sauce

GREEN PEA, APPLE, AND ARUGULA SORBET

Cut the tips off the green pea pods, blanch in a pan of boiling water, then transfer immediately to a bowl of ice water.

Cut the apple into cubes (skin on), and blend with the arugula (rocket), drained blanched peas, and ascorbic acid.

Put 250 ml of the liquefied vegetable mixture into a blender with the remaining sorbet ingredients and blend until you get a homogeneous mixture. Let sit for 12 hours, then churn in an ice-cream machine. Store in the freezer until ready to serve.

GREEN PEA JELLY

Cut the tips off the pea pods and blanch in a pan of boiling water. Transfer to a bowl of ice water. They should retain a very green color.

Drain the pea pods and put into a juicer with the arugula and apple and liquefy. Strain the juice through a Superbag.

Soak the gelatin leaf in a bowl of ice water for 10 minutes until hydrated.

Heat 10% of the obtained liquefied vegetables in a pan over low heat. When it reaches 104°F/40°C, add the hydrated gelatin. Dissolve the gelatin and salt, then combine with the rest of the liquified vegetables.

Use a dispenser to quickly spread the juice on 4 plate bowls. Let cool, then store in a cool place or a refrigerator until set.

SPICY TOMATO EMULSION

Quarter each tomato and blend in a blender. Strain through cheesecloth (muslin) and put into a Vitamix or Thermomix with the olive oil and blend until emulsified. Add the salt, hot smoked paprika, and cornstarch (cornflour). Blend for 2 minutes on high speed. The texture should be like honey, but still firm. Transfer to a squeeze bottle and leave in the refrigerator until ready to use.

VEGETABLES AND FLOWERS

Wash the flowers carefully and thoroughly, then place them on a moist piece of paper towel and place the paper in a hermetically sealed container. (Store flowers for no more than two days in the refrigerator.)

Blanch the tomatoes, then peel, halve, and store in a container with a drizzle of olive oil and a pinch of Añana's salt.

Peel the lateral thread of the green pea pod. Blanch in a pan of boiling water, then transfer immediately to a bowl of ice water and cut into thin strips on the bias. Store in the refrigerator on moist paper towels in a hermetically sealed container.

PICKLED APPLE

Mix the vinegar, bay leaves, sugar, salt, and pepper in a pan and bring to a boil. Remove from the heat and add the Txakoli. Let cool while you cut the apple into small cubes. Add the apple to the pan and let cool completely.

FATTY FISH

Remove the innards and spine from the anchovy, horse mackerel, and sardine. Clean the fillets and then marinate.

Cover the sardine fillets with Añana's salt and let stand for 5 minutes. Wash off the salt with abundant water. Put the vine shoots into a large pan. Place the fillets in a hollowed pan and then cover the large pan with the hollowed pan. Light the vine shoots with a kitchen blowtorch, then cover with a lid so the vines smoke. Cover the 2 pans with aluminum foil and let stand for 15 minutes. Remove the smoked fillets from the pan, transfer to the refrigerator, and let stand until cold (32–39°F/0–4°C). Cut the fillets into four or five ½-inch/1-cm cubes.

Cover the anchovy fillets with Añana's salt and let stand for 7 minutes. Wash off the salt with abundant water, then dry the fillet

with paper towels and rub the back with tsuyu sauce. Cut the fillet into two or three ½-inch/1-cm cubes.

Repeat with the horse mackerel but cut into two or three ½ x 1-inch/1 x 2.5-cm pieces.

TO SERVE

Lay the pickled apple over the green pea jelly, and dab on dots of the tomato emulsion.

Drain the Antzuola tomatoes, chop each half into two or three pieces, and place on the edge of the plate. Place the fatty fish, pea strips, and flowers around the plate. Place a quenelle of the sorbet in the center of the dish and top with some grains of salt flakes.

2. LEMONGRASS

SERVES 4
LEMON JELLY
- 50 ml lemon juice
- 20 g superfine (caster) sugar
- 10 g lemongrass stick, halved
CLEAN LEMONS
- 4 lemons or limes
- 12 white elderflowers, to serve
FOIE GATZATUA
- 120 g foie gras
- 50 ml whole (full-fat) milk
- 50 ml whipping (heavy) cream
- 2 g salt

LEMON JELLY

Strain the lemon juice and put into a pan with the sugar and lemongrass pieces. Heat over low heat until it reaches 240°F/115°C and becomes a dark color with a thick texture (like runny honey), then strain through a fine chinois strainer (sieve), put the mix into a pastry (piping) bag and let cool for 12 hours until it forms a jelly texture.

CLEAN LEMONS

Cut ½ inch/1 cm from the top of each lemon or lime and remove the pulp by carefully compressing it toward the center of the fruit with your hands (do not break the skin).

FOIE GATZATUA

Remove the excess fat from the outside of the foie gras and cut into ¾-inch/2-cm cubes.

Heat the milk and cream in a pan over medium heat until it reaches 158°F/70°C. Add the foie gras, reduce the heat to low, and warm through for another 5 minutes. Transfer to a blender and blend on high speed until smooth. Add the salt and strain the mixture through a fine chinois. Portion the foie inside the cleaned lemons with a piston funnel and let set inside.

TO SERVE

Cover the top of the foie gatzatua with lemon jelly. Place 3 white elderflowers on top of each filled fruit and serve immediately.

2

Gísli Matthías
Auðunsson

SLIPPURINN
Strandvegur, Westman Islands, Iceland

In the volcanic Westman Islands in the southern region of Iceland stands Slippurinn, a family-run restaurant championing seasonal and local food. With a simple and honest philosophy, chef Gísli Matthías Auðunsson and his family cook everything from scratch using seasonal ingredients. Wild herbs, seaweed, and berries are foraged daily, fish and meat are sourced from local markets, and fruit and vegetables are grown in the restaurant's on-site kitchen garden and greenhouse.

I was born in 1989 on Heimaey, the only inhabited island of Vestmannaeyjar (the Westman Islands). The archipelago was formed by volcanic activity during the last few thousand years, around the south coast of Iceland. Fishing has always been the main industry on Heimaey; I come from a hard-working family of fishermen and cooks. I'm proud of my heritage and where I come from.

In 2011, an idea came up in a family gathering to open a restaurant in Vestmannaeyjar, since my parents had recently moved back. My mother, Kata Gísla, had always dreamed of reviving this amazing old machine workshop that used to serve the slipways behind the building (where the name, Slippurinn, comes from) but which had not been used for a number of years. A year later, Slippurinn became a reality. We built it from scratch. Along with my sister Indíana and my parents, Kata and Auðunn, I have always had a clear vision of what Slippurinn should be: a place that is charming, with an amazing atmosphere. It would only open in summer. Our objective was to keep it sustainable, to work with local island produce, and to be seasonal. We want our guests to experience a strong sense of time and place while dining with us. Although the restaurant itself has changed a lot since we first opened—every year it becomes more seasonal and more sustainable—our core elements have not.

The islands are surrounded by the Atlantic Ocean and the weather makes for rough growing conditions, with high winds and saltiness in the air. Lava ash tends to settle everywhere. We have a volcanic soil that is rich in minerals and nutrients. When combined with ash, the soil becomes more acidic. It retains a lot of water so good drainage is important. We grow some of our produce ourselves but we also work closely with farmers on the mainland, who use geothermal energy to power their greenhouses all year round. We also forage on the island for wild herbs such as Arctic thyme and different types of seaweed, such as sugar kelp, dulse, sea truffles, kombu, and Irish moss. Probably 35 percent of the produce in the restaurant comes from the garden and 30 percent from foraging.

Our garden is a four-minute drive from the restaurant, on the south coast of the island. It is not very high above sea level and we use it for growing tough root vegetables such as kohlrabi, radishes, rutabagas (swedes), carrots, and potatoes. Because of the winds, and the cold climate, we cover our vegetable beds at the beginning of the season (some remain covered for most of the duration). A cover helps to create humidity.

We also grow kale and salads, such as mizuna which has a sharp flavor, a little spicy, and we have a small greenhouse for more delicate things like black currants, nasturtiums, lovage, and herbs, such as different types of thyme, rosemary, chives, and dill.

My mother takes care of the garden together with an islander called Bubba, and occasionally our cooks give a helping hand. The garden is only active from May, when we sow seeds and plant out; those crops are then harvested in July and August. On non-flowering crops, such as potatoes and other root vegetables, we use well-rotted horse manure. We stick to simple organic methods. For deterring pests, we mainly use a blend of garlic and water. We simply blend the garlic with water and spray it on the beds. It's good for aphid attacks.

We also work with local people. They know that we love wild produce and many of them let us take the rhubarb from their gardens in exchange for a voucher that can be exchanged for cocktails. We also get herbs like peppermint, parsley, and lovage from local gardens. Our cocktail program is built around locally foraged herbs; they are the main element. We wanted to create a cocktail program from only hand-foraged herbs, berries, and spices from the islands with the idea that people would sense the time and place in the first sip that they have at our restaurant. We felt that it would be more fun and unlike anything anyone else is doing.

Preserving vegetables from the garden is another key part of what we do at the restaurant. All the stems of various herbs we either turn into seasoned salts or dry and make powders and seasonings. We also pickle a lot of root vegetables, such as turnips, rutabagas, and carrots, to use early season, little over a half year after they are harvested.

We work on our menu in close connection with the garden and the wild ingredients that we are able to forage. Seasons change quite dramatically; we have many micro seasons throughout the summer. After exploring the island for produce over the past seven years, we feel that we know exactly when each herb will be hitting its prime.

FAVORITE HERBS FOR COCKTAILS
- Arctic thyme (*Thymus praecox* subsp. *arcticus*)—a foraged herb that only grows for two to three weeks over the summer. It's really aromatic with flavor notes of thyme, honey, and lavender. It's my absolute favorite. We infuse it with pear cider with burnt lemon and vodka.
- Spanish chervil (Sweet cicely, *Myrrhis odorata*) gives an anise kick, something that Icelanders love (we really like licorice).
- Birch has an herbal flavor that goes really well in a sour we make with Irish Whiskey.
- Rowanberries are bitter red berries that we infuse in our version of a negroni along with house-made rhubarb liquor that replaces the Campari in a traditional negroni.
- Sorrel is a herb that grows wild all over the island and has a very nostalgic taste for islanders.

1. RAW VEGETABLES AND OYSTER LEAF EMULSION

When new, you can't really compete with crunchy raw vegetables. But to make them work as a raw dish, the dipping sauce needs to be delicious and full-flavored. This dish of radishes, rutabaga (swede), and turnips is served with a briny, sweet, and sour emulsion with a deep herbal flavor. The parsley can be substituted for another herb. You can use 40 g raw oysters instead of the oyster leaf (*Mertensia maritima*) if you prefer.

SERVES 4
DEHYDRATED LOVAGE
– 40 g lovage leaves
OYSTER LEAF EMULSION
– 40 g oyster leaves, plus extra to garnish
– 200 g parsley leaves
– 300 ml vegetable oil
– 1 clove garlic
– 1 shallot
– 4 egg yolks
– 40 g Dijon mustard
– 10 ml apple cider vinegar
– lemon juice, to taste
– salt
RAW VEGETABLES
– 2 rutabagas (swedes), cleaned
– 4 turnips, cleaned
– 10 radishes, cleaned

DEHYDRATED LOVAGE

Dehydrate the lovage in a dehydrator or low oven for 12 hours, then blend to a powder.

OYSTER LEAF EMULSION

Put the oyster leaf, parsley, vegetable oil, garlic, and shallot into a blender and blend for about 8 minutes or until the oil reaches 170°F/75°C. Strain through a fine-mesh strainer (sieve) and then again through cheesecloth (muslin) and let cool.

Put the egg yolks, Dijon mustard, and apple cider vinegar into the clean blender and blend, then add the green oyster leaf oil and continue blending until the mixture is completely emulsified. Season to taste with lemon juice and salt.

RAW VEGETABLES

Cut all the cleaned vegetables into bite-size pieces. Reserve in ice water.

TO SERVE

Smear the oyster leaf emulsion on the side of the plates and dust the dehydrated lovage powder on top. Drain the vegetables, assemble them on the plates, and serve.

2. CURED HALIBUT WITH KOHLRABI, NASTURTIUM, MIZUNA, AND SALTED ANGELICA SEEDS

In this dish, we cure halibut with lemon thyme from the garden, rose pepper, and locally foraged Arctic thyme, then dress it with a little bit of lemon juice and plate it up with mizuna, nasturtium leaves, flowers, and salted angelica seeds (although you can use dehydrated capers instead if you prefer). The kohlrabi is dressed with sour cream and horseradish.

SERVES 4
SALTED ANGELICA SEEDS (OPTIONAL)
– 20 g angelica seeds
– 20 g salt
– 200 ml apple cider vinegar
HALIBUT
– 20 g pink peppercorns, coarsely crushed
– grated zest of 1 lemon
– 20 g lemon thyme leaves
– 20 g Arctic thyme leaves (or regular thyme)
– 120 g sea salt
– 50 g granulated sugar
– 1 x 600-g halibut fillet, cleaned
DEHYDRATED CAPERS (OPTIONAL)
– 20 g capers
KOHLRABI
– 2 kohlrabi, trimmed
– 50 g sour cream or crème fraîche
– 20 g nasturtium stems, finely chopped
– 6 g grated fresh horseradish
– lemon juice, to taste
– salt
TO SERVE
– Grated zest of 1 lemon
– 10 g lemon thyme
– 10 g nasturtium flowers and buds
– 10 g mizuna leaves

SALTED ANGELICA SEEDS

If you are using angelica seeds, pack them into a container with the salt, seal, and let stand for 2 weeks. Rinse and transfer the seeds to a container with the vinegar, seal, and keep in the refrigerator.

HALIBUT

Combine the crushed peppercorns, lemon zest, lemon thyme leaves, Arctic thyme leaves, salt, and sugar in a bowl. Coat the halibut in the mixture and chill for 24 hours in the refrigerator. Lightly brush off the mixture and air-dry the halibut for another day or two (depending on the thickness of the fillet) uncovered in the refrigerator. It should be a little dense on the outside and a little dry—similar in texture to gravlax.

DEHYDRATED CAPERS (OPTIONAL)

If you are using capers instead of angelica seeds, dehydrate them in a dehydrator or low oven at 140°F/60°C for 12 hours, or until crunchy.

KOHLRABI

Remove the tough skin and cut the kohlrabi lengthwise as thinly as possible using a meat slicer. Put it into a bowl and dress with the sour cream or crème fraîche, chopped nasturtium stems, and horseradish, and add salt and lemon juice to taste.

TO SERVE

Cut the cured halibut as thinly as possible before serving.

Place the dressed kohlrabi on plates, cover with the slices of cured halibut, and dress with the lemon zest and lemon thyme, salted angelica seeds or dehydrated capers, nasturtium flowers and buds, and mizuna leaves.

2

Greg Baxtrom

OLMSTED
Brooklyn, New York, USA

Chef and owner Greg Baxtrom heads up Olmsted, a neighborhood restaurant located in Brooklyn's Prospect Heights. The restaurant seats 50 guests, with the dining room comprising a living wall, with views to the adjoining garden. The menu is seasonal and ingredient-led, supported by the restaurant's own garden, a self-sustaining micro-farm that aims to be sustainable with zero waste.

As soon as I decided on the three things I really wanted in my first restaurant—a small dining room that was intimate but still bustling, a ten-seat bar, and some outside space—I found the perfect location on Vanderbilt Avenue close to Prospect Park in Brooklyn in 2015.

Outside we originally just had the yard behind the restaurant and we laid it out with two big horseshoe-shaped raised beds with a walking path in the middle. We problem-solved as we built it—my father, who's a carpenter, made benches and tables that hover just over the framework—this gives us 25 seats. In our first winter we added heaters and blankets and when it's cold we have a whole hot cocktail section with spiced cider and spiked hot chocolate so people are genuinely comfortable out there.

First and foremost the garden is a nice space for our guests to enjoy. The garden was never going to provide everything for the kitchen but from the start we tried to have one ingredient from the garden that featured on the menu. In the outer bed we have perennials that look good but also look after themselves including mint, fig, asparagus, rhubarb, and fiddlehead ferns, which we serve fried as nibbles with drinks.

And then in the inner bed we plant successionally for the kitchen—for example, a succession of radishes that along with their greens are used in a gazpacho—and guests can see the plants growing. We also grow peas, wild onions, artichokes, lemons, grapefruit, berries, and soft fruit, and lots of herbs including sage, thyme, and basil. There are edible flowers too, such as violets, lavender, nasturtium, and borage—we use the blue borage flowers as a decoration on top of our frozen yogurt and whipped honey dessert.

It's been a huge learning curve—the garden is only three years old. For a period of time we didn't have a farmer and I would be planting seedlings myself. After we opened, our neighbor, who's a dry cleaner, didn't need their outdoor space so we started renting their area too, adding a 10-foot (3-meter) greenhouse and more growing space, and then we took the garden from the next neighbor along, too, and now a building down the street has also given us another 1,500 square feet (140 square meters) and we have a farmer on staff who manages everything. We now have about 2,500 square feet (232 square meters) and I think it's the best we can do in New York.

Now with more space we can be more creative: we'll have enough Serrano chiles for a few weeks (we use them in a scallop dish) or a ton of heirloom tomatoes that we use all over the menu—we make an heirloom tomato schnitzel with ricotta, bagna cauda, and piperade.

We are ingredient driven so if we have kale growing and ready to be harvested we will get it on the menu and new ideas often start like that with something from the garden, like our "Crab Rangoon." We had lots of kale growing and we'd also been talking about using crab so we combined them with our own ricotta cheese, which we hang overnight—the milk comes from upstate New York. The sauce has 25 ingredients and takes two hours to make but we serve it very casually in a little box. We like to have playful things on the menu.

We have a pair of quails—they have become our mascots—that lay four or five eggs a week but we are about to get eight more and then we will have serious production. We do a French toast, *pain perdu*, which is caramelized with a quail egg on top. It's just one bite and we try to do it when we can.

I also wanted to have running water in the garden and we found an abandoned claw-foot tub underneath the bridge in Brooklyn and we now keep crawfish and other fish in there. We don't harvest them but when we have kids here they can go and feed them. We drain the fish water and spray that over the garden. We don't have the space to compost our waste on site, but we have it all composted and we now only produce one bag of landfill waste per day, which is incredible for a busy kitchen like this.

Being in the city involves some limitations; we have buildings and trees all around so we have some shady areas but we use them to grow lemon balm, angelica, paw paw, and strawberries. And birds occasionally eat our Romaine lettuce but other than that we don't have any problems growing in such an urban environment. We are still learning all the time and in no way is it a full-blown farm—it's a micro system—but to have this in the middle of a city is incredible, and it's really inspiring for us as chefs.

BOTANICAL INFUSIONS
Our garden doesn't just provide inspiration for the kitchen, our cocktails are all named after plants in the garden and we use them as botanical infusions, flavorings, or as decoration. The house Martini is made with nasturtium-infused Old Tom gin, Dolin Blanc vermouth, and a bay leaf tincture, then decorated with a nasturtium flower or leaf. Other cocktails are based around rosemary, rhubarb, or sassafras.

FAVORITE VEGETABLE VARIETIES
Kale is a key ingredient in our growing beds and we use three varieties in the kitchen:
– "Siberian" kale (*Brassica napus* var. *pabularia*) is easy to grow and very hardy. The frilly leaves are softer than some other varieties and have a tender texture and a mild flavor.
– "Red Russian" kale (*Brassica napus* var. *pabularia*) can be cut when it is young and sweet or later for a more mature robust flavor. The red leaves also look amazing growing in the winter.
– "Nero di Toscana" kale (*Brassica oleracea*) is another beautiful plant to grow, with its tall blue-green leaves. You can harvest the leaves and it will continue to grow, giving several harvests.

1. KALE AND CRAB RANGOON

MAKES 15–20
FRESH RICOTTA
- 950 ml whole (full-fat) milk
- 240 ml heavy (double) cream
- 5 g salt
- 20 ml lemon juice
SWEET-AND-SOUR CHILE SAUCE
- 500 ml orange juice
- 250 ml red pepper juice
- 1 liter glucose syrup
- 500 ml rice wine vinegar
- 250 g granulated sugar
- 250 g mirin
- 1 garlic bulb, cut in half
- ½ Fresno pepper, halved lengthwise
- 12 g Sichuan peppercorns
- 12 g coriander seeds
- 50 g ginger
- ½ bunch cilantro (coriander)
- 1½ tablespoons Calabrian chile
- lemon juice, to taste
- lime juice, to taste
- white soy sauce, to taste
- salt, to taste
RANGOON PARCELS
- 1 bunch kale
- canola (rapeseed) oil, to sauté
- 200 g picked crab meat
- 200 g fresh ricotta (see above)
- 1 package store-bought wonton wrappers
- oil, for deep-frying

RICOTTA

Put the milk, cream, and salt into a pan and bring to a boil. Add the lemon juice and let separate. Simmer for 8 minutes, then remove from the heat and strain through cheescloth (muslin).

SWEET-AND-SOUR CHILE SAUCE

Put all the ingredients except the cilantro (coriander), chili, lemon juice, lime juice, and white soy sauce into a large pan and bring to a boil. Reduce the heat and simmer until reduced by half. Remove from the heat, add the remaining ingredients, and season to taste. Let steep for 1 hour, then strain through cheesecoth (muslin).

RANGOON PARCELS

Sauté the kale in a little oil in a pan until wilted. Remove from the heat and let cool.

Once the kale is cool, chop and mix it with the crab and ricotta. Divide this mixture among 10–12 wonton wrappers.

Heat the oil in a large, deep pan to 350°F/180°C. Deep-fry the wontons for 3 minutes. Drain on paper towels. Serve with sweet-and-sour chile sauce.

2. THAI BEET SALAD

SERVES 4
CORIANDER OIL
- 1 tablespoon toasted coriander seeds
- 60 ml grapeseed oil
DRESSING
- 1 tablespoon lemon juice
- 1 tablespoon lime juice
- 1 tablespoon fish sauce
- 1 tablespoon chili oil
- 60 ml Coriander Oil (see above)
BEET JUICE REDUCTION (OPTIONAL)
- 250 ml beet (beetroot) juice
- 1 tablespoon glucose or corn syrup
SALAD
- 1.4 kg beets (beetroots)
- 120 g snow peas (mangetout)
- 1 bunch shiso leaves
- 2 g toasted sesame seeds
- salt

CORIANDER OIL

Blend the coriander seeds and grapeseed oil in a blender.

DRESSING

Combine all the ingredients in a bowl, transfer to a squeeze bottle, and set aside.

BEET JUICE REDUCTION (OPTIONAL)

Reduce the beet (beetroot) juice and glucose or corn syrup in a pan until reduced by half. Paint the inside of the salad bowl with the reduction.

SALAD

Peel the beets (beetroots) and cut them into thin slices on a Japanese sheeter or mandoline, then cut into ⅛-inch/2-cm wide strips.

Blanch the snow peas (mangetout) in heavily salted boiling water for 3 minutes, then transfer to a bowl of ice water.

Chiffonade the shiso leaves, then combine them in a bowl with the beets, snow peas, toasted sesame seeds, and dressing. Top with extra sesame seeds and serve.

1

2

Ivan & Sergey Berezutskiy

TWINS GARDEN
Tverskaya, Moscow, Russia

Identical twin chefs Ivan and Sergey Berezutskiy head up this Moscow restaurant with a modern approach to Russian cuisine. The restaurant is located in the center of the city, but they have also acquired a farm in nearby Kaluga to provide access to fresh ingredients. More than 150 kinds of vegetables, fruit, berries, and herbs are cultivated alongside goats and dairy cows for cheese production. The twins are working towards becoming completely self-sufficient.

Our restaurants are entirely sourced by our year-round farm in Russia's Kaluga region. Covering 125 acres (50 hectares) of land it includes 17 greenhouses: 15 for vegetables, one for seedlings, and a fully-automated industrial one. As well as greenhouse crops we grow around 150 different kinds of vegetables and herbs in fields. The farm also includes a cowshed, a goat shed, a chicken coop, and an apiary. We breed quails, ducks, crayfish, and five species of fish. We also planted a fruit orchard this year, which will yield pears, apples, and our favorite, thorn plums (blackthorn, *Prunus spinosa*). We grow old varieties of apples, mainly Bely Naliv (or Papirovka) and Antonovka, and we plan to make cider.

We established the farm a year before opening Twins Garden restaurant. We chose an ecologically clean location 90 miles (150 km) from Moscow. The nearest road is 6 miles (10 km) and guests are welcome to visit our location by car or on one of our tours. In time, we will offer agro-tourism accommodation for visitors.

We deliberately wanted to make our own farm because we could not always find the produce we needed because no-one grows or cultivates them, and moreover, it is essential for us to personally control the quality of the produce. The farm was developed in cooperation with Moscow Timiryazev Agricultural Academy. This is the best agricultural academy in the country and it schedules our planting and helps us keep track of production. It also advises us on soil health. Our Central Russian location means the farm has quality chernozem or "black soil." In the first year, we planted about 150 vegetables under the Academy's supervision, but only 90 of them grew. To maximize yields from crops in these open fields, the Academy advised adding highly fertile soil from Southern Russia, so we have imported about 42 truckloads.

Our mission is to get high-quality delicious produce as well as reviving forgotten varieties—and creating some new ones. Every country has classic varieties of vegetables, but in Russia they have been lost during different historical periods. The potato is one example. In Russia they are generally known simply as "red potato" or "white potato." Only small farms or private gardens might raise older, rare breeds, such as "Lorkh" from the early twentieth century, or "Sineglazka," which was once famous and is now hardly available. To discover old strains, we work closely with a specialist private breeding laboratory. Moscow Timiryazev Academy also helps us with our seed development—it currently has the largest seed collection in the country—and we also take advice on breeding and raising heritage crops from the Vavilov Institute of Plant Industry.

Sustainable production is integral to creating the high-quality produce that we are committed to growing and we want the farm to become the most environmentally friendly one in the country. There is always more to be learned in this area, but currently we use only organic fertilizers and we make our own compost from waste recycled from the restaurant and farm. All of our animals are free-range and free from antibiotics, and we employ specialists to care for the goats and cows. Our Anglo-Nubian goats, for example, require dedicated knowledge to rear properly. They are milked manually and from their quality milk we make 8 types of cheese that feature on our menu. No other restaurant in Russia has this.

The restaurant and the farm is a single entity. The quality of the farm's harvest affects the restaurant menu directly, so we work to make the union between them as strong as possible. Our restaurant, Twins Garden, uses 90 percent of the farm's vegetables, with the other 10 percent set aside for future growth. The biggest advantage of having a farm is that we can control the quality of the product from the very seed through to growing and harvest. As a result, the menu always reflects the farm's conditions. For example, abundant rain last year meant cabbages grew better than anything else in our open fields. So, we offered an à la carte menu with three or four dishes each cooked differently that illustrated its variety of flavors: cabbage with Sulguni cheese sauce, for instance. Similarly, for our salads, which always feature on the menu, we introduce up to 30 types of vegetables and herbs from the farm to showcase seasonality, texture, and taste.

Because we have an abundance of produce, we have also begun making vegetable "wine," which we now serve in the restaurant as an accompaniment to our vegetable tasting menu. The flavors of the wine bring out those of the food, and we have about 40 different wines under development at present—parsley, rhubarb, tomato, parsnip, and carrot are just a few examples.

The farm has its own seasonality. In fall (autumn), the soil is prepared. We spend summer weeding and harvesting. Spring is for sowing. We sow seeds and grow seedlings only after June 6, because frosts on the open ground are likely before then. The greenhouses offer a continuous supply of vegetables year-round. We also employ people who prepare the pond for the winter, work with fish fry, and with cows, goats, and birds. Everything is divided into different functions and areas of expertise to give the best results.

At the restaurant, we wanted to create an art object that would show the seasonality of the vegetable harvest that our guests taste. The kinetic farm is the result. We made it so that these vegetables could be highly visible from the chef's table, from the kitchen—even from the street. It has become a popular place for our guests to visit and the room also includes a catalog of our seeds, a refrigerator for cheese cultivation, and a barrel for aging our vegetable wine. Our annual farm festival each September further popularizes the natural, integrated process of the restaurant and garden. Chefs from all over Russia come, and we share some of the secrets behind the farm. We want the natural connection, which is at the heart of our restaurant, to become normal in Russia.

GARDENING NOTES

Growing potatoes is not rocket science. Sprouted potatoes give better yields than those planted un-sprouted, but sprouts should not be longer than 2 inches (5 cm) before the potatoes are put into the ground. When harvesting your crop, lay out the potatoes in the sun until the evening and then move them to a dry, shady place. Remove any that are diseased or damaged. Delay long-term storage of potatoes until at least two weeks after collection. To avoid mold, sprinkle potatoes with wood ash.

A tip for gardeners: if you don't succeed at once, don't give up. You must try again. When we started the farm, we didn't know much; we weren't farmers. But the situation with produce in Russia forced us to do it. Here, there is no tradition to grow high-quality vegetables, make proper cheese, or work with good milk. We had a great desire to give a high-quality, healthy product. In the context of globalization, we often forget about the benefits of products, but it is as important as taste—sometimes even more important. We want our products to be not only tasty, but also healthy.

The most important advice: when you open a farm at a restaurant, you must be obsessed with the idea. You have to believe that you are doing the right thing, because only then will you see the results. It's hard to start, especially in Russia. But if you want to change the industry as a whole, if you want people to come to the restaurant for food first, you need to do it. Russia is the largest country in the world with a huge territory, but agriculture is very poorly developed. We are changing that now.

We grow about 20 types of lesser-known tomatoes (*Solanum lycopersicum*), such as "Beefsteak" or "Black Prince," and this gives us a competitive advantage over other restaurants. We also grow unusual vegetables and herbs, like "chocolate" mint (*Mentha × piperita* f. *citrata*). This plant is a small nuance, a blade of grass, which can change the taste of a dish. We offer a leaf for guests to smell as part of our tasting menu; its mint-chocolate aroma colors the flavor of what they eat afterward—young green peas from our farm with black currant and parsley extract, for instance.

1. GARDEN SALAD

A third of the restaurant menu consists of vegetable dishes, which we pay great attention to. Changing the texture and temperature of even the simplest, most familiar vegetables reveals their taste again.

Garden salad is always on the menu, and it constantly changes from season to season. It is a kind of "collective image," in which we present to the guests the vegetables we grow at the farm at that particular time of the year. (The selection of vegetables below is served in August.) Depending on the season, it can include from 10 to 30 different types of vegetables. We cook them in different ways: some of the vegetables are marinated, some are baked, and some are served raw, in order to create the right balance on the plate and a variety of textures and temperatures.

SERVES 1
MARINATED TOMATOES
– 65 g beefsteak tomatoes
– 100 g large green chile peppers or 10 g small green chiles, cut in half
– 10 ml 9% white vinegar
– 20 g superfine (caster) sugar
– 20 ml sunflower oil
– 10 g parsley leaves and stems
– 50 g white onion, halved and cut into rings
RED PEPPER SAUCE
– 3 large red bell peppers, seeded
– olive oil, for drizzling
– salt and freshly ground black pepper
SALAD
– 30 g Padrón peppers
– 10 ml unrefined sunflower oil
– olive oil, for drizzling
– 40 g yellow tomatoes, cut into pieces
– 30 g black tomatoes, cut into pieces
– 10 g Red Pepper Sauce (see above)
– 5 g black carrots, peeled and very finely sliced
– 5 g white carrots, peeled and very finely sliced
– 2 g red onions, finely sliced
– 2 g radish, finely sliced
– 5 g bok choy (pak choi), thin stem removed
– 5 g zucchini (courgette), finely sliced
– 20 g pea pods
– 15 g tomato marinade (see method)
– 1 g seasonal herbs and flowers
– sea salt

MARINATED TOMATOES
Blanch the tomatoes in a pan of boiling water for a couple of seconds, then cut each tomato into 8 pieces. Warm the remaining ingredients in a pan to 122°F/50°C, then remove from the heat and add the tomatoes. Marinate the tomatoes for a day.

RED PEPPER SAUCE
Season the red bell peppers with salt and pepper, drizzle with olive oil, and wrap in aluminum foil. Preheat a Josper charcoal grill to 350–400°F/180–200°C, then grill for 15–20 minutes, let cool, peel, and blend in a blender until smooth.

SALAD
Sauté the Padrón peppers in a pan with the unrefined sunflower oil for 4–5 minutes, or until soft. Season with a generous pinch of sea salt and drizzle with olive oil. Arrange the vegetables—the marinated tomatoes, raw vegetables, and fried peppers—on a plate, add some of the tomato marinade and red pepper sauce, and finish with the herbs and flowers.

2. CATFISH BAKED IN BIRCH BARK WITH CARROTS AND HERB SAUCE

We have a pond at the farm where we breed different kinds of fish. We carefully control how our fish is grown and fed. By changing its food, we can change its flavor, too. Our guests notice, with the catfish for example, how the taste and density of the meat changes with proper feeding.

We cook catfish in the Russian oven, then smoke it on birch bark, which references the roots of Russian cuisine and gives the dish a special character. We complement it with varieties of carrot from our farm and a sauce of greens harvested that morning.

SERVES 1
HERBAL SAUCE
– 12 egg yolks
– 300 g unsalted butter, melted
– 50 g seasonal herbs, washed and prepared
– 10 g lemon juice
– 10 g Worcestershire sauce
– 2 g salt
– 2 g freshly ground black pepper
CARROT PUREE
– 530 g carrots, cut into medium pieces
– 30 g unsalted butter
– 15 g fresh ginger, peeled and sliced
– 2 g chile
– 600 ml fish stock
– 5 g salt
– 2 g freshly ground black pepper
BAKED CARROTS
– 60 g mix of carrot varieties, 10 g of them very finely sliced
– olive oil, for baking
CATFISH
– 1 x 500–600-g catfish, cleaned and scaled
– 5 g thyme (or other fragrant herbs)
– 2 x 4¾ x 3-inch/12 x 8-cm pieces birch bark
– salt
TO SERVE
– 40 g Carrot Puree (see above)
– 20 g peeled grapefruit, cut into cubes
– 2 g chervil leaves
– 20 g Herbal Sauce (see above)

HERBAL SAUCE
Whip the egg yolks with the melted butter in a heatproof bowl set over a water bath until very smooth. Add the picked herbs and remaining ingredients, then transfer to a blender, blend, and strain through a strainer (sieve).

CARROT PUREE
Sauté the carrots in the butter in a medium pan over medium heat until they get a ruddy crust. Add the ginger and chile and sauté for another 20 seconds, then add the fish stock and bring to a boil. Season with the salt and pepper. Cook until the carrots are tender, then remove from the heat, blend with an immersion (stick) blender, and strain through a strainer.

BAKED CARROTS
Preheat the oven to 350°F/180°C. Clean, peel, and cut the whole carrots into 2¼ x ½-inch/6 x 1.5-cm pieces and bake in the oven for about 7 minutes.

CATFISH
Preheat the Russian oven to 480°F/250°C. Sprinkle the outside and inside of the catfish evenly with a generous pinch of salt. Put the thyme (or other fragrant herbs) in the belly of the fish. Bake for 9 minutes. Check it near the head to see if it is cooked.

TO SERVE
Spoon the carrot puree onto a serving plate. Place the baked carrots beside the puree and sprinkle the grapefruit, raw sliced carrots, and chervil leaves on top. Take the catfish out of the Russian oven and place it on the birch bark. Set the bark on fire. Smoke the fish briefly on the birch bark to add a nice aroma, then put the fire out with a special cloth. Leave the fish under the cloth for 10 seconds. Peel off the skin, remove the fillet, and place the fish pieces on the plate and add the herbal sauce.

2

Michel & Sébastien Bras

LE SUQUET
Laguiole, France

Michel Bras inherited his family restaurant when he was 33, gaining two Michelin stars before opening Le Suquet in 1992—a modernist glass-fronted structure with views of the Aubrac countryside. In 1999, he was awarded his third Michelin star. His son Sébastien is now head chef at Bras, where three tasting menus are available, highlighting a cuisine that is very much of the moment—constantly reinvented—and Michel oversees the garden in nearby Lagardelle, which grows vegetables, fruit, herbs, and flowers for the restaurant.

The garden at Lagardelle speaks volumes about our cooking and our love of vegetables. It gets right to the source of the cook's craft, with freshly grown ingredients and seeds gathered from far afield and closer to home, and it has become a treasure trove where we now grow over 200 different varieties of shoots, stems, roots, vegetables, and fruit trees and bushes.

We initially tried to create a garden next to the restaurant but the altitude, at 4,000 feet (1,200 meters), was too high, so instead the garden was made from scratch over six years, just a few kilometers away. Along with gardeners Jean-Luc Salomon and James Gould we transformed former grazing land into a 3-acre (1.2-hectare) kitchen garden with a meticulous layout. There are 18 long zinc raised beds and some growing areas in the ground too, along with a glass greenhouse and four polytunnels where we can raise young plants or tender varieties from more tropical climates like India or South America including Mexican chiles, 12 varieties of garlic, papalo (an ancient Mexican herb similar to cilantro/coriander, *Porophyllum ruderale*), and rau ram (Vietnamese cilantro/coriander, *Persicaria odorata*).

The influence of the garden over the kitchen is never-ending as each menu is unique and changes twice a day. Our chefs go to the garden every morning, moving carefully from bed to bush, to see what they can use. Our dish *Gargouillou* is made up of around 60 separately prepared vegetables, herbs, flowers, and shoots that change all the time. It often includes *Meum athamanticum*—an alpine fennel that is quite emblematic of the restaurant—it's on the chefs' tunics and on our menus and it only grows wild where the air and soil are pure. The *Gargouillou* reflects absolutely what is growing at any particular time—for example, the nearer we get to fall (autumn), the more root vegetables we'll have in it. And each morning seven chefs will work for hours to create it.

Michel invented the *Gargouillou* in 1980 when he was out rambling in the local countryside. It was midsummer and the pastures were alive with the scents of all the flowers and plants and he thought about how he could bring all that together in one dish. It can include amaranthus, white borage, rocambole garlic (*Allium sativum* var. *ophioscorodon*), clover, cauliflower stalk, peas, tuberous chervil (*Chaerophyllum bulbosum*), nasturtium, pattypan squash (*Cucurbita pepo*), endive, pink radish, salsify, tomato, scallion (spring onion).... the list goes on. It's a true homage to nature. We first introduced a vegetarian menu in 1978, long before all things green became fashionable.

Harvesting from the garden is also one of the ways we train up our chefs. They can see, feel, taste, and understand the produce,

which is the nature and essence of our cooking. We have to know how the flavor of our plants develops over the course of the season—when they fully ripen and when we can rely on them (or not). For example, the herb *Valeriana phu* is sweeter at the start of the season and gets very bitter by the end. You've got to know what you're growing and exactly when to harvest it to get the best flavor.

Rather than grow ingredients that are common or require large-scale production, we prefer to grow specialist varieties and one of the greatest rewards is that sense of going on a journey round the garden, from Japan to Vietnam via India and South America. We love bringing interesting seeds back when we travel so we can experiment with new ingredients. Holy basil, a sacred plant with manifold benefits, came home with us after a trip to India; we discovered sansho pepper (*Zanthoxylum* species), with its lemony, woody notes and slightly spicy finish, at a restaurant in Toya in Japan; curry plant (*Murraya koenigii*) evokes the market booths of India, making for the perfect accompaniment to lamb; the South American "Violet" tomatillo (*Physalis peruviana*) is a wonderful source of acidity; then there's rau ram from Vietnam, which brings minty aromas to stocks. Almost every flavor and continent is represented in the garden. And growing them ourselves gives us the chance to watch all these plants ripen and mature, then pluck them from the earth just when their flavor is at its very best.

We take a really common sense approach to gardening and growing vegetables; we are fully organic so we only use natural fertilizers (we store manure year on year, allowing it to rot before using it to fertilize the garden). We're not into permaculture, though, because I like my garden to look tidy. It helps that James is a very meticulous gardener; the garden has a neat, architectural design with lots of clever features. For example, he has made a tepee out of bamboo shoots for beans to grow up. It's also very cleverly laid out in terms of how the soil and airflow are managed, with grass walkways, dry-stone walls that protect our crops, and a fountain for collecting rainwater to use in the garden.

The garden is entirely managed according to our climate, which can include harsh winters, so it's in action from March to November, at which point it becomes dormant until early spring. The restaurant is open from April to mid-November, so it dovetails perfectly with the garden's growing periods.

You have to have a sense of humility when you grow plants—never forget that nature is in charge. I try to follow the garden from day to day; if a certain plant is struggling, we will give it more care and attention. You can't go away for two weeks and come back expecting it not to be "out of sorts"—the whole place will be out of sorts.

KEY GARDEN INGREDIENTS
- Edible flowers have always been a central part of our menus and we use them in myriad ways. We stuff the corolla of daylilies (*Hemerocallis*); cardamine (bittercress) has a peppery flavor that we use with poultry; Silene flowers and leaves bring a flavor of spring before it has begun; and we use meadowsweet flowers for their bitter almond aroma.
- We have many favorite varieties of peas but the "Saint Fiacre" snow peas (mangetout, *Pisum sativum* var. *saccharatum*), a very old variety, produce the best beans in terms of flavor and texture. Traditional fine green beans cannot even begin to compare.

1. PORK CHOPS FLAVORED WITH HOGWEED SEED

In the garden at Lagardelle, there was always a plant that my grandmother referred to as "stuffed chard." Ever since, these simple leaves have been a feature of my cooking whenever the garden is yet to reach its peak. I have lots of varieties, one of which has broad, thick ribs that are lovely and juicy. I love just blanching this chard and tossing it with buttered shallots. I wanted to introduce you to this cousin of the Swiss chard along with a fresh look at beets (beetroots) cooked in various ways and to play with its dazzling colors.

I've always had stacks of chard, which is sometimes known as spinach beet—big, small, every color. It's a joy to extricate it from the ground to see if it's ripe. If needs be, there are usually enough of them to check a few to see how ripe they are. The garden is starting to come to life.

I pick young chard leaves from here and there so that I end up with an array of different colors. Then I dig up the beets, aiming for the smallest ones (they're the most tender). On the way back to the restaurant from the garden, clusters of common hogweed (*Heracleum sphondylium*) invade the hedges and ditches lining the road. The flavor of its first fruits always appeals to me with its citrus fruit aromas.

This delightful dish, with its harmony of confit pork and beet flavors, is finished with crunchy beets, lively young chard leaves and common hogweed seeds.

PORK
- pork chops
- salt
BEETS
- various beets (beetroots), such as yellow, white, red, and chioggia, cleaned
CHARD
- variety of colored chard leaves, cleaned
- Swiss chard
- butter
- shallots
CONFIT BEETS
- "Forono" beets
- red wine
- sugar
TO SERVE
- beet leaves
- pearled beet coulis
- common hogweed seeds
- oil

PORK
Salt the pork chops and refrigerate for 12 hours. After the 12 hours, preheat the oven. Rinse the salt off the chops and place them in the oven, lowering the temperature immediately. Let them confit for 2–3 hours.

BEETS
Slice the various colored beets (beetroots) thinly using a mandoline.

CHARD
Blanch the older, larger chard leaves, then toss them in butter and shallots. Just clean any young, soft chard leaves in running water to serve raw.

CONFIT BEETS
Confit the "Forono" beets in a sweet-and-sour dressing of red wine and sugar. Remove from the wine and sugar solution and scoop out little balls of beet with a small melon baller. Reduce the cooking juices to pour over the plate.

TO SERVE
Put the leaf and rib of the chard on the pork chop, then sprinkle the plate with the raw beet slivers and young leaves in their vinaigrette. Then add the confit beet balls with the reduced sweet-and-sour sauce, followed by the pork's cooking juices and pearls of hogweed oil. Season the dish with a few hogweed seeds, which unleash lovely, unfamiliar flavors when you bite into them.

2. ARCTIC CHAR WRAPPED IN MEXICAN PEPPERLEAF

When spring arrives, I love disappearing into the garden in search of its first treasures—I'm mad about the season's first shoots. I especially like the first crop of peas. I prise open their pods to check their sweetness and I can never resist nibbling on sugar snap peas and snow peas (mangetout), my favorite vegetable, like radishes, waiting patiently for the "St Fiacre" snow peas (the best of the best) to be ready. This was my approach the first time I rustled up this recipe.

Then, squashed against the corner of a greenhouse, the Mexican pepperleaf reaches out to me with its soft green leaves.

And I always look forward to the start of spring because that's when the Minana family sends us the first of their Arctic char. Sylvain and Najiba, my fish suppliers, have been keeping an eye on them all winter. From the time they are eggs to the moment they are sold, there's no processing whatsoever. They are fed on microorganisms from the ground and the air, along with a supplement that contains non-GM cereals and no animal bonemeal.

Everything comes together in an ensemble piece that exemplifies the lively notes of spring and blends the fresh, irresistible flavors of the garden with the refined, exotic character of fish.

- blond planèze peas
- aromatic stock
- butter
- yellow snow peas (mangetout)
- green snow peas (mangetout)
- green stick (runner) beans or lima (butter) beans
- Arctic char
- Mexican pepperleaf (*Piper auritum*)
- pea coulis
- salt and freshly ground black pepper
TO SERVE
- garden peas
- winged beans
- pea shoots
- sugar snap peas
- green or olive oil
- infused oils, such as elderberry, bedstraw, and meadowsweet

Preheat the oven to a low heat.

Cook the juiciest blond peas in an aromatic stock. When they are done, press them through a strainer (sieve) with a little butter and season the purée.

Bring a pan of very salty water to a boil. Carefully remove the flowers from the snow peas (mangetout) and green beans (lima/butter or stick/runner) and set them aside. Cook the beans quickly in the boiling water.

Fillet the char at the last minute and wrap it in the Mexican pepperleaf, then cook it at a low temperature in the oven—that way it keeps its lovely pearly white color. Remove from the oven and season with a tiny bit of salt.

TO SERVE
Lay the fish on plates on a pepperleaf alongside a smear of green pea coulis and blond pea puree, then scatter all the other peas, beans, and pea shoots around in an attractive, harmonious manner. Finish with droplets of olive oil and some infused oils.

This is a dish to cherish that blends the fresh, irresistible flavors of the garden in spring with the refined, exotic character of fish.

Note from the chef: A recipe for me is like a walk in the garden, it is to be interpreted not followed verbatim. Depending on how many guests you have, where you are, what ingredients are available, who you are, and your tastes, you can add some vegetables, take others out, and adapt these recipes as you like.

Common hogweed (Heracleum sphondylium) is edible but giant hogweed (Heracleum mantegazzianum) is not.

1

2

Manoella Buffara

RESTAURANTE MANU
Curitiba, Paraná, Brazil

Restaurante Manu keeps true to its roots and experiments with indigenous Brazilian produce from the surrounding region of Paraná. Chef Manu Buffara's menu tells the story of the land, sea, garden, and farm from which it was created. Working closely with local producers, Manu has created an agroecological community garden to promote the region's traditional ingredients, farming methods, and biodiversity.

I always wanted a garden or a farm. I was born in the middle of a field and was raised by my parents on their farm, so I have a long-standing connection with horticulture and the land. But I didn't want a vegetable garden only for me, or my restaurant Manu. I wanted something that I could share, that would show the local community how we can eat better and change the landscape of our city.

The plot that sustains Manu is the Community Garden of Rio Bonito, which is in the Tatuquara district of Curitiba. This temperate region of Brazil has regular rainfall throughout the year and generally doesn't suffer from extremely high or low temperatures. Approximately 40 percent of the neighborhood is vegetated, which points to the naturally arable conditions of the local soil. We established the project on land donated by a private company, which is also concerned with the importance of access to good food and the future of Curitiba. In total, the vegetable garden covers 2½ acres (1 hectare) and was built entirely by our community.

The gardens involve 100 families; each has an area of 1,000 square feet (just over 100 square meters) to plant in, using seeds that are primarily donated by me, as well as by Curitiba city and by an organic seed producer, Isla. To continue our investment in seeds for the gardens, I also have a 100-square-meter garden within the main Rio Bonito plot that we use solely for plant development. Here, after a crop reaches its full harvest, we simply let produce go to seed. We then harvest and dry the seeds, and use them for planting the following season. This reinvestment in seed production creates a continuous, self-perpetuating cycle of growth. Our husband-and-wife team Delso and Nilda Moretti oversee the garden and the community's participation, and are there daily. All the families agree to our rules of participation and visit at least once a week. The community takes part in many aspects of the garden, including growing, maintaining soil quality, new plantings, seed selection, classroom education, and feeding the community.

Andrey da Silva and I care for the garden most closely and work between the plot and the kitchen. I'm there almost every day; Andrey is responsible for harvesting, planting, and taking care of all Manu's vegetables. We use crop rotation. After a productive cycle, crops such as sorghum, millet, or sunflowers are intentionally planted to deliver nutrients back to the soil and restore it for food production the following season. We believe that this is the most appropriate technique to maintain the quality of our land, and minimize environmental aggression that can result from agricultural practices.

We use compost to nourish the garden's growth. This was a deliberate choice so that our restaurant could recycle all its biodegradable waste. Much of the food waste that people usually throw away can become incredible compost. We use any organic residue such as fruit peel, pulp, coffee grounds, or leftover restaurant food,

and the community has also learned how to turn kitchen waste into food for the garden. We apply the compost directly onto the soil across all 1,000 square feet (100 square meters).

Composting is part of our overall organic and sustainable approach. I understand sustainability in its fullest sense. It is the ability of humans to interact with the world and preserve the environment, so that our impact does not compromise the natural resources of future generations. I also adhere to the established measure of sustainability as being socially just.

Each season has its own characteristics, and seasonality is a very important factor in planning our garden; it influences which varieties we decide to cultivate. Every year we follow a planting schedule, planned in advance. We look at the plants we want to grow and see which ones will adapt to lower winter temperatures, which will look beautiful in the fall (autumn) with their fallen leaves, and which will grow well in the summer at higher temperatures.

The planting schedule also reflects our research into the use of particular species of flowers, such as false acacia (*Robinia pseudoacacia*), Pitkin marsh lily (*Lilium pardalinum* subsp. *pitkinense*), or white ipe (*Tabebuia roseoalba*), which we cultivate. The flowers are a distinctive part of our menu as they give dishes such amazing color and flavor. We are careful to grow plants in their appropriate seasons, so the flowers become attractive pollinators for our native bees, which also live in the garden. The effect of this cross-pollination has transformed the garden into a more productive place.

In the garden, our "treasure" is seeing the changing relationship between people and the earth—the daily knowledge and understanding of sustainable values. By working in the garden, we learn to wait; we lose products because of a lack of rain or its excess; we have learned that the land feeds on itself. Our restaurant work becomes even more rewarding when we are part of the garden's whole life cycle: sowing, planting, and harvesting.

Time, Mother Nature, and of course human work, give us the ingredients that we take into the kitchen. All my inspiration for cooking comes from my garden, and I discover most of my creative ideas there, whether through conversations with people, through the products we grow, or by discovering new tastes. I draw on what is in the garden for Manu's menu, and also experiment with old cooking methods, such as fermented vegetables and leaves. Because the food at Manu relies almost entirely on produce from our garden, we often change the menu daily to reflect what is happening in the plot.

The garden is the key to what happens at Manu: we involve everyone in the process, whether it's front house or kitchen staff—even restaurant guests are welcome to visit. The garden is our way to share, not only produce and cuisine, but knowledge and friendship with the community and encourage a better future for them.

GARDEN TIPS

Have you noticed that if you "forget" a clove of garlic, the buds soon begin to appear? These little alliums, that make all the difference in the seasoning of dishes, are in themselves true seeds that grow well in water. Their "shoots" when they begin to sprout, can be used in many dishes, such as salads and sauces.

One of the most nutritious foods, the potato, also has a very simple planting method: just cut one in half and leave it buried in the soil. In about seven weeks you can see the first signs of new potatoes coming through. Just water them regularly and in a short time you will have a source of vitamins C and B, zinc, and magnesium, to grow in a pot at home.

Carrots are a good source of pectin, and also a digestive. To see them grow naturally, cut off the top

and just leave it in water. When the cutting begins to grow, transfer the shoots to the soil so that the plant receives enough nutrients to sprout completely. This works better still if it is an organic carrot.

Queen of the Brazilian Salad, the lettuce is practically an X-Man: it has the power to regenerate itself from its own pieces. Just put some leaves into a water basin and place it where it will have lots of sunlight. You will quickly see roots form, and then you can transfer it to the earth to receive more nutrients.

To guarantee a supply of avocado takes very little effort. Just wash the seed, punch it with toothpicks, and suspend it over water; do not submerge the entire seed. The root growth process will take time (about six weeks). After the seed begins to grow, transfer it to soil. Soon you will have a harvest of avocados.

Fresh ginger can also be easily planted. Take a piece of ginger and place it on the ground with the rhizome facing up. Within a week, you will see shoots, which can be dug up and replanted.

FAVORITE VEGETABLE VARIETIES

– Cambuci chile (*Capsicum baccatum* var. *pendulum*), a sweet Brazilian chile.
– Mandioquinha salsa (*Arracacia xanthorrhiza*), a Brazilian root, super sweet and with a unique flavor.
– Purple araçá (*Psidium cattleyanum*), a very acidic, sour fruit that looks like a guava inside.
– Purple yam (*Dioscorea alata*) is a root that we use to make yogurt, or you can serve it raw.
– Purple okra (*Abelmoschus esculentus*) are full of flavor but mature quickly and harden.

1. SPINACH AND PINK LIME

This dish was inspired by the big city, the rush, the lack of contact with nature. Then the poor spinach trying to free itself from the tempura, and growing again in the stone city in the great metropolis.

MAKES 4 SNACKS
SUGAR SYRUP
– 120 ml water
– 100 g superfine (caster) sugar
LIME GEL
– 2 sheets leaf gelatin, cut into small pieces
– 75 ml lime juice
RADISH MAYONNAISE
– 5 radishes, 1 finely sliced
– 100 ml cold whole (full-fat) milk
– 100 ml cottonseed oil
SPINACH TEMPURA
– 200 ml pork fat or cottonseed oil, for deep-frying
– 80 g rice flour
– 20 g all-purpose (plain) flour
– 150 ml sour beer
– 2 g fresh yeast
– 4 spinach leaves
TO SERVE
– 4 slices cooked Canadian (back) bacon, cut into thin 1¼ x 2 inch/3 x 5-cm rectangles
– 4 small basil leaves
– salt

SUGAR SYRUP
Put the water and sugar into a pan over low heat and simmer gently until it has reduced to 75 ml but remains colorless.

LIME GEL
Put the pieces of leaf gelatin into a bowl of ice water for 2 minutes, then squeeze out the excess water. Put the drained gelatin into a pan over low heat and heat gently to fully melt. Add the sugar syrup and the lime juice and mix well. Pour into a container and refrigerate until set firm. Sift through a sifter (sieve) and transfer to a small bottle.

RADISH MAYONNAISE
Put the 4 whole radishes and the milk into a blender. Blend and gradually pour in the cottonseed oil.

SPINACH TEMPURA
Heat the pork fat or cottonseed oil for deep-frying in a deep pan to 300°F/150°C.

Put the flours, sugar, and sour beer into a bowl and mix well. Dip each spinach leaf into the mixture to coat. Deep-fry the spinach leaves for 2–3 minutes until golden on both sides.

TO SERVE
Put the bacon pieces on top of the tempura and put a pinch of salt, 3 drops of radish mayonnaise, and a speck of lime gel in the middle. Top with 2 slices of radishes overlapping 2 basil leaves to finish.

2. FLOWER, CORN, AND YOGURT

When we installed the boxes of native bees in the garden, we also needed a flower garden. This recipe was created in honor of both our flower garden and the native bees.

SERVES 10
FERMENTED CORNMEAL FLOUR
– 8 corn cobs (about 800 g)
MARIA-PRETA POWDER
– 200 g maria-preta fruit berries (*Eugenia candolleana*)
FROZEN YOGURT
– 2 liters whole (full-fat) milk
– 1 jar plain yogurt
– 100 ml native honey (Mandaçaia or yellow Uruçu)
CANDIED FLOWER PETALS
– 10 untreated edible rose petals, carefully washed and dried
– 1 egg white, beaten until frothy
– 50 g superfine (caster) sugar
MACARONS
– 3 egg whites
– 110 g superfine (caster) sugar
– 110 g confectioners' (icing) sugar
– 3 tablespoons Fermented Cornmeal Flour (see above)
FLOWERS
– edible flowers from your garden
TO SERVE
– Maria-Preta Powder (see above)

FERMENTED CORNMEAL FLOUR
Remove the raw kernels from the fresh corn cobs. Put the raw corn kernels in a glass container or in a vacuum bag, seal well, and let stand for 1 week at room temperature.

Preheat the oven to 140°F/60°C.

Open the bag or container, transfer to a lipped baking sheet, and let dehydrate in the oven for 2 hours. Blend the dehydrated, fermented corn in a food processor or blender until it resembles flour.

MARIA-PRETA POWDER
Dehydrate the maria-preta fruit in a dehydrator at 127°F/53°C for 4 hours, then grind to a powder in a mortar with a pestle.

FROZEN YOGURT
Reserve 240 ml milk. Heat the rest of the milk just until it begins to boil, then turn off the heat and let cool.

Mix the yogurt with the reserved milk, stir well, then add the mixture to the hot milk, stirring thoroughly. Transfer the milk mixture to a glass bowl with a lid. Wrap the bowl with a thick cloth or a very thick towel and put into a Thermos box. Leave for 10 hours.

Line a chinois or fine-mesh strainer (sieve) with cheesecloth (muslin) and put a pot underneath. Place the yogurt in the cloth-lined strainer and let drain in the refrigerator for 4–5 hours. The more it drips, the thicker the yogurt gets. Discard the drained liquid and put the thick yogurt from the strainer into a pot, add the native honey, and churn in an ice-cream machine to make the mixture creamy. Store in the refrigerator until ready to use.

CANDIED FLOWER PETALS
Preheat the oven to 95°F/35°C and line a baking sheet with parchment (baking) paper. Brush both sides of the petals with the egg white. Sprinkle the petals lightly with sugar, covering them completely, then let dry in a place without humidity, or place on the prepared sheet in a single layer and put in the oven for 4–6 hours.

MACARONS
Put the egg whites and refined sugar into a pan and warm over medium heat until all the sugar has dissolved. Remove from the heat, transfer the warmed egg whites to a stand mixer or bowl and beat with the whisk attachment or hand whisk until it starts to become fluffy, then start gradually adding the confectioners' (icing) sugar. Continue beating until the mixture is firm. Put the macaron mixture in the refrigerator for about 2 hours.

Preheat the oven to 275°F/140°C.

Beat the fermented cornmeal flour into the macaron mixture and transfer to a piping (pastry) bag. Pipe into a silicone mold. Let dry for 20 minutes, then bake for 13 minutes until dry and crunchy. Turn off the oven and leave the macarons inside for 1–2 minutes before removing.

FLOWERS
Meanwhile, dehydrate several edible flowers from the garden in a dehydrator at 145°F/63°C for 40 minutes.

TO SERVE
Sandwich the macarons in pairs with the frozen yogurt and decorate with the candied flower petals and dried edible flowers. To finish, sprinkle with maria-preta powder.

1

2

Jen Castle
& Blake Spalding

HELL'S BACKBONE GRILL & FARM
Boulder, Utah, USA

Located in the wilds of Utah, Hell's Backbone Grill & Farm emphasizes regional food along with locally sourced ingredients. Chef-owners Jen Castle and Blake Spalding prepare a seasonal and sustainably sourced menu that follows Buddhist principles of environmental ethics, and community responsibility. Across two gardens on a 6-acre (2.5-hectare) farm, the pair grow much of the kitchen's organic produce. Food waste is fed and composted back to the land, or feeds their chickens, which are reared to lay eggs for the restaurant.

When we opened Hell's Backbone Grill in the year 2000, one of our main objectives was to grow our own produce for the restaurant. Not only was doing so congruent with our ethics, it was also a necessity: we're located in Boulder, Utah, on the edge of the Grand Staircase-Escalante National Monument. Our town, with a population of just 250, is considered one of the most remote in the nation, and Salt Lake City—the nearest "big" city with grocery stores offering organics—is over 4 hours away.

In the first few years, we grew as much as we could in a small corral garden across from the restaurant, along with separate plots at our houses. But as our restaurant grew, we needed to expand our growing capacity, so 13 years ago we bought a parcel of land about 3 miles (5 kilometers) from the restaurant. It was a played-out horse pasture without a single tree on it, but after years of planting fruit and ornamental trees and cultivating the soil, the farm now produces more than 20,000 lb (9,000 kg) of fruits, vegetables, and herbs annually.

Our farm is 6½ acres (2.5-hectares), about 4 acres (1.6 hectares) of which are devoted to vegetable and fruit production, and the remaining 2½ acres (1 hectare) function as an animal pasture for our chickens, goats, alpacas, and llamas. As chefs, we care deeply about the quality of the ingredients we cook with and serve to our guests, so we work with our farm managers, Tony Jacobsen and Kate McCarty, to determine what the farm grows each season. We grow more than 130 varieties of vegetables, fruits, herbs, flowers, and trees, many of which we love and grow year after year, and many that are experimental. Our staples include garlic, lettuce, greens (spinach, collard/spring greens, kale, tatsoi), asparagus, radishes, carrots, beets (beetroots), beans, summer squash, cucumbers, cabbage, broccoli, potatoes, bell peppers, tomatoes, tomatillos (*Physalis philadelphica*), and winter squash. We also grow strawberries, rhubarb, blackberries, grapes, and several varieties of apples, cherries, peaches, plums, apricots, and pears.

But it hasn't always been easy. Farming in Utah's high mountain desert is not exactly a stress-free endeavor. (We like to say that Mother Nature is a very fickle business partner.) At over 6,300 feet (1,920 meters), our farm is subject to unexpected cold snaps and extreme temperature fluctuations. Our typical last frost is in early May and first frost is late September; however, it's not unheard of to get a freak snowstorm in June. But our biggest challenge, by far, is the wind. Every year we have several windstorms with gusts of almost 100 mph (160 kph), which have destroyed six different polytunnels on our farm. So: no more polytunnels for us. We grow our starts in a strawbale greenhouse and a converted RV, but the rest of our growing now happens exclusively outdoors, uncovered. We focus on soil cultivation (applying compost and manure, and inoculating the soil with fungi) to protect the topsoil from the winds and to promote healthy plants that are more resilient to adverse weather.

And, of course, having a farm is an ongoing exercise in learning to be flexible. Our team of farmers (we generally have three to four full-time farmers every season) constantly adapts to the unpredictable conditions that arise. When there's a break in the irrigation line, they use a pump to water from our back-up irrigation pond. If peas refuse to grow once it gets hot, there's no use in hoping they'll change their minds; it's better to till in the peas and plant lettuce instead. If tomatoes haven't ripened and a frost is coming, we pull the tomatoes and put fried green tomatoes on the menu. Every year on our farm is different—some crops are prolific one year and mediocre the next. The most important aspect of farming is being curious about what works and what doesn't, and recognizing that there is always more to learn.

The farm is central to our identity. Owning and operating our own farm is definitely more expensive than simply ordering produce from far away to be delivered, but many people choose to visit our restaurant (and return year after year) *because* we have our own farm; they want to eat and support local, organic, high-quality, sustainably grown food. They know good, clean ingredients that have been picked from healthy soil, often just hours earlier, taste better.

Because of our food ethics and the high cost of running a farm, it's critically important to us that the restaurant uses every ounce of produce we grow. In addition to serving farm vegetables and fruits fresh on the plate, we also focus on preservation in order to be able to serve our own produce during the farm's less productive months. We're open seasonally, closing from November to March, and during those months, we're continually pickling, jamming, freezing, and dehydrating, so that when the restaurant opens in March and the farm is just waking up again, we can still serve our very own crab apple jam or "Blue Hubbard" squash (*Cucurbita maxima*) soup. It's more along the lines of how the pioneers cooked, and at HBG, we call it "true seasonal." We also return our food to the farm, so any food waste that the restaurant produces (scraps, onion peels, coffee grounds) goes back to the farm, either as chicken and goat treats or compost material.

Our menu is as local as we can get, but being in the middle of nowhere means there are certain items we can't source locally, such as grains and some dairy. And while we raise laying hens and keep rescue goats and llamas for soil fertilization, we don't raise animals for meat. Instead, we source our meat as locally as possible, too—the beef and lamb we serve come from local Boulder ranchers, and the pork and elk come from elsewhere in Utah. Whatever our farm can't provide, we seek from the most local, sustainable source possible.

We see ourselves as educators. Our restaurant staff are trained to teach customers about our farm and the importance of eating locally sourced, organic, humanely raised food. And the farm has visiting hours every day from 10.00 a.m. to noon. We encourage all our guests to stop by and take a tour and ask questions—because not only is it the beating heart of our business, it's also our passion, and our favorite topic of conversation.

FARMING WITH COMPASSION

Blake is Buddhist (and Jen calls herself a Buddhist enabler); we're a "no-harm farm." This means pests are deterred without being killed. And though we've not gone through the official organic certification process, we use only organic practices on our farm. Weeds are managed using earth-friendly means, and natural nutrients and products such as leaves, manure, and composted food are built into the soil to fertilize plants without the use of chemicals. Artificial products such as petroleum-based fertilizers, herbicides, and pesticides are strictly avoided.

Essentially, everything used on the farm to promote healthy plant growth comes from the earth and won't pollute, harm, or imbalance the environment, contaminate the water supply, or hurt beneficial organisms.

KEY VARIETIES

– "Scarlet Nantes" carrot (*Daucus carota* var. *sativus*)—This carrot grows particularly well in our sandy soil and is wonderfully sweet after a light frost. It's important to thin them when the greens are 3 inches/8 cm tall.

– "Sungold" tomato (*Solanum lycopersicum*)—When you grow outdoors, not every year can be a good tomato year. However, this exceptionally sweet cherry tomato variety guarantees we'll have at least some fresh tomatoes during the season.

– "Ute Indian" squash (*Cucurbita maxima*)—We grow over 25 varieties of winter squash, but this is a favorite. Native to our area, it has thick skin, a small seed pocket, and stores well, so if we harvest in late September we can serve it at our Thanksgiving feast.

1. MINTED PEA SOUP WITH GOOSEFOOT

SERVES 4–6 AS AN APPETIZER
– 1 tablespoon butter
– 1 clove garlic, minced
– 1 shallot, minced
– 2 tablespoons white rice
– 120 g onion, diced
– 750 ml water (or chicken broth if you prefer)
– 270 g fresh or frozen peas
– 175 g wild goosefoot (*Chenopodium berlandieri*), coarsely chopped
– 1 tablespoon mint leaves, coarsely chopped
– juice of 1 lemon
– salt and freshly ground black pepper
– sour cream, to serve

Put the butter, garlic, and shallot in a soup pot over medium heat and sauté for 2–3 minutes until fragrant. Add the rice and onion and cook for another 5 minutes until the onion softens, then add the water (or chicken broth) and simmer for 15 minutes, until the rice is cooked.

Remove the pot from the heat and add 1 teaspoon of salt, a dash of black pepper, the peas, goosefoot, mint, and lemon juice. Carefully blend with an immersion (stick) blender until smooth. If you're serving the soup hot, you may need to reheat it. If you're serving it chilled, let cool, then refrigerate for at least 2 hours.

When you're ready to serve, top each bowl with a spoonful of sour cream and some freshly ground black pepper.

2. PIÑON AND SAGE-STUFFED SUMMER SQUASH

At the height of summer when we're juggling squash, we do everything we can with them. In this stuffed squash recipe, we take inspiration from the surrounding land by incorporating piñons (pine nuts). We call these Zuke Canoes. We use our famous black pepper biscuits (like a savory scone in the UK), but you can substitute with 80 g bread crumbs with ½ teaspoon each of salt and pepper.

SERVES 6
– 1 tablespoon salted butter, plus extra for greasing
– 6 medium-large summer squash (about 8 inches/ 20 cm in length)
– 2 tablespoons water
– 1 teaspoon salt
– 120 g onion, diced
– 60 g piñons, toasted
– 80 g biscuit crumbs, toasted
– 120 ml white wine
– 2 tablespoons chopped sage
– ¼ teaspoon ground nutmeg
– 200 g Monterey Jack cheese, grated
– 50 g cream cheese, cut into ¼-inch/5-mm chunks

Preheat the oven to 350°F/180°C. Grease a shallow baking dish.

Place the squash on a cutting board. Create a "boat" to stuff by cutting off a quarter of a squash along its length (from top to bottom) and scraping out the seeds and most of the flesh from the remaining three-quarters of the squash. Repeat with the remaining squash and set the "boats" aside. Finely dice the "lids," seeds, and flesh.

Place the squash boats cut side down in the greased baking dish and add the water. Roast in the oven for 15 minutes, to soften.

Meanwhile, put the diced squash lids, seeds, and flesh into a pan with the butter, salt, and onion over medium heat and sauté for 15–20 minutes until quite soft.

Once the squash boats are cooked, remove them from the oven, remove the water from the dish, and flip them over. Let cool for 30 minutes.

When the diced squash and onion mixture is cooked through and soft, remove from the heat and add the piñons, biscuit crumbs, white wine, sage, nutmeg, and 80 g of the grated Monterey Jack cheese. Stir until combined. Add the cream cheese chunks at the end and stir gently. It's lovely for people to find a cream-cheesy bite, so don't combine it too thoroughly.

Divide the filling equally among the 6 squash boats in your baking dish and top with the remaining grated cheese. Cover with aluminum foil and bake for 10 minutes. Uncover and bake for another 10 minutes until the cheese is browned.

3. SOUTHWESTERN-STYLE PEACH CRISP

A Navajo family in Canyon de Chelly taught Blake this recipe. In Boulder, we have many varieties of peaches and apricots in our heirloom orchards, and some trees are more than 100 years old. This fruit crisp is one of our favorite ways to use them.

SERVES 6–8
FILLING
– 150 g cold unsalted butter, cut into small cubes, plus extra for greasing
– 1.5 kg fresh ripe peaches, peeled and cut into ½ inch/1 cm slices
– 200 g granulated sugar
– 30 g all-purpose (plain) flour
– 2 tablespoons lemon juice
TOPPING
– 120 g all-purpose (plain) flour
– 80 g medium yellow cornmeal
– 135 g granulated sugar
– 1 teaspoon salt
– 60 g toasted pine nuts

Preheat the oven to 375°F/190°C. Grease an 8 x 10-inch/20 x 25-cm baking dish.

FILLING
Combine the peaches, sugar, flour, and lemon juice in a medium bowl. Use your hands to really mix it well so no little lumps of flour lurk anywhere. Spread the fruit mixture evenly in the greased baking dish and set aside.

TOPPING
Mix together the flour, cornmeal, sugar, and salt in a medium bowl. Using your fingers or the paddle attachment of a stand mixer, work the pieces of butter into the dry ingredients until the mixture looks like coarse crumbs. Mix in the pine nuts.

Cover the fruit mixture evenly with the topping. Set the dish on a baking sheet to catch any juices that spill over and bake for about 45 minutes until the fruit is bubbling and tender to the prongs of a fork and the topping is golden.

1

2

Damian Clisby

PETERSHAM NURSERIES CAFÉ
Richmond, London, UK

In 2002, Gael and Francesco Boglione bought the plant nursery next door to their home in Petersham, which sits on the River Thames just southwest of London. Two years later, after a major overhaul, they reopened it along with the Petersham Nurseries Café—a charmingly casual yet sophisticated restaurant, set within a glasshouse. Respecting the Slow Food philosophy, the café serves seasonal, inspired food, with a focus on quality ingredients and Italian flavors. Chef director Damian Clisby uses fresh ingredients produced at Petersham Nurseries as well as Haye Farm in east Devon run by the Bogliones' son, Harry.

As a chef I have often worked in windowless kitchens, which are downstairs, and inspiration comes from what you read or what you see. At Petersham Nurseries, because we are surrounded by nature and flowers, inspiration comes directly from the seasons and we respond to them all the time. We could arrive at work with the sun shining and think "let's change the menu." It's a very creative place to cook and that comes from the environment, the gardens, the plants, and the interaction with everyone there. It provokes you to cook much more intuitively.

From the earliest days of the restaurant and adjoining teahouse, the chefs would start their day in the walled kitchen garden picking fresh herbs, salad greens, and vegetables before planning the menu. When Gael and Francesco Boglione bought the nursery, Lucy Boyd became head gardener and increased production, planting crops that would do well in the soil or were expensive or difficult to source, including puntarelle, purslane, and chicory. Several years on, the kitchen garden is now overseen by head gardener Rosie Bines and herbs, leaves, and edible flowers, including borage and nasturtium, continue to feature heavily on our menus. One of our signature dishes is "Scallop Crudo," which has finely sliced sea scallops, with green chile, horseradish, nasturtium flowers, and our own Zisola olive oil, which are all quite peppery. We also make a wonderful pesto with nasturtiums, parsley, basil, pine nuts, pecorino cheese, garlic, and olive oil.

Our food is very beautiful; it's delicate and simple without being overly fussy. Edible flowers are engrained into our DNA—we use nigella, viola, primrose, calendula, as well as pelargoniums or roses, which are used to flavor dishes and to decorate cakes and desserts, as well as rose petal bellinis, which have become a Petersham Nurseries classic. The kitchen garden provides cut and edible flowers for as much of the year as possible so we plant successionally to extend the growing season and plant varieties with long flowering and cut-and-come-again potential.

In 2012 a new vegetable patch with raised beds was added and it has grown and expanded each year. In 2015 an orchard was planted, including a variety of fruiting and flowering trees. This gave us a long flowering and harvesting period of mulberries, crab apples, plums, damson plums (damsons), pears, apples, cherries, and sloes. The garden is also home to four beehives that provide us with delicious floral honey.

We are not certified organic but we follow the principles of organic horticulture and its methods almost entirely. There's always been a focus on minimizing waste, so using as much of the plant as possible is fundamental to the approach in the kitchen, and any kitchen waste is then composted along with all our herbaceous garden waste to make our own liquid fertilizer. Woody materials are chipped and added to grass cuttings for compost. The vegetable beds are no-dig beds.

We are in a river basin and the sandy soil in the vegetable beds is free draining, and has poor nutrient content, so we add our own homemade compost to the beds to improve the structure, water retentiveness, and nutrient quotient. The soil in the kitchen garden is rich in nutrients and organic matter after years of lovingly applied mulch and compost. The soil in these areas has a lovely friable texture, it is moisture retentive but free draining. The garden is sheltered and warmer than many other parts of the UK. We use biological controls and non-chemical methods to control pests and diseases. We have also started to experiment with following a biodynamic calendar for our seed sowing, pricking out and potting on, and propagation in general, with the aim of maximizing potential.

As the restaurant has expanded we now get much of our organic produce from Harry Boglione's Haye Farm, a 66-acre (27 hectares) mixed organic farm in east Devon. The farm is still in its infancy, but it's wonderful as a chef not only to have our own eggs, chickens, and lambs, but to really have input into produce, too. We will grow crops that might be very expensive to get from Italy like *agretti* (monk's beard) or zucchini (courgette) flowers, but our starting point will always be the environment in Devon and what grows best there. If there's something seasonal that grows really well, then we celebrate it in the restaurants—when zucchini is in season we will make zucchini risotto at our restaurant, La Goccia Bar in Covent Garden, London. We are planning to experiment with growing some additional interesting and obscure varieties of culinary herbs and fruit to use in botanical infusions for cocktails at La Goccia.

Everything we do in the kitchen goes back to that idea that Petersham Nurseries is very much in tune with the time of year. If you look at the colors of the food, they echo the colors in the garden, and the menus are constantly changing with the weather and the seasons. When you walk through those gates in Richmond you just naturally relax because of the environment. You can while away a whole day there as it's such a creative and inspiring place. So many restaurants stay the same, whether you are there in May or November, but at Petersham Nurseries everywhere you look it's always different, it's always evolving.

GARDEN TIPS
We have been experimenting with making biochar to add to the vegetable beds as a soil conditioner and to increase the biodiversity of the soil. It's a great way to use up woody waste that is difficult to compost, and improve the health and vigor of your plants. We dig a trench and fill it with woody waste and then burn it, but in more of a controlled way than a normal fire. It's covered with soil and then left to cool. When dug into beds it increases the carbon content.

We also increase biodiversity through willful negligence of various areas of the garden, for example, leaving the grasses and wildflowers to grow in areas, leaving some woody compost to decompose naturally, providing a habitat for insects, bacteria, and fungi, and leaving seed heads to overwinter as a food source for birds.

We sow our edible flower seed in small batches successionally throughout the year to maximize the flowering season—for example, planting hardy annual crops in September for early spring flowers.

FAVORITE VEGETABLE VARIETIES
– Borage (*Borago officinalis*)—Vivid blue edible flowers that have a sweet honey taste are grown for decorating dishes or deep-frying.
– "Pan di Zucchero" endive (chicory; *Cichorium intybus*)

A mild broad-leafed endive, used to create Francesco's favorite salad that takes him back to his idyllic Italian childhood.
– Nasturtium (*Tropaeolum majus*)—Wonderful for making nasturtium butters and pestos, adding to salads, and decorating platters.
– Zucchini (courgette, *Cucurbita pepo* var. *cylindrica*)—The restaurant uses the flowers in abundance between May and September for fried stuffed zucchini flowers.

1. ZUCCHINI FRITTI
FRIED ZUCCHINI FLOWERS
SERVED WITH CRISPY SAGE
LEAVES

SERVES 3 AS AN APPETIZER
- 150 g "00" flour, plus extra for dusting
- 100 g cornstarch (cornflour)
- 1 teaspoon baking powder
- 500 ml very cold sparkling water
- 2 liters sunflower oil
- 5 sage leaves
- 6 medium zucchini (courgette) flowers
- pinch salt
- large lemon wedges, to serve

Thirty minutes before you want to serve the fritti, gently mix the flour, cornstarch (cornflour), baking powder, and sparkling water together in a bowl using your hand. Keep the batter in the bowl over a bowl of ice, to keep it cool.

Heat the sunflower oil in a large, deep pan to 338°F/170°C. Deep-fry the sage leaves in the oil for about 20 seconds—they will cook quickly. Remove with a slotted spoon and drain on paper towels. Set to one side.

To cook the zucchini (courgette) flowers simply dust them in a little extra "00" flour, then dip them in the batter. Make sure that the flowers are very lightly covered in batter. Deep-fry all at once for 2–3 minutes until golden brown and crispy. Remove with a slotted spoon, drain well, and season with a pinch of salt.

Serve on a plate with the fried sage leaves and the lemon wedges.

2. SCALLOP CRUDO
RAW SCALLOP SALAD WITH
RADISH, CHILE, AND LEMON

The inspiration behind this dish was the nasturtium flowers. Walking through the gardens, they are a striking color and have an amazing peppery, fiery taste, which balances so well with the sweetness of the raw sea scallop.

SERVES 2
- 6 very fresh, medium sea scallops, cleaned and roe removed
- ½ large lemon
- 1 white radish
- 1 watermelon radish
- ½ bird's eye green chile, finely chopped
- extra-virgin olive oil, for drizzling
- 2 pinches sea salt, plus extra for seasoning
- 2 pinches Togarashi powder
- 16 primrose, nasturtium, or viola flowers, cleaned gently with a damp cloth

Thinly slice the sea scallops into rounds (each scallop should yield about 5 slices). Arrange the slices on 2 plates.

Using a microplane (fine) grater, grate lemon zest over the scallops, then squeeze the juice from the lemon over the top of both plates.

Thinly slice the radishes and put them into a bowl of ice water.

Put the finely chopped green chile into a bowl and cover with a drizzle of olive oil.

To assemble, season the scallops with a pinch of sea salt and a pinch of the togarashi powder, then spoon over the green chile and olive oil dressing.

Drain the sliced radishes and dry them with paper towels. Season with salt and a good drizzle of olive oil and place over the scallops.

Finish with the picked flowers.

1

2

Mauro Colagreco

MIRAZUR
Menton, Côte d'Azur, France

Argentinian-born chef Mauro Colagreco opened his first restaurant in a glass-fronted 1930s building in the French Riviera in 2006 at just 29 years old. Within a few years he transformed the surrounding gardens into "the spiritual heart" of his two-Michelin-starred restaurant. The constantly evolving menu is inspired by the location on the Italy–France border, the Alps, and the Mediterranean Sea, along with the herbs, vegetables, and fruits that are harvested daily.

The garden at Mirazur is typical of the region that stretches along the Côte d'Azur from Nice all the way to Bordighera, just across the border in Italy. The restaurant sits on a hilltop above Menton, and the garden runs from just above sea level, sweeping up to an immense cliff, offering 180-degree views over the Mediterranean Sea and across to Cape Martin. I find it truly spectacular.

The only way to transform that sort of landscape is to have terraces, or *restanque* as they are known here. They closely overlap, giving the impression of a labyrinth and it's a pure moment of magic when you're on one of the upper terraces and you suddenly don't know if you'll find your way down. Originally, it was a formal, ornamental garden of a luxurious villa—said to have belonged to the King of Belgium—featuring fountains, pools, and flower beds, but when I first came here, nature had reclaimed its rights and it was a true jungle.

The garden is at the back of my house and just a five-minute walk from the restaurant. Seven years ago, Laure, the gardener, started the kitchen garden with five containers and it has been extended every year, transforming the overgrown terraces, one after the other, into plots. The latest addition is a small greenhouse we use to grow our own seedlings, even in winter.

We grow the vegetables I love to incorporate into my dishes: leeks, peas, tomatoes, potatoes, garlic, onions, carrots, turnip, beets (beetroots), cabbage, green beans, squashes, and then herbs and flowers, some of which grow wildly: oxalis, rosemary, yarrow, borage, mint, cilantro (coriander), dandelion, and nasturtiums. Each day, one cook is responsible for harvesting flowers and herbs, and for overseeing their transformation in the kitchen.

It's an incredible place to get creative; the original features have been transformed into an edible oasis. We grow mint, garlic, and purslane in former fountains. We let squashes spread in the former ponds, in the 50-year-old mandarin trees, up and over the stone balustrades; I am especially fond of "Tromba d'Albenga" squashes (*Cucurbita moschata*), which grow beautifully shaped fruits and have a very delicate taste. We also use the small streaks of shade created by the balustrades to grow rhubarb and cover some walls with strawberries, or we let beans and peas climb up them.

Menton Garavan, where we are located, has the reputation of being the only place in France where bananas can ripen and this tropical microclimate is ideal for physalis, which seeds itself freely and gives us delicious fruits in winter, or tomatoes, which are a particular passion of mine. We grow 40 varieties including "Green Zebra" and "Andine Cornue." They remind me of my childhood, making homemade tomato sauce with my Italian grandmother using home-grown tomatoes and basil.

Chickpeas, historically cultivated in the region, don't need a rich soil and also grow well. Green peas grow quite early in the season, thanks to the exceptionally mild winters, and our citrus, including mandarins and clementines, grow marvelously. And, finally, come the exotic produce that we test on small plots: for example, we are trying to acclimatize a variety of corn I brought back from the Andes. I love bringing seeds back from my travels and seeing how they feel in my garden.

However, the heavy clay soil and the south-facing terraces, which get sizzling hot in summer, aren't suitable for all plants; we have had to improve the soil for years with compost and manure and we've planted fruit trees to give shade, so we can grow root vegetables such as beets or heavy feeders such as raspberries.

Growing in close proximity to the kitchen you can taste a plant at all stages of its development: cilantro's leaves, flowers, green seeds, and dry seeds all taste very different. And it's the same for nasturtium, arugula (rocket), and onions. Many vegetables, including green peas, also have a delicate sweet taste when they are young. But the kitchen also influences the garden: recently we decided to try and grow strawberries next to rhubarb. They taste good together . . . so why wouldn't they grow well together?

We can't produce everything for the kitchen but each month we try to be autonomous in one seasonal vegetable. For example, cabbage in February, leeks in March, green peas in April, young chickpeas in May.

I love saying there are not four seasons but 365 seasons in the Mirazur's garden. Harvest season can be really short for some herbs and flowers so we need to keep a close eye on them to make sure not to miss them, and our daily routine changes all the time as we need to adapt to nature. We are lucky enough to have a short winter; the restaurant is closed from the end of December and during January while nature rests, and then the garden is productive from February all the way to November.

Our horticultural approach is inspired by a number of different practices including agroecology, permaculture, biodynamics, and natural agriculture. We mulch as much as possible, grow in layers (cultivating under the trees, for example), use companion planting, and we don't use any chemical fertilizers, herbicides, or pesticides. We use our own compost, which is made with the restaurant's vegetable waste and finally, leave wild patches to boost biodiversity.

I continue to learn every day with this garden. I don't really think in terms of failure and successes in my garden, as they are just the two sides of the same coin. Some crops don't work, other exceed our expectations. What's important is the surprise, and the knowledge we gather on how nature works here, in this small patch of paradise.

GARDEN TIPS

Enriching the soil is an ongoing process. The entire restaurant team comes for a few hours every month, to lend a hand when it comes to larger projects such as mulching large areas. We use our own compost, which is made with the restaurant's vegetable waste and we are also experimenting with *terra preta*—a very fertile soil enriched with biochar that was originally developed in the Amazonian basin by pre-colonial civilizations.

Always be curious in the garden; chickpeas are supposed to be an annual in France but we decided to keep some of the plants through the winter just to see. Not only did they survive the winter, but they also are the ones producing the most.

Don't be afraid to plant densely: we plant small tomatoes between green peas at the beginning of the season. It allows us to enjoy the end of the pea season, while the tomatoes take their time to grow, and it keeps the ground covered, which helps to reduce weeds and retain moisture.

FAVORITE PLANT VARIETIES
- "Trombetta d'Albenga" zucchini (courgette, *Cucurbita moschata*)—a local variety of squash with beautiful shapes and delicate taste.
- Arugula (rocket, *Eruca sativa*)—it has an incredible taste. It grows wild all over Southern Europe and was taken to Argentina by European settlers. It has perfectly acclimatized to the garden. And you should try the flowers as well.
- "Dragon Feathers" Indian mustard (*Brassica juncea*): green and red leaves with a stingy taste.

1. GREEN BEANS, CHERRIES, PISTACHIOS

This is one of my oldest recipes and one of the most heartfelt dishes I have ever created. There are so many memories in this dish. It reminds me of my childhood when my mom used to cook green beans for dinner and put some pistachios on top to decorate the dish. I grow various varieties of green beans in my garden and get my cherries from an incredible producer just 20 minutes from Mirazur in la Vallée de Gorbio, a small town in the mountains. The idea for the dish came to me when I grew green beans for the first time in my garden: I remember having so many ideas for how I could use them. I wanted to share these memories with my customers in a unique dish.

SERVES 4
VINAIGRETTE
– extra-virgin olive oil
– white balsamic vinegar
– 50 ml pistachio oil
VEGETABLES
– 200 g green beans
– 100 g lima (butter) beans
– 100 g yellow wax beans
– 1 Tromba d'Albenga squash
– small piece of fresh ginger, peeled
– olive oil, to taste
– fleur de sel, to taste
– salt
TO SERVE
– 1 shallot, finely diced
– 100 g cherries, pitted
– oxalis
– chickweed flowers
– ¼ red onion, finely diced
– 20 shelled pistachios
– wild arugula (rocket) leaves

VINAIGRETTE
Make a vinaigrette with some olive oil, white balsamic vinegar, and the pistachio oil.

VEGETABLES
Blanch the three types of beans in a pan of salted boiling water for a couple of minutes. Drain, then refresh in a bowl of ice water.

Use a mandoline to cut the squash lengthwise into long, thick slices.

Drain the beans from the ice water, put them into a bowl, and flavor them with freshly grated ginger, olive oil, and fleur de sel.

TO SERVE
Place the beans on plates in an arrangement that creates volume. Add the squash slices, shallot, cherries, oxalis, and chickweed flowers, and sprinkle the salad with the vinaigrette and fleur de sel. Finish with the diced red onion, 5 pistachios per plate, and the wild arugula (rocket) leaves.

2. MANDARIN, PUMPKIN, GRANITA, HONEY, AND VANILLA

Winter is not the best time for gardens in general, but I am lucky to be in Menton, which benefits from a favorable microclimate. It's a small heaven for all sorts of citrus trees. However, one year the winter season was particularly difficult and we only had fruit from the old mandarin trees and some pumpkins. I was trying to think what I could do with them when I remembered that my father used to make pumpkin marmalade—it is the inspiration behind this dish.

SERVES 10
PUMPKIN PUREE
– 200 g butter
– 1 kg fresh pumpkin, chopped
– 50 ml simple syrup
PUMPKIN CONFIT
– ½ pumpkin, cut into ¼-inch/5-mm cubes
– 200 ml simple syrup
MANDARIN GRANITA
– 2 g leaf gelatin sheets
– 1 liter mandarin juice
– 150 g superfine (caster) sugar
MANDARIN POWDER
– 100 g mandarin skin
– 1 liter water
– 30 g superfine (caster) sugar
HONEY AND VANILLA CHANTILLY
– seeds scraped from 1 vanilla bean
– 500 ml heavy (double) cream
– 45 g acacia honey
– 10 g confectioners' (icing) sugar
MANDARIN SEGMENTS
– 4 mandarins

PUMPKIN PUREE
Melt the butter in a pan and add the pumpkin. Cover the pan with parchment (baking) paper and cook over low heat until the pumpkin is cooked. Turn up the heat to dry up the pumpkin, then put the pumpkin into a blender, add the simple syrup, and blend.

PUMPKIN CONFIT
Put the pumpkin cubes into a pan with the simple syrup and cook for 3 minutes. Remove from the heat, transfer to a container, and put in the refrigerator until needed.

MANDARIN GRANITA
Put the gelatin into a bowl of water and leave to soften at room temperature.

Pour 250 ml of the mandarin juice into a pan and add the sugar. Heat over low heat until the sugar dissolves. Remove from the heat, drain the softened gelatin, and add it to the pan, stirring until it dissolves. Pour the remaining juice into the pan and let cool, then transfer to the freezer and grate with a fork. Keep the granita in the freezer.

MANDARIN POWDER
Blanch the mandarin skin in a pan of boiling water, then drain. Heat the water in a pan, add the sugar, and stir until melted. Add the blanched mandarin skin. Cook the skin in the

syrup for 30 minutes. Drain the skin and leave to dry for 24–36 hours, then mix to a powder.

HONEY AND VANILLA CHANTILLY
Whip the vanilla, cream, honey, and sugar until it becomes Chantilly cream. Put into a airtight container and place in the refrigerator.

MANDARIN SEGMENTS
Separate the mandarin segments and cut each segment into three pieces.

TO SERVE
Put a layer of pumpkin puree in small glass bowls, make a hole in the puree, and put a few mandarin segments and cubes of pumpkin confit in the hole. Top with Chantilly cream and sprinkle with mandarin powder. Lightly cover with granita and sprinkle with more mandarin powder.

3. TOMATO MARTINI, GARDEN FLOWERS, SAFFRON

I love tomatoes—the different flavors, colors, shapes—raw, cooked, sweet, in a sauce... there are so many possibilities. I grow more than 35 varieties. Every season I create new dishes but this is one of my favorites.

SERVES 10
TOMATO MARTINI
– 1 kg ripe tomatoes
– 6 basil leaves
– 5 g salt
– 7 g leaf gelatin sheets
SAFFRON OIL
– 3 saffron threads
– 150 ml grapeseed oil
TO SERVE
– olive oil
– basil leaves
– fleur de sel
– seasonal edible flowers

TOMATO MARTINI
Put the tomatoes, basil leaves, and the salt into a blender and blend. Transfer to a fine-mesh strainer (sieve) placed over a bowl and let drain overnight.

The next day, reserve 500 ml of the collected tomato water and set it aside.

Put the gelatin sheets into a bowl of very cold water and leave to soften at room temperature, then drain.

Heat a little of the remaining tomato water in a pan and add the softened gelatin. Pour this into the reserved tomato water, then pour 50 ml of that into each martini glass. Refrigerate for 1 hour.

SAFFRON OIL
Put the saffron threads in the grapeseed oil and leave to infuse.

TO SERVE
Decorate the chilled tomato martinis with a drizzle of olive oil, basil leaves, saffron oil, a pinch of fleur de sel, and seasonal flowers.

1

Kyle Connaughton

SINGLETHREAD FARM
Healdsburg, California, USA

Opened in 2016 to great acclaim, SingleThread combines a restaurant, luxurious inn, and 5-acre (2-hectare) organic farm in Northern California. The unique vision of husband and wife team Kyle and Katina Connaughton, all elements of SingleThread reveal the couple's passion for Japanese culture and design. Head chef Kyle majors in inventive modernist cooking. Kaiseki, a traditional Japanese cuisine that focuses on nature, inspires his 11-course tasting menu. Dishes are created using the best seasonal produce from the farm, which is overseen by Katina.

We established SingleThread farm in 2015, a year before opening the restaurant. Home-grown produce was integral to our vision, and Katina had the experience and the expertise, having studied Horticulture and Sustainable Agriculture.

Sited a few kilometers from the restaurant, the farm is part of an historic vineyard property that flanks the Russian River as it flows through Sonoma County toward the sea. Katina chose a piece of fallow land for the farm between the vines and the river, and started from scratch: digging a well, installing electricity, preparing the soil. The farm now boasts a large greenhouse, polytunnels, raised beds, fields, chicken coops, an orchard, olive trees, beehives, and a cattle paddock. It supplies most of the restaurant's produce, including vegetables, fruit, herbs, edible flowers, honey, eggs, and olive oil, as well as cut flowers for the dining room and inn.

Sonoma is in the heart of Northern California wine country, about 45 minutes east of the Pacific Ocean. We are blessed with a Mediterranean climate, with low-lying fog in the mornings, warm days, and cool nights almost all year round. The soil is rich and mineral-dense from the water table of the river. All this enables us to keep growing throughout the year.

Our intention has always been to grow with nature. We employ organic methods, and follow a Japanese farming almanac system that breaks the year into 72 "micro seasons," or *kō*, of just a few days each. Each *kō* is associated with an occurrence such as the last frost or the ripening of wheat. We have adapted this to our own seasons and climate and find it is an effective way to track and respond to the changes that constantly occur in the fields. We can look back over previous years and compare what's happening. The system helps us decide on the best time to sow, plant, or harvest different varieties, depending on weather, temperature, and so on.

Katina manages the farm day to day, sharing the role of Head Farmer with colleague Jonny Wilson. Together they oversee a staff of four other full-time farmers. Their day starts early—at least one person arrives around 5.00 a.m.—and is filled with weeding, planting, preparing seeds, prepping beds for the next rotation of crops, and also beekeeping (the pollinating activity of the bees from our four hives is very significant to the biodiversity of the farm). In the late morning, the farm team begins the daily harvest, which they deliver to the kitchen as the chefs are arriving. They then return to the farm and keep working, pretty much until the sun goes down.

We also have rooftop gardens at the restaurant itself, growing vegetables, herbs, edible flowers, citrus fruits, and apples. The produce is used in the kitchen but these gardens are also for our guests: they can begin or end their meal there.

We use the Japanese term *shun* to refer to the moment when a fruit or vegetable is at its peak of ripeness and flavor. Our menus are driven by what is in *shun* and are constantly evolving to use these items, often changing day by day. At any given time we have more than 100 varieties of vegetables, fruits, and herbs flourishing on the farm but some of these appear only fleetingly. In a way, these are the most exciting foods for us: they remind us to appreciate the moment. Mulberries are a good example. We get only two or three small harvests and the first picking is served unadorned so guests can enjoy them just as they are. As the berries become softer and deeper in flavor, we turn them into a pre-dessert: a kind of mulberry sorbet, with aerated fresh soy milk infused with the herb shiso.

We offer an 11-course tasting menu each day. The dishes are modern and technical, but beautifully fresh: we are strongly influenced by Japanese cuisine but of course the food is Californian too. Our main methods of cooking are in the open hearth or in traditional Japanese clay pots called *donabe*. Dishes might include artichoke hearts simmered in dashi, olive oil, and citrus, or a range of tomato varieties, some marinated in tomato *ponzu* (a sharp sauce), some semi-dried and stuffed with herb puree, all of them dressed in smoked tomato dashi and frozen cucumber *amazake* (a fermented rice drink). We often serve fish cooked in the *donabe*, such as black cod veiled in a croute of fresh herbs, with that day's farm vegetables. Dessert might be parsnips fried in brown butter, with a bay laurel sorbet on crème fraîche.

Just like the menu, the farm is constantly developing and we are continually trialing new varieties. It's an ongoing learning process. Sometimes things don't work out: we've had cucumber varieties that have been too bitter, melons without sweetness, greens that were astringent, and pumpkins that looked beautiful but were ultimately flavorless. Some seeds can be problematic but we find it generally comes down to conditions: many vegetables and fruits are incredibly sensitive to soil and environment. Often, seeds can produce amazing results in one location but not another. That's what makes farming so challenging, but at the same time so exciting. Like cooking, it is about experimenting until you find the perfect combination.

BUILDING HEALTHY SOIL

Our best advice to any gardener would always be to focus on the soil. If you look after it, it will give you great produce and beautiful flowers. We are constantly "amending" our soil. This means feeding it with what it needs, always putting back what we've taken out, and letting it rest sometimes.

Compost is a good basic soil-enhancer, boosting nutrients and building structure. Natural fishmeal is another good feed that we particularly like for tomatoes, which are hungry plants: we save up fish heads, freezing them until it's time for tomato-planting, then dig them into the soil before the young tomato plants go in. The fish slowly breaks down and gives the plants the array of nutrients they need.

Crop rotation is also extremely important. Growing the same crops in the same place year after year can really deplete the soil. We alternate hungry plants such as corn and squashes with less demanding ones, like root vegetables, that take less from the soil. In addition, it's important to understand how certain crops use up certain nutrients and others put them back. Brassicas are very nitrogen-hungry, for example, so we plant them on a patch where we've previously grown legumes such as peas or beans—these are crops that absorb nitrogen from the air and "fix" it in the soil. Clover also fixes nitrogen and we use it as a cover crop (ground cover), growing it for a few months, then turning it over into the soil as a type of green manure.

KYO-YASAI

Everything we grow is really exciting to us but we particularly love unusual types of vegetable that we can share with our guests. We specialize in unique Japanese varieties, particularly those from the Kansai region, called kyo-yasai:

- Kujo negi (*Allium fistulosum*)—We love this Japanese scallion (spring onion) for its long white stem and mild onion flavor. It's one constant on a farm that is always in flux: we grow it all year round. In fact, it is so important to us that its flower is the basis of the SingleThread logo.
- Kamo nasu (*Solanum melongena*)—This is a type of round eggplant (aubergine). We use it in lots of ways, including lightly frying it, then simmering it in duck consommé with mirin, sake, and tamari.
- Shishigatani (*Cucurbita moschata*)—After roasting this crazy-looking, sweet winter squash whole until blistered, we scoop out its delicious, deep orange flesh for purees.
- Shogoin kabu (*Brassica campestris* subsp. *rapifera*)—This is a creamy, sweet turnip that we often use raw.

1. COAL-ROASTED BEETS WITH BEEF RIB AND SIMMERED GREENS

Kampyo is a dried gourd from Japan that is cut into strips for simmering. It is traditionally used in some sushi preparations, such as *futomaki* and *ehonmaki*.

SERVES 4
COAL-ROASTED BEETS AND BEET JUS
- 8 large red beets (beetroots), about 1.2 kg
- 300 ml plum wine
- 50 g granulated sugar
- salt
BLACK RICE SOIL
- 300 g black rice
- grapeseed, or canola (rapeseed) oil, for frying
- dehydrated beet pulp (from juicing)
- 25 g black sesame seeds, toasted and ground
- salt and pepper
SIMMERED GREENS
- 2 bunches (about 200 g) mizuna, cleaned
- 100 ml sake
- 100 ml mirin
- 500 ml dashi
- 50 ml white tamari
TURNIP-TOP PUREE
- 500 g turnip greens, cleaned
- 200 ml dashi
- salt
BEEF AND BEET JUS
- 100 g beet and plum base (from Coal-Roasted Beets and Beet jus, see above)
- 250 g reduced beef stock
- salt
- micro tatsoi greens, to garnish
KANPYO
- 50 g dried kanpyo gourd
- 200 g beet and plum base (from Coal-Roasted Beets and Beet jus, see above)
BEEF
- 500 g boneless American Wagyu beef rib, cut into a rectangular block
- sea salt

COAL-ROASTED BEETS AND BEET JUS
Peel 4 of the beets (beetroots) and juice them in a juicer. Reserve the juice and spread the pulp in a thin layer on a dehydrating mat and dehydrate at 140°F/60°C for 12 hours.

Preheat the oven to 350°F/180°C.

Build up a fire in a hearth or grill and let it burn down to embers. Carefully bury the remaining 4 beets in the hot coals for 40 minutes, then remove and arrange in a single layer in a baking pan and cover with aluminum foil. Place in the oven and continue to cook until tender, then remove from the oven and peel away the skins. Reduce the oven temperature to 140°F/60°C, return the peeled beets to the oven in the baking pan (uncovered) and dehydrate for 12 hours.

Meanwhile, combine 300 ml of the reserved beet juice with the plum wine and whisk together with the sugar. Place the roasted, dehydrated beets in the plum and beet juice mixture and season with salt.

BLACK RICE SOIL
Cook the black rice in a pot of boiling water until it becomes overcooked and begins to split. Strain, let cool, then spread it out in a single layer on a dehydrating mat. Dehydrate for several hours until completely dried.

Heat oil in a pan to 375°F/190°C, then fry the rice in batches until puffed up. Remove them with a slotted spoon and drain on paper towels.

Fry the beet pulp in the oil for about 30 seconds or until crispy, and drain separately on paper towels.

Combine 100 g of the puffed black rice and 100 g of the fried beet pulp with the ground sesame seeds, and season with salt and pepper. Reserve in a sealed container.

SIMMERED GREENS
Keep all the stems in the bunches of mizuna running in one direction. Blanch in a pan of boiling water for 10 seconds, plunge into a bowl of ice water, then drain and press out the excess water.

Combine the sake and mirin in a pan and bring to a simmer. Reduce by half, then add the dashi and tamari. Add the blanched greens, remove from the heat, and let cool.

Once cooled completely, place the mizuna in a sushi rolling mat with the leaves overlapping in the middle of the mat and the stem ends of each bunch on the outsides. Pull tight into a bundle, slice into 8 pieces, and set aside.

Strain the dashi liquid and reserve to re-heat the greens.

TURNIP-TOP PUREE
Blanch the turnip tops in a pan of boiling water for 10 seconds, then drain and plunge into ice water. Drain and place in a blender. Blend with just enough cold dashi to create a puree, then season to taste with salt. Strain the puree through a fine-mesh strainer and transfer to a squeeze bottle.

BEEF AND BEET JUS
Combine the beet and plum base with the beef stock in a small pot. Heat and reduce slightly to a sauce consistency and season with salt. Reserve and keep warm.

KANPYO
Wash the dried kanpyo in cold water, draining and repeating with fresh cold water until the water is clear and the kanpyo softened. Let soak overnight.

The next day, drain and cut the kanpyo into 2-inch/5-cm long pieces. Simmer in the beet and plum base for 30 minutes, then let cool in the liquid. Cut into julienne strips and return to the liquid.

BEEF
In a hearth or grill, bring coals to a glowing flame. Season the beef and grill it on all sides until medium rare. Set aside and let rest for 5–8 minutes before carving.

TO SERVE
Using a 2¼ inch/6 cm metal ring cutter, spoon the black rice soil onto each plate to form a perfect circle.

Heat the remaining beet juice base in a small pan and add the 4 beet pieces, then bring to a low simmer for 2–3 minutes.

Re-heat the greens in the seasoned dashi in a shallow pan and place onto the plates. Top with micro tatsoi greens. Add a small spoonful of the turnip-top puree.

Slice the rested beef into 4 tranches and season with salt. Place them on the plates.

Remove the beets from the liquid and place each on top of the black rice soil. Spoon a little beef and beet jus onto the plates, place a small pile of the kanpyo onto each piece of beef and serve.

1

Rafael Costa e Silva

LASAI
Botafogo, Rio de Janeiro, Brazil

Opened in 2014, Lasai holds a strong connection to its Brazilian roots. Rio-born chef Rafael Costa e Silva bases his cuisine around the ingredients supplied by a rich network of farmers, fishermen, and artisans of his hometown. As Lasai has evolved, two company-run gardens have been set up: a small one in the city supplying eggs, and another larger plot, which grows a high percentage of the restaurant's fruit and vegetables.

In 2012, after working in New York and Spain for ten years, I came back to Rio de Janeiro to open Lasai. I wanted to have the best vegetables we could, so I got to know the local organic street markets, the Circuito Carioca de Feiras Orgânicas, very well. It was clear that I could buy excellent produce but there were ingredients I loved from working abroad that we would have to grow ourselves.

We now have two gardens that jointly produce at least 40 percent of the items used in the daily menu at Lasai. The larger garden is next to my parents' house in the hills, at Vale das Videiras, a couple of hours from the city but still in the state of Rio. It began as a small family garden in 2005, where my mother grew greens and raised chickens, and it has grown to about 2½ acres (1 hectare). There are now 120 chickens that produce our eggs and take up about 20 percent of the garden, also doing the important "work," which is to produce manure. The rest of the garden is used for growing varieties of vegetables that we cannot acquire from the market. I'm particularly excited about growing tomatillos (*Physalis philadelphica*), from Mexico: they look similar to tomatoes but are different in texture and flavor—they're used commonly in salsas, and I like them both super sour and when left to sweeten. Recently, I fried them in tempura batter with spicy sauce. When a little sweeter we make salsa out of it with Brazilian chiles and Brazilian olive oil.

Other favorites that we grow include Mexican mini-watermelon (a cucumber, despite its name), Mexican peppers, and colorful rainbow chard—they taste super fresh and in each season they have different characteristics. The garden gives us the opportunity to grow interesting varieties of common vegetables too: I love the look of yellow and purple French beans, and many of them have exceptional flavor and texture. I have been growing them for a few years and given seeds to one of the producers at the organic market so he can grow more for us. Green beans are very common in Brazil and hence sell the best, so we guarantee we will buy any purple or yellow beans the grower doesn't sell at the market. Ninety-five percent of the dishes on our menu don't have a recipe, we decide on the day: last time I used the yellow and purple beans toasted, with Brazilian organic rice cooked in squid ink, fresh grilled squid, and a herb cream.

We have two people working full time and one part time in this garden, and I visit once a week to pick produce and to plan the next steps on the garden. We may not have organic certification, but there is nothing that we put on the soil that doesn't come from our own production—no pesticide or any kind of chemical is used. It is an agroecological garden.

The smaller garden is in the city. My parents lived in the same place in Rio for 35 years and had a small patch of land next to where they lived, which we kept when they moved out. It is about 7,500 square feet (700 square meters) in size, in a green part of the city and close to the mountains. When my wife Malena (also maître and partner with me at Lasai) and I came back to Rio, we built the garden together. There, we grow only potatoes and sweet potatoes collected from around the world, which means even the "plainer" ingredient in recipes like "Slipper lobster, potatoes from our garden, and hearts of palm" are as good as they can be. Potatoes almost look after themselves too, taking very few visits during the growing season, so it suits us perfectly. The city tends to be hotter and drier than the hills, so we sometimes need to water through dry spells, and we have an automatic watering system that takes care of it. We also keep about 30 chickens there, again for eggs, and to produce manure.

We are very thoughtful about what we grow in each garden. The main principle is not to plant anything that we find at the local organic street market: those producers can do it more easily, cheaper, and better than us. We concentrate on broadening our options in the kitchen by growing vegetables and varieties that can't be bought. When I was in New York and Spain, I collected seeds and exchanged with others so that I returned with lots of different varieties, many unavailable here in Brazil, that I have grown. Since being back I am still exchanging with others, expanding what we can try in my search for new flavors and textures.

At Lasai, we usually have 40 people dining a night, so throughout the day all the little details of the menu are worked out among the 10 chefs that work with me in the kitchen. Both gardens are the main source of inspiration for me as well as the sous-chefs when creating new dishes and ideas—we have a produce-led menu that changes every day, based on the produce available from the gardens and around the markets.

The restaurant is very young, and with the gardens we just do what we do in the time and space we have. We are learning as we go. I ask those I get seeds from if they have any growing advice, and our gardeners have some knowledge, but finding people to work on the land, especially in the city, is hard these days; I'm just happy to find people who want to be part of what we do. I don't know if our techniques are good or bad—we search the internet to get some information in the limited time we have and go from there, learning from our experience. For example, celery root (celeriac) isn't common in Brazil and slowly we are getting the knowledge about how to get it to a good size. At first, we couldn't get it beyond being apple-size, but now we understand it needs more water at certain stages of its growth to keep it developing. In ways like this, our evolving knowledge of growing benefits the kitchen and in turn our customers.

GROWING UNUSUAL VARIETIES

I don't grow anything we can buy from the market; instead, I focus on vegetables and varieties with different flavors and textures. For example, in Brazil, our sweet potatoes are white, whereas I know from having worked in the States and in Europe that other colors are more common, so I grow orange and purple kinds, from seeds collected on my travels and from friends. The ones I'm growing at the moment are from the US and UK. Guests often ask if the sweet potato in our dishes has been cooked with orange to give it that color, which opens the conversation about what we are doing for our customers, too. It is the same with potatoes—I'm growing varieties from Peru and Mexico among others.

Growing varieties not native to Brazil also means that after a few years we produce an excess. I've given some products to the person I deal with most at the market, who now grows them on a bigger scale, which gives us greater volume as well, so it works for everyone.

1. SLIPPER LOBSTER, POTATOES FROM OUR GARDEN, AND HEARTS OF PALM

SERVES 4
LOBSTERS
– 2 x 500-g live slipper lobsters
– 40 ml extra-virgin olive oil
– sea salt
POTATOES
– 20 ml extra-virgin olive oil
– 2 cloves garlic
– 3 sprigs thyme
– 200 g in total of 3 varieties of potatoes, scrubbed clean
HEARTS OF PALM SAUCE
– 500 g fresh hearts of palm, coarsely chopped
– 1 liter heavy (double) cream
– coarse sea salt
SPEARMINT OIL
– 500 g freshly picked spearmint leaves
– 150 ml extra-virgin olive oil
TO SERVE
– watercress

LOBSTERS
Bring a pan of water to boil with 10% salt. Kill the lobsters in the boiling salted water.

Preheat the sous vide water bath to 136°F/58°C. Remove the lobster meat from the shells using scissors, and divide the meat between 2 vacuum bags. Divide the olive oil equally between the 2 bags.

Place the bags in the water bath and cook for 8 minutes, then immediately transfer to ice water and let cool completely.

POTATOES
Bring the oil, garlic, and thyme to 198°F/92°C, then add the potatoes once the oil is at the correct temperature. With the help of a thermometer, cook for 40 minutes or until the potatoes are soft. Remove from the oil and keep the oil for later.

When the potatoes are warm but not hot, peel them carefully using a cloth or tweezers, then return them to the cooling oil.

HEARTS OF PALM SAUCE
Preheat the oven to 350°F/180°C. Put the pieces of palm heart into a roasting pan and roast for about 30 minutes or until they get nicely caramelized.

Transfer the roasted palm heart pieces to a pan and cover them with the cream. Place over low heat, cover with a lid, and simmer for 1 hour.

Pass the palm heart pieces through a strainer (sieve) and reserve the cream (keep the sauce warm until ready to use).

SPEARMINT OIL
Put the leaves and oil into a Thermomix and blend at 176°F/80°C for 10 minutes, then pass it through a strainer (sieve) lined with cheesecloth (muslin).

TO SERVE
Preheat the oven to 350°F/180°C. Warm the lobster in the oven for 2 minutes, then place the meat in the center of each plate with the potatoes next to it. Use an immersion (stick) blender to make the hearts of palm sauce foam up. Cover the lobster with the hot hearts of palm foam. To finish, top with 15 drops spearmint oil, garnish with watercress, and and season with coarse sea salt.

2. AMBERJACK, BEETS, MUSTARD

SERVES 4
BEETS (BEETROOT)
– 2 egg whites
– 750 g coarse rock salt
– 8 white beets (beetroots), just washed and stems removed
MUSTARD SAUCE
– 2 larges bunches mustard leaves
– extra-virgin olive oil
– 5 ml lemon juice
– sea salt
AMBERJACK
– 320 g amberjack, skin on and boneless
– lemon juice, to taste
– sea salt
TO SERVE
– 32 fresh mustard flowers
– 20 fresh mustard sprouts
– 5 ml organic apple cider vinegar

BEETS (BEETROOTS)
Preheat the oven to 400°F/200°C.

Whip the egg whites in a large bowl, then gradually add the salt until the mixture forms firm peaks and the salt is fully incorporated.

Place the beets (beetroots) in a roasting pan and cover with a thick layer of the egg-white mix. Make sure they are completely covered and bake for 1 hour 20 minutes. Remove from the oven, let cool, then carefully peel away the salt crust with a cloth. While still warm, peel the skin off the beets.

MUSTARD SAUCE
Put the mustard leaves and some olive oil into a blender, blend, then strain through cheesecloth (muslin).

AMBERJACK
Preheat the charcoal grill to its highest heat; usually we start the fire 1 hour before using. If you do not have a charcoal grill I would recommend using a sauté pan with some vegetable oil. Sear the fish for 2 minutes on the skin side, then let rest close to heat.

TO SERVE
Season the freshly picked mustard flowers and sprouts with apple cider vinegar, to taste, and season the mustard sauce with the lemon juice and salt. Heat the sauce for 30 seconds—it should be warm, but not hot otherwise it will turn brown.

Season the fish with lemon juice and salt, and place on plates with the salt-baked beets, seasoned leaves and flowers, and the warm mustard sauce on the side.

3. SORREL, WHITE CHOCOLATE, RICOTTA

SERVES 4
SORREL FROZEN YOGURT
– 500 ml raw sheep milk yogurt
– 100 g granulated sugar
– 200 g sorrel leaves
WHITE CHOCOLATE CRUMBLE
– 150 g white chocolate, broken into pieces
– 50 g unsalted butter
– 100 g powdered milk
– 20 g cornstarch (cornflour)
– 50 g all-purpose (plain) flour
– 2 g sea salt
– 20 g regular sugar
RICOTTA CREAM
– 500 g ricotta
– 100 g crème fraîche
– 60 g regular sugar
SORREL POWDER
– 100 g sorrel, stems removed
RANGPUR LEMON JAM
– 12 Rangpur lemons
– 1 liter water
– 1 kg granulated sugar

SORREL FROZEN YOGURT
Mix all the ingredients in a bowl, transfer to a Pacojet beaker, and freeze overnight or until hard. Process twice, refreezing each time.

WHITE CHOCOLATE CRUMBLE
Preheat the oven to 200°F/100°C.

Melt the chocolate with the butter.

Put all the dry ingredients into a bowl and mix thoroughly. Add the melted butter and chocolate and stir to combine, then transfer to a Silpat mat. Bake for 30 minutes, then remove from the oven and let cool. Once cool, break into pieces with your hands.

RICOTTA CREAM
Blend all the ingredients in a bowl with an immersion (stick) blender, then refrigerate.

SORREL POWDER
Put the sorrel into a Pacojet beaker. Freeze, then process twice, refreezing it each time. Once it is a powder, keep in the blast freezer.

RANGPUR LEMON JAM
Peel the lemons, removing any pith. Set the peeled lemons aside for juicing later. Put the lemon peel into a pan of cold water and bring to a boil, then strain and repeat the process 8 times, using fresh, cold water each time.

Heat the water and sugar in a large pan over high heat until the sugar dissolves. Add the blanched lemon peel, reduce the heat to low, and cook for 1 hour. Transfer to a Thermomix (not set to a temperature and at full speed) and blend with the juice of 8 peeled lemons. Adjust the consistency and flavor of the jam—it should be like light (single) cream—and pass through a tamis strainer (sieve). Let set in the refrigerator.

TO SERVE
Put the ricotta in the center of each plate, top with the yogurt, then the jam, the crumble, and finally the sorrel powder.

1

Enrico Crippa

PIAZZA DUOMO
Alba, Langhe region, northern Italy

Creating a platform for the dialogue between guest and kitchen is central to Chef Enrico Crippa's food philosophy. At his three-Michelin-starred restaurant, Piazza Duomo, the chef curates an almost personalized experience for every diner, with the produce from his farm and garden making the journey from plot-to-plate in a matter of minutes. The land hosts greenhouses, vegetable patches, and herb beds where Crippa visits daily to collect only the best ingredients for his menu.

I opened Piazza Duomo in the heart of the Langhe region, northern Italy, in 2005. My experiences working at groundbreaking restaurants including El Bulli in Spain and with Michel Bras in Laguiole, France, where local horticultural traditions guided and shaped the dishes created, inspired me to create a light, vegetable-based menu at Piazza Duomo. I knew I could produce more interesting dishes if I grew the salads, herbs, flowers, vegetables, and even some fruit myself, and this has proven to be the case.

The owners, the Ceretto family, have a biodynamic vineyard at their headquarters, just a few kilometers from the restaurant, and offered us space to grow some of our food. We started with a wonderful glass greenhouse, made according to what we thought would be enough to supply our needs, but the importance of vegetables at Piazza Duomo grew exponentially, and so the garden expanded, the number of people who deal with it increased, and the way of working in it changed substantially. The garden is 10 acres (4 hectares) three-quarters of which are cultivated at the moment. The wonderful bespoke 4,300-square foot (400-square-meter) greenhouse has since been joined by a 1-acre (4,000-square-meter) plot of land, as well as two polytunnels. Our climate gives us hot summers, but also long winters when the temperature falls dramatically during the night, sometimes to -4°F/-20°C, so the greenhouse and polytunnels are vitally important to ensure we have crops such as Asian greens, herbs, and edible flowers, during those lean winter months. The soil is mostly clay, but we keep adding our own compost and manure.

We currently grow about 400 different types of fruit, vegetables, flowers, and herbs, though this number is always increasing. While we cultivate the usual varieties you might expect to see in a productive garden, we try to find the more interesting heritage varieties, too, such as "Corno di Bue" chiles (*Capsicum annuum*), "Fiolaro" broccoli (*Brassica oleracea* var. italica), and "Tromba d'Albenga" squash (*Cucurbita moschata*). We also enjoy discovering lesser-known edibles, and specialize in halophytes (plants that naturally grow in water with a high salinity) and plants with a flavor that evokes the sea, including sea kale, samphire, atriplex, oyster leaf, and ice plant. Using these flavors gives dishes a marine note without us necessarily having to use fish and crustaceans. Our cultivated crops are complemented by the plants that grow wild here, such as violets, dandelions, primulas, elderflowers, purslane, and black locust flowers. The complexity of flavor and the range of textures in vegetables is mind-blowing: plants can be dry, sinewy, succulent, fleshy, or gooey—they provide gratification to all the senses.

Our philosophy is to offer dishes every day that are made with local and seasonal raw materials: we focus heavily on *terroir* and on excellent local products including meats and cheeses, and having our own chosen vegetables, herbs, and flowers ensures we have the highest quality available to us. Over the years, the restaurant's strength has increasingly become the attention we pay to the freshness of the ingredients: I like to harvest when the crops are young and tender, often when just sprouting, which often gives the best flavor and texture. When an ingredient is no longer available or at its best, we rethink the dish: the feature vegetable may be too large, too long, more bitter, or more leathery, so another ingredient replaces it, or its role in the dish changes.

Every day, I rise early to be in the garden before 8.00 a.m., to help my team select and collect the vegetables, herbs, and flowers we need. The team of gardeners and I grow using a biodynamic approach—a holistic, ecological, and ethical growing method where the relationship with the seasons and the cycle of the moon is inextricably linked—to growing food that goes beyond organic. It's a rewarding (though time-intensive) method of growing, that enriches the garden and gardener alike. We plant and sow crops according to their variety and during specific weeks: the week of the leaves, the week of the roots and so on. If you plant carrots in the week that should be dedicated to leaves, they will put their energy into producing top growth as opposed to roots.

Ninety-eight percent of dishes on the menu begin with the name of a vegetable, and the garden dominates even when meat is featured, for example: "L'orto e la Fassona" ("The Garden and the Fassona," Fassona is a locally prized beef), and "Evasione e Territorio" ("Evasion and Territory"), which was created when only the hearts of the radicchio survived the incredibly harsh winter of 2017. "Insalata 21-31-41-51," our signature dish, refers to how many ingredients feature in the dish each season: all are listed on the menu; in spring these may include the regional favorite "Senise" pepper (*Capsicum annuum*, a sweet pepper that looks like a chile) and Malabar spinach (*Basella alba*, a fleshy-leaved, highly nutritious vegetable also known as Chinese spinach, which is usually eaten raw); in winter, perhaps marsh samphire (*Salicornia europaea*), mizuna (*Brassica rapa* subsp. *nipposinica*, a spicy-leaved Asian green), and ice plant (*Carpobrotus edulis*).

In the first years of its life, the garden played a secondary role at the restaurant, but in the last two years it's considered to be a key part of the experience. Guests can visit the garden and those who experience it are always amazed, but even if they don't see it, we hope they perceive its presence in our dishes as a strong and indispensable protagonist.

FLAVORS OF THE SEA
- Marsh samphire (*Salicornia europaea*)—This succulent is common on our coasts. Its fleshy, bright green stems contain a considerable percentage of salt, which helps give the dishes a strong sea flavor. In the greenhouse, its cultivation requires watering with water and salt.
- Oyster leaf (*Mertensia maritima*)—This small plant grows naturally in cliff environments permanently misted by seawater. Its blue-green leaves have the taste—anything but mild—of oysters.
- Sea fennel (*Crithmum maritimum*)—A herbaceous perennial that is typically found on rocky shores and has gradually been domesticated because of the pleasant taste of its tender leaves and shoots. It has a slightly salty flavor and its perfume is very similar to that of fennel. It becomes an excellent seasoning if preserved in vinegar.
- Ice plant (*Carpobrotus edulis*)—A South African succulent with leaves that give extreme freshness to dishes and salads and are covered with tiny blisters full of water, which serve as a water reservoir for the plant.

1. EGGS AND EGG SALAD

SERVES 4
MARINATED EGGS
– 40 g salt
– 10 g sugar
– 100 g unsalted pinto (borlotti) beans, pureed
– 5 egg yolks
CONSOMMÉ
– 1 x cod
– 200 g unsalted butter
– 2.5 liters water
– salt
CREAM BUTTER
– 800 g chopped mixed cuts of veal
– 600 g unsalted butter
– 10 sage leaves
– salt
TO SERVE
– 4 small bunches fresh seasonal salad greens, such
   as lettuce, bok-choy (pak choi), Treviso radicchio
– 4 Marinated Eggs (see above)
– 40 g caviar
– 40 g pressed caviar
– 1 lemon, peeled and cut into 20 x ⅛-inch/
   2-mm cubes
– 4 teaspoons sour cream

MARINATED EGGS
Add the salt and sugar to the pureed beans
and mix well. Put the egg yolks into a bowl
and cover with the pureed beans. Let the
yolks marinate for 12 hours at room temperature, then gently wash the yolks with cold
water and leave in the refrigerator for 5 days,
turning them every day. They are ready when
the consistency of bottarga (easy to grate).
CONSOMMÉ
Cover the cod with salt and let stand at room
temperature for 4 hours. Remove the salt and
extract the skin and flesh from the fish. You
will need 500 g—half skin, half flesh. Cut the
cod skin and flesh into small pieces and put
into a pan. Toast it, then add the butter. When
it is well browned, put it in a high-sided skillet
or frying pan and cover with ice. When the
ice has melted, bring it to a gentle boil and
cook for 3 hours. Remove from the heat and
let infuse for another 3 hours. Drain in a colander lined with cheesecloth (muslin) to obtain
a clear broth.
CREAM BUTTER
Brown the meat in a large skillet with the
butter and sage over low heat for about 1½
hours until the meat is hazelnut in color and
the butter takes on the flavor of the meat
and sage. Pass the butter through a strainer
(sieve), press the meat to release its juices,
then discard the meat and sage.
   Whisk the butter in a bowl set over ice
until it has a texture resembling buttercream.
TO SERVE
Spread the salad greens with the cream butter. Put them on a large flat plate and spread
them out, arranging them with grated marinated egg, the caviar, pressed caviar, and
lemon cubes.

Finish with some drops of sour cream and
serve with a small, hot cup of the consommé
on the side.

2. SALAD 21…31…41…51…

For the mixed salad greens we use a combination of: gentilina leaves, parella leaves,
valerian leaves, watercress, poppy, dandelion, primrose leaves, spinach, Treviso
radicchio, field salad (trusot—a typical
Piedmontese salad similar to spinach), red
beet (beetroot) greens, beet greens, salad
burnet, tarragon, sorrel, summer savory,
marjoram, red mizuna, green mizuna,
Chinese mustard, chervil, scarlet pimpernel greens, celery, lovage, green shiso, red
shiso, dill, raw fennel fronds, and nasturtium leaves.
   For the mixed flowers we use a combination of red, white, purple, orange, and yellow
marigolds, violet flowers, primrose flowers,
borage flowers, cornflower, chive flowers,
and garlic flowers.

SERVES 4
HERB-FLAVORED OIL
– 50 g parsley
– 50 g tarragon
– 250 ml extra-virgin olive oil
AMARANTH CHIPS
– 200 g amaranth seeds
– 13 g instant dashi
– 12 liters water
– peanut (groundnut) oil, for frying
SALAD
– 160 g mixed salad greens (see intro)
– 50 g mixed flowers (see intro)
DRESSING
– 4 teaspoons Herb-Flavored Oil (see above)
– Barolo wine vinegar
– 2 teaspoons white sesame seeds
– 2 teaspoons black sesame seeds
– nori, finely chopped
– candied ginger, diced, and ½ teaspoon of
   the syrup

HERB-FLAVORED OIL
Blanch the herbs in a pan of boiling water for
just under a minute, then squeeze dry with
your hands. Put the herbs into a blender with
the oil and blend until homogenous. Filter
the herb oil through a colander lined with
cheesecloth (muslin). This makes more than
is needed for this recipe but you can use the
rest another time.
AMARANTH CHIPS
Cook the amaranth as a risotto with the
instant dashi and water for about 40 minutes. The consistency should be similar to
that of a risotto. Remove from the heat and
spread the cooked amaranth out on a sheet
of parchment (baking) paper. Cover with
another sheet of parchment paper and
let dry for 24 hours in a warm room (104°F/

40°C). When it is completely dry, break into
irregular pieces.
   Heat the peanut (groundnut) oil in a deep
pan to 320–340°F/160–170°C. Add 1 piece at
a time and deep-fry until the amaranth seeds
pop. Remove and drain on paper towels.
SALAD
Clean and wash all the herbs and salad greens.
DRESSING
Combine the dressing ingredients.
TO SERVE
Season the herbs and greens with the dressing. Place the amaranth chips on the plates,
top with the dressed herbs and greens, and
garnish with the mixed flowers.

3. SEASONED VEGETABLE

SERVES 4
– 1 daikon, peeled
– 500 g white miso paste
TO SERVE
– black pepper
– extra-virgin olive oil
– lemon juice
– Parmesan cheese shavings
– arugula (rocket) leaves

Cut the daikon widthwise into 3 equal parts.
Put the daikon pieces into a container, coat
with the white miso paste, cover with a cloth,
and let marinate at room temperature for
10 days.
   After 10 days, rinse and dry the marinated daikon pieces. Use a mandoline to
cut them into very thin slices and put the
slices on the plate as though you were serving bresaola, curling them with your fingers.
   Garnish the plate just before serving:
grind over some black pepper, drizzle over
some extra-virgin olive oil and lemon juice,
and finish with some shavings of Parmesan
cheese and arugula (rocket) leaves.

1

2

Mary Dumont

CULTIVAR
Boston, Massachusetts, USA

Located in the center of bustling Boston, chef Mary Dumont's restaurant Cultivar has a menu driven by hyper-local cuisine, and a desire to express the very best of the surrounding Massachusetts countryside on a plate. Her on-site, hydroponic garden lies within a shipping container on the restaurant's patio. With innovative climate technology and growing equipment, the container allows plot-to-plate to exist in the most urban of landscapes.

I have always been a gardener and a forager. I live with my family in Groton, a little way outside Boston, and I spend a great many mornings, before I head to the restaurant, foraging for foods such as rose hips, wild garlic, mushrooms, miner's lettuce, and sea beans (also called glasswort). Our garden at home supplies the restaurant with peas and beans, heirloom tomatoes, squashes, grapes, blueberries, raspberries, and many varieties of herbs.

But that wasn't enough for me. I also wanted to harvest fresh produce as close to the restaurant as possible. Cultivar is adjacent to the busiest intersection in downtown Boston—not the obvious site for a garden—but I didn't see this as an obstacle. The idea of having a fully functional garden in the middle of the city always appealed to me and with hydroponics, it was more than possible.

We are the first restaurant in Boston to utilize a hydroponic garden attached to the restaurant itself. The farm was designed and built by Freight Farms—also located in Boston. They are an innovative company who have developed a hydroponic growing system that can be housed in an upcycled shipping container. At Cultivar, the container is located on our raised terrace, and was hoisted into place with a crane.

My farm is fully enclosed, climate-controlled, and can grow all year round, no matter how harsh the outdoor conditions. Each plant grows in a cocoa and peat plug, and these are housed within vertical growing towers, to maximize the use of space. The hydroponic system delivers nutrient-rich water directly to the plants' roots, and is computer-programmable. The pH is also controlled, for perfect growing conditions. There is no natural light; instead, high-efficiency LED lights provide the crops with just the blue and red light required for photosynthesis. The disco-esque effect of these "grow lights" is a big hit with the restaurant guests and adds to the interest and intrigue around the farm.

The farm is equipped with environmental sensors that measure water, climate, and lighting conditions. I am able to monitor everything with an app on my phone: two cameras feed images to me, and I also get notifications on temperature, humidity, and nutrient levels. I do go in every day to check on everything though—it's a welcome, quiet respite from the city.

A hydroponic plant can grow faster than a garden plant because it has consistent light, water, and nutrients. And there is less waste—for example, I find that with hydroponically grown lettuces, fewer leaves need to be pruned due to insect or water damage. The system is very efficient: there are zero food miles and the farm uses 98 percent less water than a traditional plot. There is no pollution and no chemicals are needed.

The beauty of a hydroponic farm from a business, culinary, and menu-planning point of view is that I can be precise in how much I plant and harvest and I know how long the plants will take to grow. I can really depend on certain crops at specific times instead of fearing that a cold snap or heat wave will kill my plan. In other words, the farm always has my back. However, even though I can grow virtually anything at any time of the year, I defer to proper seasonal varieties and flavors. For example, I grow nasturtiums all year round for the adorable leaves, but I reserve the edible flowers for the summer months.

Despite its small size, the farm is extremely productive, giving us 1½ acres (0.6 hectares) of crops in a year. I've learned what grows best and also what to avoid or what takes too much room away from other crops. The best choices for us are lettuces, herbs, flowers, and micro greens. We grow heirloom greens, such as "red veined" sorrel (*Rumex sanguineus*), as well as micro fennel and bronze fennel (*Foeniculum vulgare 'Purpureum'*). Pea greens grow wonderfully, and are used in many of our spring dishes. Edible flowers such as pansies, calendula, and arugula (rocket) are all favorites, too. I also grow several varieties of root vegetables that I harvest when they are only about 4 inches/10 cm long. These include crimson carrots, turnips, and kohlrabi. Things that don't work are really tall plants like corn, or rangy herbs like borage.

I spend time at the farm every day but also have a dedicated gardener, Christina Erving, who plans, plants, harvests, and makes sure it is running smoothly. As with any other farm or garden, we plan weeks in advance for different crops. We can't grow everything we need for the restaurant here, so I focus on it as a means of producing more specialized or unusual plants. We go to local farms and suppliers for other fresh produce.

I describe the food at Cultivar as modern American garden cuisine. It's an expression of New England's finest foods—lots of fantastic fresh fish and seafood, plus dry-aged meats, hand-made pasta, lovely desserts—and the cooking is always informed by homegrown or foraged produce. Herbs, leaves, and edible flowers appear in most of the dishes. That might be yakitori kale with our rib-eye steak, chive oil on our fish chowder, snail toast, or wild nettles to flavor bucatini pasta. Hydroponic herbs even find their way into our house cocktails.

As well as being a hyper-local source of fresh ingredients for the restaurant, I also want the farm to be an experience for my guests. I take diners on tours through the farm so they can witness the entire process, from germination to harvest. Most people are fascinated by it, and they love the fact that part of their meal has been grown within feet of where they are dining. For me, this is a way of closing the loop—I am now involved with every part of my guests' food experience. It is also an adventure and an intersection between the things I love: food, sustainability, and technology.

FAVORITE VARIETIES
- Tuscan kale (*Brassica oleracea*)—This grows amazingly well in our system. We are currently pairing it with venison for the fall (autumn) season.
- Radishes (*Raphanus sativus*)—These also grow incredibly well, and very quickly. We use the entire plant, root to leaves, either fresh, grilled over the yakitori grill, or butter braised. "Breakfast" and "Icicle" radishes are two favorite varieties.
- Viola "Helen Mount" (*Violaceae*)—This pansy gives us lots of tiny, purple-and-yellow edible flowers.
- "Red veined" sorrel (*Rumex sanguineus*)—A really beautiful leaf, with strong red veins running through the green, this is full of sour, lemon-apple flavor.
- "Rouxi oakleaf" lettuce (*Lactuca sativa*)—A favorite lettuce, this has handsome, burgundy-edged leaves and a full, sweet flavor.
- "Thumbelina" carrots (*Daucus carota*)—Like radishes and other small root vegetables, these carrots grow very well and quickly in our farm. It's so much fun to use baby vegetables in this way. Not to mention the fact that they are very cute.

1. FARM SALAD WITH ALL THE SEEDS, ALL THE FLOWERS, AND GREEN GODDESS

SERVES 4
DEHYDRATED MUSHROOM POWDER
− 400 g puffball mushrooms (or mushrooms of your choice such as button mushrooms), cleaned and thinly sliced
DEHYDRATED LEEK POWDER
− 400 g blanched and cleaned leeks, cut into 1-inch/ 2.5 cm-thick rings
"ALL THE SEEDS"
− 250 g puffed black rice
− 100 g sunflower seeds
− 50 g dill seeds
− 100 g black sesame seeds
− 25 g white sesame seeds
− 10 g caraway seeds
− 10 g celery seeds
GREEN GODDESS
− 100 g dill fronds, chopped
− 200 g parsley leaves, chopped
− 50 g oregano leaves, chopped
− 100 g mint leaves, chopped
− 200 g chervil, chopped
− 100 g white sesame seeds (not toasted)
− 15 g yuzu kosho
− grated zest of 4 limes
− 10 g ascorbic acid
− 100 ml cold water
− 1 g dehydrated leek powder (see above)
− 400 g extra-virgin olive oil
− salt, to taste
TO SERVE
− 100 g fresh baby head lettuce
− edible flowers, such as chive blossoms, nasturtiums, pansies
− 4 g dehydrated mushroom powder (see above)
− thinly sliced radish
− "all the seeds" (see above)
− freshly picked foraged greens, such as wild garlic leaves and nasturtium

DEHYDRATED MUSHROOM POWDER
Put the mushroom slices into a dehydrator and dehydrate at 135°F/57°C for 48 hours, then grind to a powder in a spice grinder.

DEHYDRATED LEEK POWDER
Put the leek slices into a dehydrator and dehydrate at 135°F/57°C for 48 hours, then grind to a powder in a spice grinder.

"ALL THE SEEDS"
Toast all the seeds separately. We like to toast our seeds in a mini air popcorn popper: it toasts them perfectly and they do not burn. Combine the toasted seeds in a spice grinder and pulse six times.

GREEN GODDESS
Blanch all the herbs in a pan of boiling salted water. Drain and squeeze out any excess water. Put everything except the olive oil and salt into a blender and slowly drizzle in olive oil and season to taste with salt. Transfer to a bowl and chill immediately.

TO SERVE
Gently toss the baby head lettuces in the green goddess dressing and season to taste with salt. Plate the dressed leaves and garnish with flowers, dehydrated mushroom powder, sliced radish, seeds, and wild herbs.

2. "SNAIL TOAST"

SERVES 4
SEEDED BRIOCHE (MAKES 2 LOAVES)
− 350 ml warm whole (full-fat) milk
− 80 g fresh yeast
− 175 g sugar
− 80 g honey
− 12 eggs
− 175 g all-purpose (plain) flour
− 225 g high gluten flour
− 225 g toasted sunflower seeds
− 3 teaspoons salt
− 12 oz soft unsalted butter
− 1 egg, beaten, for brushing
SNAILS CONSERVA
− 225 g white onion, finely diced
− 225 g celery, finely diced
− 10 cloves garlic, finely diced
− 2 fresh bay leaves
− extra-virgin olive oil, to sweat and cover
− 120 ml dry white wine
− 60 ml Pernod
− 225 g poached and drained Burgundy snails
− 1 tablespoon sea salt
FAVA BEAN PUREE
− 225 g shelled and blanched fava (broad) beans, cooled in ice water
− 120 g crème fraîche
− grated zest of 1 lemon
− 50 g mint chiffonade
− sea salt, to taste
TO SERVE
− unsalted butter, for spreading
− edible flowers such as chive blossoms, allium flowers, locust flowers
− foraged greens, such as wild garlic leaves, nasturtium
− fruity extra-virgin olive oil

SEEDED BRIOCHE
Put the warm milk into the mixing bowl of a stand mixer with the yeast. Once the yeast has dissolved, add the sugar, honey, and eggs and whisk until combined, then add both the flours, along with the seeds and salt. Use the dough hook and knead the dough on low speed for 5 minutes until it forms a smooth ball. Scrape the bowl to make sure there are no pockets of flour. Add the soft butter and knead for 5–10 minutes until the butter is fully incorporated and the dough is smooth.

Place the dough in a container and allow to rise overnight or let prove until about double the size if making it the same day.

Preheat the oven to 350°F/180°C.

Shape 1.7 kg of the dough and place into two 13 x 4 inch/34 x 10 cm Pullman loaf pans. Let prove on top of the oven for about 1 hour or until the dough has doubled in size.

Brush the top of the loaves with beaten egg and score. Bake in the oven at 15% humidity for 15 minutes, then reduce the oven temperature to 325°F/160°C (15% humidity) and bake for another 15 minutes. Reduce the oven temperature again, to 300°F/150°C (0% humidity), until the internal temperature is 350°F/180°C.

SNAILS CONSERVA
Sweat the onion, celery, and garlic with the bay leaves in a lightly oiled heavy-based pan over medium heat until tender. Deglaze the pan with white wine and Pernod. Add the snails and pour over enough extra-virgin olive oil to just cover. Season to taste and let steep over low heat for 30 minutes.

FAVA BEAN PUREE
Put all the ingredients in food processor, blend, and season to taste with salt.

TO SERVE
To plate, cut a ½ inch-/1 cm-thick slice of seeded brioche and generously spread both sides with butter. Griddle on both sides until golden brown in a hot pan on a plancha grill. Spread about 50 g of fava bean puree across the bread, then spoon 50–80 g of snail conserva evenly on top. Repeat with more brioche slices, puree, and snails conserva. Garnish each serving generously with edible flowers, herbs, and greens, and drizzle with a fruity extra-virgin olive oil.

1

Rodney Dunn
& Séverine Demanet

THE AGRARIAN KITCHEN COOKING SCHOOL
Lachlan, Tasmania, Australia

In 2007, Rodney Dunn and his wife, Séverine Demanet, moved from
Sydney to Tasmania, where they transformed a schoolhouse into
a cooking school surrounded by 5 acres (2 hectares) of farmland.
They later opened The Agrarian Eatery restaurant in New Norfolk.
Celebrating local and seasonal produce, The Agrarian Kitchen is
committed to reconnecting its customers with the surroundings.
Many of the ingredients at The Agrarian Eatery come from the sub-
stantial organic vegetable garden, orchard, and herb garden.

I often start my classes at The Agrarian Kitchen Cooking School by saying, "I like to cook, because I like to eat." For me, food is about a craving for the next rush of flavor. After eating in the best restaurants in this country, and around the world, as Food Editor of *Australian Gourmet Traveller* magazine, the only logical step seemed to be to go back . . . back to the source, back to the earth, for this is where all flavor begins. After my first feeble attempts at gardening, it became blindingly obvious to me that man couldn't surpass what Mother Nature achieved in the flavor department. My job was to respect that, not stuff it up by messing around with it too much, so I find the food I cook is becoming simpler, relying on the harmonious marriage of flavors, and balancing work done in the garden with work done in the kitchen.

We moved to Tasmania in 2007 to create The Agrarian Kitchen Cooking School, a cooking experience on a farm where participants could harvest and cook directly from the garden. We purchased an old 1887 schoolhouse and 5 acres (2 hectares) of surrounding land and set to work, extending the small existing vegetable garden into what is now more than an acre of growing space. We did this with the guidance of Lee Farrell, our head gardener. The first step was using pigs to root up the ground and eat the weeds, leaving a relatively clean soil in which to form raised beds and begin growing. We planted a large orchard of 40 fruit trees, including peaches, pears, and quince, and set up five 100-foot (30-meter) long rows of many berry varieties: raspberries, blueberries, currants, boysenberries, loganberries, silvanberries, marionberries, youngberries, and tayberries.

The garden continues to evolve; since the initial set-up we have extended it to include the old chicken yards as well as two 100-foot (30-meter) long polytunnels. We have also added beehives and 15 olive trees. Given our cooler temperate climate in Southern Tasmania the tunnels allow us to properly ripen melons, and grow heat-loving Solanaceae plants, such as eggplants (aubergines) and chiles, more easily and quickly. We call it an insurance policy. Because we are located inland, the temperature here can be up to 43°F/6°C cooler in winter than the nearby coastal capital of Hobart; however, summer temperatures are the opposite, with hotter summer days. In the cooler months the polytunnels allow us to begin sowing seeds of frost-tender plants earlier before planting them outside. In general, the warmer soil keeps the winter plants moving a little quicker. Crops are rotated around the beds and it is always interesting to look back in the garden diary to compare the difference in seasons each year.

We are located on a valley floor, 330 feet (100 meters) above sea level, with a top layer of alluvial sandy loam with a clay base. It is beautiful soil to work and we find it drains well. The main problem we have encountered is that it washes a lot of nutrition through to the subsoil clay. Therefore our mission is always to build the level of humus on top. We do this by creating large amounts of our own compost. We always have several large piles of compost on the go but also we use our paths as a composting system. They are made up of wood chips that break down over time. Once broken down they go into the beds and are replaced with fresh wood chips. We find this is also a good incubator for mycelium, which extends the nutrient area of fungus.

We also built worm farms, which produce a nutrient-dense liquid that we dilute 10 parts water: 1 part juice. We then water the plants with this super worm juice and it has an immediate effect, making plants look happier and healthier only a day after watering. We run the garden and surrounding paddocks according to organic principles—they are free from chemicals—and an abundance of wildlife including frogs are happy to make their homes there.

Where possible we like to save our own seeds, but given our thirst for new varieties we are always buying and growing new seeds from around the world. At last count we have tried over 150 varieties of tomato (*Solanum lycopersicum*). We keep and save the varieties that do well in our garden, such as "Periforme Abruzzese," "Black Cherry," and "wild currant," (*Solanum pimpinellifolium*) and introduce a few new varieties each year. Of particular interest are summer crops that we can use in winter: dried varieties of corn or beans, or crops that do well over winter, such as roots or brassicas.

The biggest lesson I have learned from the garden is not to fight Mother Nature. It is not worth the effort trying to establish a plant that doesn't want to grow in a particular spot; it is far easier to find the right place for the plant to grow happily and where it will produce abundantly. Though failures might initially seem a disappointment, I have learned not to be disheartened by them because from each failure we have learned a valuable lesson.

We began our cooking experiences in 2009, and the garden provides our guests with the majority of ingredients for their cooking. Several years on from this we found our garden and orchards maturing and providing an abundance of produce above and beyond the needs of our cooking-class guests. We decided to open The Agrarian Kitchen Eatery in a nearby abandoned mental asylum, built in 1925. All the excess produce unused in classes now makes its way into the restaurant kitchen along with produce sourced from many local small growers and from the community garden across the road. Both the Cooking School located in Lachlan and The Eatery located in New Norfolk are restricted to use only produce from the garden and surrounding areas. So the menus are directly influenced by the seasons and all the nuances that come with the local climate. Menus change from class to class at the Cooking School and weekly at The Eatery. We could now cook no other way. However difficult it is to cook with the restriction of the garden's source, the rewards are ten-fold in flavor. Once you experience cooking with garden-fresh produce it ruins you forever.

GROWING ADVICE
- To make life easier in your garden, set up a dripper watering system. This will mean you use less water and the water you do use actually goes to the roots of the plants you want to grow, instead of creating weed growth around the plants.
- Get your garden soil tested. This will help you understand your particular type of soil and will then help you decide what your soil needs in order to improve its growing ability.
- Ask for, and heed, good advice. Neighbors, and especially those with well-established gardens, are often a great source of gardening knowledge and they are working the land in a climate that is similar to your plot.

WORM FARMS
A simple way to improve soil quality and productivity is to incorporate the use of waste from worm farms. Readymade double-layered containers for farms are widely available and offer a way to turn excess produce or scraps into garden nourishment. After laying down shredded, damp newspaper or cardboard in the bottom of the container, add food. Avoid oil or animal products like bone, meat, fat, or dairy; as a guide to quantity, worms consume their own weight in food each day. Introduce the worms on top, with a final layer of damp paper/card and the lid. In a couple of weeks, you'll begin to see the harvest: worm casts inside the upper layer, and concentrated juice in the lower layer.

1. ROAST BABY CARROTS AND BEETS WITH CHICKPEAS AND YOGURT TAHINI DRESSING

When I first started a garden the vegetables that were truly surprising were the root vegetables, in particular the carrots and beets (beetroots). The depth of flavor and sweetness blew me away. Providing they are given the time to get started in fall (autumn) they will hold right through winter and if anything only get better with the cold weather. To that end, they are the vegetables we grow all year round. One tip I learned was to remove the leaves when harvesting the vegetables, to stop them sucking the sugar from the roots when storing.

SERVES 8
- 500 g baby beets (beetroots)
- 50 ml olive oil
- 500 g baby carrots, tops trimmed
- 1 tablespoon cumin seeds
- 200 g dried chickpeas, soaked overnight in cold water
- 100 g buckwheat
- vegetable oil, for frying
- sea salt and freshly ground black pepper
YOGURT TAHINI DRESSING
- 250 g thick plain yogurt
- 3 cloves garlic, finely grated
- 1 tablespoon tahini
- 100 ml extra-virgin olive oil
TO SERVE
- 4 scallions (spring onions), thinly sliced
- 20 g loosely packed mint leaves
- 20 g loosely packed basil leaves, torn
- sumac

Preheat the oven to 350°F/180°C.

Drizzle the beets with a little olive oil and season, then wrap in aluminum foil and place in a roasting pan. Roast for 50–60 minutes, until tender. Remove from the oven, peel, and cut into wedges.

Place the carrots in a large roasting pan, scatter with the cumin seeds, drizzle with olive oil, season with salt and pepper, and roast for 35—40 minutes until tender.

Drain the chickpeas and transfer them to a large pan of fresh water. Bring to a boil over high heat and cook for about 1 hour or until tender. Drain, season to taste, and set aside until required.

Put the buckwheat into a pan of water, bring to a boil, then reduce the heat and simmer until the buckwheat is just tender. Drain and pat dry with paper towels.

Pour vegetable oil into a large pan or deep-fryer to a depth of 2 inches/5 cm and heat to 350°F/180°C and line a plate with paper towels. Add the buckwheat and fry until golden, then remove with a slotted spoon and drain on the lined plate.

YOGURT TAHINI DRESSING
Put the yogurt, garlic, and tahini into a bowl and stir to combine. Beat in the olive oil in a thin, steady stream, and season to taste with salt and pepper.

TO SERVE
Arrange the chickpeas on a serving plate, scatter with the roasted carrots and beet wedges, and drizzle with the yogurt tahini dressing. Scatter with the scallions (spring onions), mint, basil, buckwheat, and sumac.

2. CHIVE FRITTERS WITH SMOKED PAPRIKA AIOLI

A lot of our recipes come about by necessity, to use up abundance of an ingredient or to replace another of which we have run out. This dish uses a lot of chives, which are abundant in spring and are too good to waste. It is a good example of how a balance of textures, flavors, and colors makes a beautiful dish.

SERVES 10
- 2 bunches chives, thinly sliced
- 200 g all-purpose (plain) flour
- ½ teaspoon chili powder
- 1 teaspoon ground turmeric
- 1 teaspoon baking powder
- 1 teaspoon ground cumin
- 2 green chiles, seeded and finely chopped
- 50 g cilantro (coriander) leaves, finely chopped
- sparkling water
- vegetable oil, for frying
- sea salt and freshly ground black pepper
SMOKED PAPRIKA AIOLI
- 4 cloves garlic, finely chopped
- 3 egg yolks
- 1 tablespoon lemon juice
- 125 ml extra-virgin olive oil
- 125 ml vegetable oil
- 1 ml sweet hot smoked paprika
PICKLED RADISH
- 300 ml apple cider vinegar
- 110 g superfine (caster) sugar
- 2 teaspoons caraway seeds
- 20 red round radishes, cut into quarters
TO SERVE
- 1 large iceberg lettuce, leaves separated
- 200 g cilantro (coriander) and mint leaves

SMOKED PAPRIKA AIOLI
Put the garlic into the bowl of a mortar, add a pinch of salt, and crush to a fine paste with the pestle. Add the egg yolks and lemon juice and whip until light and frothy, then whip in both oils in a thin steady stream until emulsified. Season to taste, stir in the paprika, and refrigerate until required.

PICKLED RADISH
Combine the cider vinegar, sugar, and caraway seeds in a pan and stir over medium heat until the sugar dissolves. Remove from the heat and let cool to room temperature. Place the radishes into a large bowl. Season with sea salt, toss, and set aside for 30 minutes, then transfer to a colander and rinse under cold running water. Spin in a salad spinner to dry. Pour the pickling liquid into a container and immerse the radishes in the liquid.

In a large bowl combine the chives, flour, chili powder, turmeric, baking powder, ground cumin, green chiles, and cilantro (coriander). Add about 200 ml water—enough to make a thick batter—season to taste, and mix to combine.

Line a baking sheet with paper towels. Pour vegetable oil into a large frying pan or skillet to a depth of 2 inches/5 cm and place over high heat. Add several tablespoons of fritter batter and cook over high heat for 2 minutes until golden brown, then turn and cook for another 2 minutes or until golden brown on both sides. Do this in 2–3 batches to avoid over crowding. Transfer the fritters with a slotted spoon to the lined sheet and repeat with the remaining batter.

TO SERVE
Put the fritters into the lettuce leaves with pickled radish and aioli spooned over, then wrap the leaves around the fritters and serve.

3. BRAISED ZUCCHINI, BEANS, AND PINK-EYE POTATOES WITH SAVORY

Anyone who grows zucchini (courgettes) will know the agony of discovering those extra-large fruit hidden among the leaves. Sadly, many of these end up on the compost as they tend to be very watery and benign in flavor. Interestingly, minus the water the flesh is meaty and delicious. This dish uses the water in the zucchini as the braising liquid. Feel free to change the other vegetables in the dish; sometimes we have used freshly shelled dried beans instead of potatoes.

SERVES 8
- 125 ml olive oil
- 1 brown onion, thinly sliced
- 6 large zucchini (courgette), cut into large pieces
- 1.5 kg small pink-eye potatoes
- 300 g French beans, trimmed
- 1 tablespoon finely chopped tarragon
- 1 tablespoon chopped savory
- sea salt and freshly ground black pepper

Heat the olive oil in a large deep pan over medium heat, add the onion and sauté gently for about 8 minutes, or until the onion is soft and translucent. Season with salt, add the zucchini (courgette) pieces, cover, and simmer gently for 45 minutes or until cooked through. Remove the lid, add the potatoes, and cook uncovered for another 15–20 minutes until the zucchini braising liquid is reduced and the vegetables are tender. Stir through the beans and cook for 5 minutes, or until the beans are tender. Add the herbs and adjust the seasoning to taste with salt and pepper. Serve warm in bowls.

1

2

Alexandre Gauthier

LA GRENOUILLÈRE
La Madelaine-sous-Montreuil, France

Alexandre Gauthier is one of France's most inventive chefs, and La Grenouillère, located near sleepy Montreuil-sur-Mer, northern France, is certainly out of the ordinary. Set in a centuries-old building with a sleek, glass-fronted dining room that opens out onto the kitchen garden, the restaurant is known for serving modernist cuisine. Rooted in his local area, Gauthier works with everything that can be fished, hunted, or gathered nearby, along with the herb, fruit, and vegetable bounty of the on-site garden.

Our garden surrounds us at La Grenouillère, at the foot of the ramparts of Montreuil-sur-Mer. We are 4.3 miles (7 kilometers) from the sea, on the Opal Coast in northern France. The garden provides us with herbs and plants that we use in the kitchen for our dishes, our lemonades, and our hot and cold infusions. It's also part of the visible landscape, from the dining room and kitchen. When the weather is fine, drinks and coffee are served on log tables beneath the apple trees. We wanted to create a non-ostentatious garden—a different version of luxury for our guests. It's about stewarding nature and working in tandem with it, while bringing out the poetry of each season or the light of each day.

We are on marshland on the banks of the River Canche, which flows into the Channel. The soil is damp, and temperatures are moderate, typical of northern France. The landscape is always a lively green, with a diverse range of plants and herbs. The plots are not regular. The plants might look wild and unruly, but the cane structures and bulrush walkways are examples of how the space has been "borrowed" rather than subdued. The garden's designer, Tiphaine Hameau, has a relationship with plants that is rather like mine with produce: there's no such thing as a bad plant or herb—they're all natural and beautiful and wild. You simply need to look at them from a different angle and find some kind of harmony. Our garden stops where our neighbors' gardens begin. I'm very attached to the idea of closeness with your neighbors and living in harmony together.

When the restaurant was being remodeled, our aim was to reorient the house, which had looked out onto the courtyard, and open up views over the garden, the hill and the fortified ramparts of Montreuil-sur-Mer. The entrance is still through the centuries-old farmhouse, via the courtyard, which is dominated by a pair of slanting thuja trees. The entrance hall is still fairly untouched and rustic. The light creeping in from the end of an ancient, narrow, and dark corridor beckons you to the dining room and kitchen beneath two pagoda-style roofs. The space, with its work counters, forges, and chimneys looks out on nature, letting in equal measures of light and greenery. The restaurant is lined with huge floor-to-ceiling windows offering views of the garden at every turn. The space is at once very architectural and very free.

My cooking uses seasonal produce, 80 percent of which is sourced locally from the Opal Coast. We have created a special garden of herbs and aromatics on the opposite bank of the River Canche. Guests are free to take a walk "across the bridge" among the inviting aromas of lemon balm, thyme, mint (including lemon, Moroccan, purple, and peppermint), verbena, black currant, marjoram, geranium, absinthe, thyme, sage, lemongrass, and more. We don't use any chemical products or artificial fertilizers.

Our garden isn't big enough to supply the whole restaurant. We have rhubarb in the garden, but not enough to use in the kitchen, so we buy it from local suppliers who grow more than 100 different varieties. Our 14 apple trees and 2 pear trees produce enough fruit to make our homemade winter compote. We have fruit bushes, including red currants, gooseberries, and black currants. We make jams that are a blend of fruit and herbs, for breakfast. Our bees pollinate the garden and the orchards, and give us honey and pollen.

We also use herbs for making pitchers (jugs) of sweet drinks. I like to use fresh, zingy herbs such as lemongrass, lemon balm, and various mints. I throw in sparkling water, fruit, or maybe a homemade (but not too sweet) syrup of some kind. We have wild marrows growing among the herbs: salad burnet, sorrel, sage, chamomile. Aromatics also include nasturtium flowers and the leaves of black currant and red currant. They are all part of the DNA of our kitchen. We experiment with our home-grown produce in the same way that our produce experiments with our cooking . . . . The same goes for our passion and our energy. It makes us happy and inspires us to try new things.

The seasons dictate what we cook, or rather our garden does, along with the gardens of our local producers. Nature sets the tempo, the rhythm—it determines the colors and shades on the plate. This approach to cooking also affects the way we tend and plant our garden, ensuring that we enjoy the finest, most aromatic ingredients all year round. It's a forward-looking garden that seeks to inspire and educate people of all ages.

1. VEGETABLE ANEMONE

SERVES 10
"SEAWATER" JELLY
– 500 ml mineral water
– 20 g sea lettuce
– 10 g nori
– ¼ lemon
– 3.5 g iota carrageenan
SEA LETTUCE OIL
– 30 g sea lettuce
– 200 g peanut (groundnut) oil
LEMON VERBENA EMULSION
– 500 g whole (full-fat) milk
– 2 bunches lemon verbena
– salt
ZUCCHINI ROLLS
– 5 yellow zucchini (courgettes), trimmed
– 2 g sucro (emulsifying agent)
TO SERVE
– 5 lemon verbena shoots

"SEAWATER" JELLY
Make the "seawater" jelly the day before by blending the mineral water, sea lettuce, nori, and the lemon in a blender. Transfer to a container, seal, and keep somewhere cool. The next day, strain, add to a pan with the iota carrageenan and bring to a boil. Let cool.

SEA LETTUCE OIL
Toast the sea lettuce on a grill, then blend it with the peanut (groundnut) oil.

LEMON VERBENA EMULSION
Warm the milk in a pan and add the lemon verbena leaves. Cover the pan with plastic wrap (clingfilm) and let infuse for 30 minutes. Strain into a bowl and season to taste with salt.

ZUCCHINI ROLLS
Preheat the steam oven to 200°F/100°C.
Slice the zucchini (courgettes) into ⅛ inch/2 mm-thick strips on a mandoline. Roll each strip into 1¼–1½-inch/3–4-cm-wide rolls. Tie them with kitchen string and cook in the steam oven for 2–3 minutes. Remove the string and slice each roll at an angle.

TO SERVE
Put a bit of sea lettuce oil on each plate. Arrange the zucchini rolls in staggered layers and place them on the seaweed oil. Place a spoonful of "seawater" jelly on the side, garnish with some lemon verbena shoots, and serve alongside a small bowl of the lemon verbena emulsion.

2. RHUBARB AND BINDWEED

SERVES 10
RHUBARB SORBET
– 10 large rhubarb stalks, sliced
– 50 g unsalted butter
– 165 ml water
– 250 g white sugar
– 20 g maltodextrin
– 2 g sorbet stabilizer
RHUBARB STRIPS
– 750 g superfine (caster) sugar
– 50 ml water
– 5 large rhubarb stalks
CREAM
– 250 g heavy (double) cream
RHUBARB LEAF OIL
– 150 g peanut (groundnut) oil
– leaves from the 15 rhubarb stalks
TO SERVE
– 1 bunch bindweed leaves

RHUBARB SORBET
Stew the 10 sliced rhubarb stalks in a pan without any sugar to make a compote. Keep the remaining stalks (for the strips) fresh in some water.
Weigh out 500 g of the rhubarb compote into a bowl and add the butter a little at a time, mixing it in as it melts. Set aside.
Bring the water to a boil in a pan with the sugar, then add the maltodextrin and sorbet stabilizer to stabilize the syrup. Fold the buttery compote into the syrup, mix well, pour into a Pacojet beaker and freeze.

RHUBARB STRIPS
Make a syrup by heating the sugar and water in a pan and simmering for 2 minutes or until all the sugar has dissolved, then remove from the heat and let cool. Chill in the refrigerator. Slice the rhubarb stalks on a mandoline: you're looking for strips that are about ¾ inch/2 cm wide, 2¼ inches/6 cm long and ⅛ inch/2 mm thick. Leave somewhere cool.

CREAM
Whip the cream in a bowl as much as possible to firm peaks.

RHUBARB LEAF OIL
Blend the peanut (groundnut) oil with the rhubarb leaves (choose the greenest, youngest leaves), then strain to leave the oil.

TO SERVE
Plunge the raw rhubarb strips (removing and retaining a few strands) into the cold syrup, then put them into a vacuum bag and put into a sous vide machine for 2 minutes. Remove and drain the rhubarb strips, then stand 5 of them on top of a little of the whipped cream, building up a rhubarb "millefeuille." Place a quenelle of rhubarb sorbet next to it, drizzle with some rhubarb leaf oil, and lay some bindweed leaves on top along with a few strands of rhubarb.

3. POTATO, SEA ROCKET, PRALINE

SERVES 10
SAVORY PRALINE
– 250 g white almonds
– 250 g hazelnuts
– 50 g salted peanuts
– salt and ground black pepper
MUSTARD LEAF OIL
– 250 g green broadleaf mustard greens
– 75 g peanut (groundnut) oil
POTATOES
– 6 large Agata or Bintje potatoes, peeled
– 2 liters peanut (groundnut) oil, for deep-frying
TO SERVE
– 150 g clarified butter
– fleur de sel
– 2 bunches arugula (rocket) leaves

SAVORY PRALINE
Preheat the oven to 338°F/170°C.
Spread the nuts out on a lipped baking sheet and gently roast in the oven for 30 minutes. Remove, let cool, then blend to a paste. Chill in the refrigerator for 1–2 hours, then blend again until it becomes smoother and runnier. Season with salt and pepper and set aside in a sealed container.

MUSTARD LEAF OIL
Blanch the green mustard greens in a pan of boiling water for a few seconds, then remove and plunge into a bowl of ice water. Once cool, drain the leaves and dry them. Blend in a blender with the peanut (groundnut) oil.

POTATOES
Slice the potatoes on a mandoline and immediately put the slices into a bowl of cold water. Roll a few slices together into a relatively tight tube about 1¼ inches/3 cm in diameter. Tie up with kitchen string so it holds its shape. Repeat with the remaining slices to form 10 rolls. Allow one roll per person and keep them in fresh water.
Heat the oil for deep-frying in a large pan to 347°F/175°C and preheat the steam oven to 200°F/100°C.
While the oil heats, cook the rolls in the steam oven for 8–10 minutes. Use a skewer to make sure they are cooked through. As soon as you take them out of the oven, cut them in half lengthwise and carefully place them in the hot oil. Deep-fry until they have a good color, then remove with a slotted spoon, drain on paper towels, and cut each into one big piece and one small.

TO SERVE
Reheat the potato rolls in the oven, slather generously with clarified butter, and season.
Place a few spoonfuls of green mustard leaf oil on each plate and put the potatoes on top, with the thin layers facing upward. Scatter with arugula (rocket) leaves and place a spoonful of the savory praline on the far side of each plate.

Robin Gill

THE DAIRY
Clapham, London, UK

Irish chef Robin Gill grew up in Dublin, spending his summers in the Cork countryside, and after working in a series of restaurants with kitchen gardens, he was eager to bring his long-held farm-to-table ethos to an urban environment. The Dairy opened in Clapham, London, in 2013, complete with a rooftop garden that supplies all the restaurant's herbs and salad greens; the fertilizer used is created from the restaurant's food waste.

When we opened The Dairy in 2013, my vision was to create an experience as close to "farm-to-table" as possible in a central London location. We are what we like to call a modern bistro; a place with charm and atmosphere, but without fuss. We cook in a primitive fashion, where everything revolves around the fire, using wood from different trees depending on our produce. I have been lucky enough to work in establishments that have their own farms and gardens, so although I'm not based in a rural location like the restaurants that inspired me, I knew I wanted to grow my own produce.

The garden is on the rooftop of The Dairy, and around 1,000 square feet (93 square meters), and it's where we grow all of our herbs and salad greens. Unusually, it came slightly before the restaurant opening, as our small kitchen team was already on hand and keen to get cracking, but the build was delayed. It just made sense to use the time to get to work clearing the rooftop. With virtually no budget, we looked at what materials we had available and got creative with repurposing. We had some deep plastic trays from deliveries, for example, which had holes in the base that meant they were perfect containers. What started off as a budget-friendly solution turned into an advantage in working out the best locations for the plants—you could transfer them in and out of shade.

We have a simple approach. It's all about the health of the soil; we have made mistakes in the past by harvesting too much, which has resulted in the plant not recovering, so we rotate them every year and avoid over-picking. We also try to use natural techniques. For example, we soak nettles in water and then use the infused water to spray plants affected by fly—it's a way of preventing it spreading. Watering is taken care of by an irrigation system utilizing rainwater. The majority of what we grow has been planted from seed, but the rest—and it's slightly cheating—we source from a herb farm called Foxhollow in Sussex, South East England. Buying young plants is a great way of getting a head start.

I grow herbs that fit into one of five flavor profiles: mint, pepper, allium, anise seed (aniseed), and aromatic herbs. We choose the plants based on things that we struggle to find, or plants that have a short shelf life and really pack a punch, such as black peppermint, lemon verbena, and "Blue Pepe" nasturtium (*Tropaeolum majus*). We also cultivate wild herbs, such as sheep sorrel (*Rumex acetosella*), buckler leaf sorrel (*Rumex scutatus*), three-cornered garlic (*Allium triquetrum*), borage, and onion cress (*Alliaria petiolata*); seeing them return the next year is a beautiful thing.

Our garden is attended to by the chefs; we spend a short spell of time just before each service in teams of two snipping herbs. The benefits are twofold, as we can manage weeds and do deadheading at the same time. I believe the garden has a real therapeutic value for our staff. Even if it's just a snatched ten minutes, it's important to have a quiet oasis available.

The garden very much influences the kitchen, but what I see happening now is that the influences bounce off each other. When you have too much of something growing in the garden, and you're unsure what to do with it, something magical happens that is a one-off creation. A carrot-top pesto springs to mind, and a wild sorrel granita.

What we are doing at The Dairy has always been my goal; the "farm-to-table" feel is very much part of my past. I grew up in county Dublin, Ireland, but my Auntie Emer lived in Mallow, West Cork, with the charming Doctor Miles Frankel at Kilbrack Farm, and I used to spend my summer holidays there. I will never forget that mad kitchen; stone floors, an old wood-burner heating the place, and something delicious always bubbling away on the stove. My brother Earl also worked there. It's now been turned into one of the most respected organic farms in Cork. Living in a city, it was important to me to retain my connection to this legacy, and its progression. The garden helps me recreate that time, and define our approach to cooking.

We've made developments with our gardening practices, too. We used to buy compost, but that all changed when we started to work with Tom, who owns Full Circle Farms—what he has helped us achieve is remarkable. He takes our food waste, and, using a Japanese method known as *bokashi*, turns it into compost. It's organic, and made with a type of fermented molasses and naturally occurring microorganisms that turn kitchen scraps into safe, nutrient-rich compost. He has a farm in Sussex that is currently growing produce exclusively for The Dairy, Sorella, and Counter Culture (my other restaurants). We now also have what we call a guerrilla urban farming set up. Dean Parker (head chef and co-owner of Sorella) has claimed unwanted ground near the restaurant, and is aiming to grow as much as he can from there.

WHAT TO GROW IN A HERB GARDEN
- Grow herbs that aren't readily available, such as Black peppermint (*Mentha* x *piperita*), bronze fennel (*Foeniculum vulgare* "Purpureum"), and Corsican mint (*Mentha requienii*).
- Use moveable containers, which allow you to experiment and see where in the garden will be best for each plant.
- When picking, snip the herbs straight into an ice water bath, then store on a damp cloth in an airtight container in the refrigerator.

FAVORITE HERB VARIETIES
- Black peppermint (*Mentha* x *piperita*) has a strong, very clean flavor compared to more common varieties, so it's a good one to use when you want sharpness without floral notes.
- Bronze fennel (*Foeniculum vulgare* "Purpureum") is visually appealing due to its rusty golden, at times purple hue, and yellow flowers in summer. The fronds are great with fish.
- Buckler leaf sorrel (*Rumex scutatus*) packs a real citrus punch, so is great for adding some interest to summer salads.

1. FRESH PEAS, ROOFTOP MINT, AND FRIED BREAD

Everyone has food memories and most of us remember eating fresh peas from a pod. Sweet and juicy, the taste and bouncy texture alert you to summer just round the corner. As a chef, the last months of winter can be challenging, so the appearance of fresh peas is a welcome sign that soon the crates from the farm will be full and plentiful. Most of our dishes start with a conversation about what we have. This dish, with peas from our farm and mint from the rooftop, was created during a team brainstorming session while we worked together to pick, shell, wash, and trim the morning delivery.

SERVES 8–10
NORI OIL
- 350 ml grapeseed oil
- 5 x 3-g sheets dried nori, cut into small pieces with scissors
- 30 g parsley, leaves picked
- 30 g chervil, leaves picked
- 30 g tarragon, leaves picked
- 30 g dill, leaves picked
FRIED BREAD CRUMBS
- 150 g yesterday's sourdough
- 25 ml Arbequina olive oil
- ½ clove garlic, crushed
- grated zest of ½ lemon
- 1 sprig lemon thyme, leaves picked
- Maldon sea salt
PEA MOUSSE
- 1½ x 2.5-g leaf gelatin sheets
- 500 g frozen garden peas
- 10 g Sosa ProEspuma Cold
- salt
LEMON GEL
- ½ leaf gelatin sheet
- 35 g superfine (caster) sugar
- 75 ml lemon juice
MINT GRANITA
- 2 bunches mint (about 60 g in total), leaves picked
TO SERVE
- 500 g podded fresh peas
- 1 head celery
- Nori Oil (see above), to taste
- lemon juice, to taste
- 15 g chives, chopped
- 100 g Fried Bread Crumbs (see above)
- Maldon sea salt
- pea shoots
- celery pollen

NORI OIL
Put the oil into the freezer to chill for 2 hours.

Preheat the oven to 400°F/200°C. Toast the nori on a baking sheet in the oven for 5 minutes.

Blanch the herb leaves in a pan of boiling water for 2 minutes, then refresh in ice water and drain well. Coarsely chop the herbs.

Put the oil and toasted nori into a blender and blend for 2 minutes. Add the herbs and blend again for 2 minutes. Strain the mixture through a fine-mesh strainer (sieve) into a bowl set over ice (keeping the oil cool helps to retain the bright green colour).

Store the nori oil in a sealed container in the refrigerator for up to 1 month or in the freezer for up to 3 months.

FRIED BREAD CRUMBS
Chop the bread into pieces, then dry out completely in a dehydrator, or in the oven on its lowest setting, for 3–4 hours. Blend the dried bread in a food processor to a bread crumb consistency.

Set a wide-bottomed pan over medium heat and add the olive oil followed by the bread crumbs. Toast, using a whisk to stir the crumbs, for about 10 minutes or until golden brown. Add the crushed garlic, lemon zest, and thyme with a pinch of salt and mix. Tip the mixture onto a flat tray lined with paper towels and let cool. Store in an airtight container for up to 5 days.

PEA MOUSSE
Soak the gelatin in a bowl of cold water.

Bring a medium pan of water to a rolling boil with a generous pinch of salt. Blanch the peas in the water for 2 minutes, then drain. Tip into a blender and blend until smooth.

Drain the softened gelatin, then warm it gently in a small pan with a splash of water to melt it. Add the gelatin to the pea puree along with the ProEspuma and blend to incorporate. Pass the mixture through a fine-mesh strainer (sieve) onto a flat tray set over ice to cool the mixture as quickly as possible.

Decant the mixture into a whipping siphon so that it is three-quarters full. Add two charges and give the whipping siphon a strong shake. Refrigerate until required.

LEMON GEL
Soak the gelatin in a bowl of cold water.

Dissolve the sugar in the lemon juice by warming it in a pan to just under boiling point. Remove from the heat. Drain the softened gelatin, squeezing out excess water, and add to the pan. Stir until the gelatin has melted into the mixture. Let cool, then decant into a squeeze bottle or disposable pastry (piping) bag and refrigerate until required.

MINT GRANITA
Blanch the mint leaves in a pan of boiling salted water for 4 minutes. Drain, reserving the liquid, and refresh the mint in a bowl of ice water. Drain the mint and squeeze out as much of the water as possible. Blend the drained mint with a little of the reserved blanching liquid in a blender until smooth.

Pour the blended mint into a metal tray or other freezerproof container to make a thin layer. Freeze until solid, then run a fork through to break it up and create a granita texture. Keep in the freezer until required.

TO SERVE
Separate the small, sweeter-tasting shelled peas from the larger ones. Leave the small, sweet ones raw. Blanch the larger ones in a pan of boiling water for 30 seconds, then refresh in a bowl of ice water. Keep all the peas in the refrigerator until required.

Peel the strings from the celery, then cut into ½-inch/1-cm dice. Weigh the diced celery and calculate 1% salt to season.

Dress the peas and celery with a little nori oil, lemon juice, and salt to taste. Stir through the chopped chives. Spoon this mixture around each plate. Pipe some of the lemon gel around the plates. Sprinkle over the fried bread crumbs and add a generous mound of pea mousse. Scatter the pea shoots and celery pollen over the plates and finish with some of the mint granita.

1

Peter Gilmore

QUAY
The Rocks, Sydney, Australia

With a menu that reads like an ode to Australia, Quay remains one of the world's most celebrated restaurants. Chef Peter Gilmore works exclusively with artisan growers to harvest bespoke produce for his nature-inspired cuisine at the restaurant, which is set in the heart of Sydney Harbour. Gilmore's own garden, where he grows more specialist ingredients, is his playground for experimentation.

I've been growing vegetables in my home garden at Bayview in Sydney's Northern Beaches, for about 14 years now. I refer to it as my test garden, as it's where I trial vegetables. In four 10 x 1 m (33 x 3 ft) railroad tie (sleeper) beds, I plant new and old varieties of mainly open pollinated vegetables—perhaps 15 kinds each season. I never know what part of the vegetable I will end up using or at what point in its life cycle it will be picked: it may be the young shoots, seed pods, flowers, stems, roots, or leaves. It may be that I use it at an immature stage or when it is fully developed. I evaluate each on the merits of its flavor, texture, and heritage, and I then have the best varieties grown on a much larger scale by one of the three dedicated organic gardeners who supply my restaurants, Quay and Bennelong.

The garden also has space for an orchard, planted into hollow water tanks to mitigate against the very steep slope and poor soil. There are figs, pomegranate, Seville orange, West Indian lime, a purple-fleshed peach, apricots, a Cox's orange pippin (*Malus domestica*) and, right down the bottom, a white mulberry tree.

For mass production, I work with gardeners two hours north of Sydney that have a coastal climate, and gardeners that are based two hours west of Sydney in the Blue Mountains. They have quite different elevations and growing conditions, which allows me to extend the seasons and produce different vegetables that are suited to the different climates. I also work closely with a farmer based in Byron Bay who has a more subtropical climate that allows for more exotic vegetables like bamboo shoots, angled gourds, and snake beans. They practice organic principles, two of them have a no-dig policy, and each aims to be sustainable and practice composting, worm farming, and other related techniques.

Working closely with these farmers to supply my restaurants requires a lot of advance planning and commitment, and that is where my own garden comes into its element. For example, if I wish to put my "Tennouji white turnip, blue swimmer crab, and Jersey Wakefield cabbage with fermented cabbage juice and brown butter dressing" dish on the menu, I have to commit in advance to the numbers of that heirloom turnip I require, give specifications of the size I would like them grown to and for how long I intend to keep them on the menu. At Quay I would be looking at 1,000 turnips per week, so it is necessary for me to be planning my menus up to two seasons in advance to ensure supply. Each grower may be supplying me with several vegetables, herbs, and flowers each season, and sowing to harvest can take anywhere between 6 and 15 weeks depending on the vegetable: this process is not an exact science and if you want to work this way you have to be flexible, you have to understand that there will be crop failures and weather issues, but the rewards of growing in this bespoke manner are clear in flavor,

quality, and uniqueness, and far outweigh the negatives. The biggest benefit is working with like-minded passionate growers on a personal level that gives greater meaning and value to your produce.

My home garden has been a great source of inspiration for me over the years. I feel it has connected me to nature in a far deeper and more meaningful way. Observing the life cycle of plants and appreciating how wonderful the process of nature is has informed and influenced my cuisine. I find the garden is a place where I can meditate and be inspired to create new dishes. Growing vegetables has also given me an appreciation of the effort my farmers, producers, and suppliers go to: it makes you want to respect the ingredients even more and bring out the best in them.

Working in this way allows me to use any part of the plants from their different stages of life: it may be that I use the flowers and the immature shoots in a dish, or I might leave the vegetable to go to seed and use the seed pods. In my "Lamborn peas, green miso, and lemon" recipe, for example, I use pods, growing tips, and flowers from the pea plant. It's not always about when the vegetable is at full maturity; often it is while reaching maturity that it's the most tender and the shoots are the most flavorsome.

With gardening in general, I think you are also learning. The biggest successes are crops that are rare and not available in the general market place, ones that have a unique flavor, texture, or appearance. One of my great passions is growing heirloom vegetables. "Red Kyoto" carrots (*Daucus carota* subsp. *sativus*), "Country Gentleman" corn (*Zea mays*), Italian black chickpeas (*Cicer arietinum*), and "Burback" white sprouting broccoli (*Brassica oleracea* Italica Group) are among the many varieties that are no longer grown commercially and I find it exciting to rediscover them. Many yield as highly as the modern varieties but they often have a unique appearance, color, flavor, and texture. They could easily be lost unless they are grown and appreciated by passionate gardeners: some have been saved from extinction by just one area, a single valley, or even an individual or family. If a vegetable is not grown each year and its seeds saved, the genetics that may have taken hundreds of years to develop through chance happenings of nature or observation and selection by man could be lost in no time.

Uniqueness, diversity, flavor, and heritage is at stake. Chefs and cooks can play an important role here by keeping these unique vegetables alive on our menus and our guests appreciating their unique qualities. There is a trickle-down effect to promoting these heirlooms: customers and the wider public start asking for them at farmers' markets, passionate home gardeners seek the seeds out from specialist seed companies around the world. These vegetables are our shared cultural and culinary inheritance and it is up to us to preserve them.

SUCCESSIONAL HARVESTS
You can plan to grow either for gluts—large harvests, ready at once—or successionally, where the crop comes in a steady supply over a longer period: the latter takes careful planning. For example, my growers in the Blue Mountains, Epicurean Harvest, will sow every two weeks to maintain the steady supply of fava (broad) beans through late spring and early summer; as one batch of plants becomes tired, there are more to follow.

GARDEN TIPS
Of course, gardening is a learning process. I wish I had realized the importance of composting early on; I believe it really is so important to the health of your garden. Crop rotation is vital too, so that you aren't growing the same variety in the same bed year after year as you will strip that bed's nutrients and increase the risk of diseases. Mulching is similarly important as it not only helps build and enrich the soil, but also keeps the soil at the right moisture level for the particular vegetable.

FAVORITE HERITAGE VARIETIES
These two have particularly interesting colors, flavors, and textures:
- White sprouting broccoli (*Brassica oleracea* Italica Group), while similar to other sprouting broccoli, is much more tender and delicate in flavor.
- "Red Kyoto" carrots (*Daucus carota* subsp. *sativus*) have an intense red color and dense texture that means you can cook them for longer without them breaking up.

1. LAMBORN PEAS, GREEN MISO, LEMON

The late Dr Calvin Lamborn developed nu-
merous new varieties of peas throughout his
career. These pea varieties are only available
from a few specialized growers around the
world and they are grown under licence by
the Lamborn family. In this recipe I use two
varieties: the speckled red variety and the
Lamborn snap peas. This salad is placed on
a bed of green soy miso with unsalted butter,
lemon zest, and dehydrated anchovy sauce.

SERVES 2
– 16 Lamborn snap pea pods
– 2 teaspoons Korean green soybean miso
  paste (doenjang) or other high-quality miso
– 4 teaspoons softened unsalted butter
– pinch of dehydrated anchovy sauce
– grated zest of ½ lemon
– 24 red speckled snow peas (mangetout),
  trimmed
– 8 Lamborn pea shoots
– 4 teaspoons extra-virgin olive oil
– 12 red speckled snow pea flowers

Shell the Lamborn snap pea pods. Blanch
the peas in a pan of boiling water for 10 seconds, then remove and refresh in a bowl of
ice water.

Mix the miso paste, butter, anchovy
sauce, and lemon zest together in a bowl,
then spread out on 2 serving plates.

Place the blanched peas on top of the
miso, dress the snow peas (mangetout)
and pea shoots in the extra-virgin olive oil,
then place them on top of the peas and
miso. Garnish with the red speckled snow
pea flowers and serve.

2. TENNOUJI WHITE TURNIP, BLUE SWIMMER CRAB, AND JERSEY WAKEFIELD CABBAGE WITH FERMENTED CABBAGE JUICE AND BROWN BUTTER DRESSING

This recipe features heirloom Tennouji kabu
white turnips and Jersey Wakefield cabbage
accompanied by blue swimmer crab claw
meat and a dressing made from fermented
cabbage leaves and brown butter. The dish
is about the purity of flavors and unique
textures of the white turnip and Wakefield
cabbage stems.

SERVES 4
– 1 Jersey Wakefield cabbage
– 4 Tennouji white turnips
– 2 x 800 g live blue swimmer crabs
– 50 g unsalted butter, melted
– fine sea salt
BROWN BUTTER
– 100 g salted butter

Four days before you want to serve the dish,
remove and discard a couple of the outer
green layers of the cabbage. Peel away another 6 or 7 layers of the cabbage, reserving
the heart. Wrap the heart in plastic wrap (clingfilm) and store in the refrigerator. Weigh
out 200 g of the cabbage leaves, place them
in a vacuum bag, and add 4 g of sea salt. Seal
the bag and leave out at room temperature
for 4 days to enable fermentation.

After the cabbage leaves have been fermenting for 4 days, remove the plastic wrap
from the reserved cabbage heart, cut it in
half, and peel away 4 central stems with
some leaf attached. This part of the cabbage
should be pure white in color and very tender.

Peel the white turnips and cut a central
disk from each turnip about 1¼ inches/3 cm
thick. Set them to one side.

Place the live swimmer crabs in a large
tub of ice water for 15 minutes to numb them,
and bring a large saucepan of salted water to
the boil. After they have had 15 minutes in the
ice water, immediately transfer the crabs to
the boiling water. Blanch for 4 minutes, then
transfer the crabs back to the tub of ice water to cool. Crack the shells and remove the
meat from the claws. Reserve the meat from
the rest of the crab for another use.

BROWN BUTTER
Place the butter into a medium pan over
high heat until the butter starts to brown.
Pour off the butter, leaving behind the solids.
Remove any scum off the top of the butter
and let cool.

Open the fermented cabbage bag and
squeeze all of the juice from the cabbage
into a small pan. Place over high heat and

let it boil until reduced by half, then beat in
the brown butter, remove from the heat and
set aside.

Set up a steamer over a pan of boiling
water. Heat a nonstick skillet or grill in preparation for the cabbage. Place the disks of
Tennouji turnips in the steamer and steam
for 3 minutes. Place the crab claw meat in
the steamer for about 1 minute, to reheat
and finish cooking. Lightly brush some of
the melted butter on the cabbage stems
and briefly pan-fry or grill.

TO SERVE
Brush the steamed white turnip slices with
the remaining melted butter and season
with sea salt. Place the white turnip slices, grilled cabbage stems, and crab claw
meat on each serving plate. Dress with the
fermented cabbage juice and brown butter
and serve.

1

Bertrand Grébaut

D'UNE ÎLE
Rémalard, Normandy, France

Far from an island, as its name suggests, French country house D'une Île lies southwest of Paris in Normandy, in the stunning yet relatively unspoilt conservation area of Le Perche. Surrounded by woodland, the restaurant sources its ingredients from local farms and markets, as well as its own kitchen garden; as a result, chef Bertrand Grébaut's menu abounds with local, seasonal, and sustainable produce, with all the rustic charm of its rural location.

D'une Île is a country guesthouse with eight bedrooms, and a restaurant seating 25 guests. We arrived here in spring 2018. Moving to the Basse-Normandie region seemed like the most natural thing in the world for us. The Perche Nature Reserve is only a two-hour drive from Paris: when you come off the motorway, you suddenly find yourself in a thriving, market-garden region, full of committed small producers growing fruit and vegetables, and dairy farmers firmly rooted in a true farming tradition. The farmhouse stands on the edge of a wood and is built in yellow stone dating back to the seventeenth century, lovingly renovated by the two previous owners. The property is surrounded by 20 acres (8 hectares) of land, which used to produce cider apples and grain crops, and where cattle once grazed.

D'une Île is our own small patch of countryside: it represents these woods where we pick wild blackberries, elderberries, and sweet vernal grass; it is our orchard where old varieties of cherries, apples, and pears grow, these fields that we sickle once a year. We also have our own beehives and we grow champignons de Paris (white button) mushrooms in the old cider cellar. The kitchen garden lies right at the heart of the property. It has been there since the farm was first built. It's the ideal spot: on a slight incline, well drained, south-facing, standing beneath a large tree to provide shade in the mornings. A dry-stone wall runs along one side of the garden, stores all the heat absorbed in the day, then gently radiates it back out at night. To make the most of these balmy conditions, our project for next year is to plant small fruits along the garden wall, such as raspberries, black currants, and red currants.

The Perche region has a cold, changeable climate: the whole area is acidic and damp. Our fig trees only produce leaves—which luckily we love, as their flavor works wonders infused in *îles flottantes* (floating islands) or vegetable *velouté*. We grow all our produce outdoors in the open air, which means we are forced to plant quite late in the year, starting in February for the first turnips. So we are thinking of building a greenhouse on one of the meadows to grow our seedlings, and keep harvesting right up into the cold season.

The whole team worked together on designing the garden, which is divided into five main plots of raised soil beds. Our approach is based on permaculture. To avoid soil erosion we have set up an annual "crop rotation" system for four of the plots—namely, every year we leave one plot fallow to rest for growing flowers, while the other three plots are planted with vegetable crops and the fifth is permanently kept aside for testing out different varieties.

We follow the natural cycle of the seasons: from spring through to fall (autumn) we produce leafy vegetables such as Swiss chard, sorrel, and cabbage; come summer, it is time to pick the fruit vegetables such as zucchini (courgettes) and eggplants (aubergines). Finally, we produce root vegetables, such as potatoes, to help keep us going through the winter. We also have two raised planters where we grow 20 or so different aromatic herbs, such as savory, basil, and lovage, to name but a few.

As far as first years go, we have been extremely lucky: we had an unprecedentedly warm and sunny summer, and the garden grew at an incredible rate. Our zucchinis and tomatoes did particularly well; however, our cabbages did very badly, having been attacked by the cruciferous flea beetle and slugs, before deer came along and dealt the final blow: we produced next to nothing.

I have always dreamed of having a little place where I could connect with nature, ever since 2006, the year I began working for chef Alain Passard at L'Arpège, just as he was becoming practically self-sufficient, sourcing his ingredients almost solely from his gardens. Whereas at our restaurants in Paris—Septime and Clamato—the menus are often thought up in our offices, at D'une Île the menus are inspired by a stroll through the gardens. Our eye will fall on some "Jack Be Little" pumpkins (*Cucurbita pepo*) that are just ripe, and we'll have some dried sweet vernal grass—just what we need to infuse a soup. Some new beets (beetroots) will be ripening at the same time as the black currants, whose purple tones blend perfectly in a crunchy salad.

It is a whole interplay of harmony, ripening, and colors, where vegetables that grow well together also complement each other on a plate. It is natural, common sense. This is raw, no-frills cuisine with authentic ingredients and we ensure our menus give pride of place to the Perche region and all its natural wealth. The menus change less frequently than in our Paris restaurants because they take their cue from developments in the garden. Here, we follow the slow pace of nature. Our kitchen garden provides a constraint that is an unfailing springboard for creativity, continuously forcing us to come up with new recipes but also new ways to conserve surplus fruit and vegetables or make up for a shortage of produce in the winter.

Our garden continues a long tradition that goes back generations of supplying the needs of the household, even if today the people who tend the garden are no longer those who eat at the table. When we first arrived, the land had long been left to its own devices. All we did was to bring it back to life, and expand it. The kitchen garden is only 6,458 square feet (600 square meters), but that is enough for us: we have never been so bold as to try to be fully self-sufficient; however, we do aim to ensure that the garden graces the plates of our 25 guests. The restaurant is small enough to allow us to garden with an eye to abundance rather than productivity, while still using natural techniques such as hand-weeding, without applying any chemical treatments or using heavy machinery.

It will take another four to five years for the garden to fully come into its own. We have a lot to learn from all the farmers who have been here for years: in the short time we've been in the Perche, we have tasted more vegetables than we could have ever imagined. And it is only the beginning. Here at D'une Île we are still laying down our roots.

TIPS FOR GARDENING WITH RAISED BEDS
- On small areas such as ours, follow the key principles of permaculture, especially companion planting: plant carrots at the foot of tomato plants, and co-plant radishes, lettuces, and leeks in the same bed.
- Straw mulch: this brings undeniable benefits, namely helping the soil to hold in moisture so you don't have to water as often, plus staving off weeds.
- Treat weeds as your allies: we use chickweed and wood sorrel to liven up a mesclun salad. And don't let any part of your vegetables go to waste: beet (beetroot) greens work well with pickles, green celery leaves are good in salad, and radish and carrot leaves make great soups.

FAVORITE VEGETABLE VARIETIES
- Red sorrel (*Rumex acetosella*)—This plant produces very little, but it is low-maintenance and grows back several times between spring and fall (autumn). With a strong acidic taste, it is a delight wilted in semi-salted butter.
- "Rouge Crapaudine" beet (beetroot, *Beta vulgaris*)—This variety is ready to pick later in the year compared to other beets, and is a robust vegetable that is easy to grow. We particularly like its almost meaty flesh, and we cook it with marrowbone, roasted and smoked.
- Lovage—This is an old kitchen garden variety, also known as perennial celery. It is a hardy plant that flourishes at high altitudes. We prefer using it at the end of the summer for its anise seed aroma that is almost crustacean-like. We use it to infuse our creams and stocks.
- "Monarch" celery root (celeriac, *Apium graveolens* var. *rapaceum*)—The moment this vegetable matures, it sounds the start of the fall season. Planted in July, it can grow 6 inches/15 cm in diameter by the end of September. We like using it as an ingredient when it is still quite young and tender, whole-roasted in the oven in the last leaves from the fig tree, and then sautéed until caramelized.

1. CAULIFLOWER IN BUTTER-GLAZED BRIOCHE WITH FRESH AND DRIED SEEDS, BERRIES, AND HERBS

The wild garlic seeds need to be pickled at least a month before you make the dish, and the lacto-fermented red currants up to three weeks ahead.

SERVES 6
PICKLED WILD GARLIC CAPERS
– 60 g wild garlic seeds, picked a few days after the blossom has come out
– sea salt, to cover
– 15 g bouquet of aromatic herbs, such as thyme, laurel, and tarragon
– apple cider vinegar, to cover
LACTO-FERMENTED RED CURRANTS
– 120 g red currants
– spring water, to cover
– sea salt
BRIOCHE DOUGH
– 6 eggs, plus 1 egg, beaten, for glazing
– 50 g granulated sugar
– 8 g salt
– 380 g all-purpose (plain) flour, plus extra for dusting
– 10 g fresh yeast
– 300 g softened unsalted butter, diced
CAULIFLOWER
– 600 g cauliflower
– 50 g unsalted butter, plus extra (melted) for glazing and frying
– 50 g whole grain mustard
– fleur de sel
TO SERVE
– 20 g parsley seeds
– 60 g Lacto-fermented Red Currants (see above)
– 60 g Pickled Wild Garlic Capers (see above)
– 20 g leek flowers in bud
– 20 g marjoram flowers
– 100 ml canola (rapeseed) oil

PICKLED WILD GARLIC CAPERS
Immerse the wild garlic seeds in salt for 12 hours, then rinse off the salt with clean water and dry the seeds. Put the dry seeds in a clean glass jar, add a bouquet of aromatic herbs and cover with vinegar. Seal and store for at least 1 month at 59°F/15°C before using.

LACTO-FERMENTED RED CURRANTS
Fill two-thirds of a 200 ml glass jar with red currants, then fill to the top with spring water and add 2% of the total weight in salt. Cover with the lid and let ferment for 3 days at 72°F/22°C, then transfer to a cool place (59–64°F/15–18°C) for a minimum of 3 weeks.

BRIOCHE DOUGH
To prepare the dough, put the eggs, sugar, and salt into the bowl of a stand mixer, beat, then gradually add the flour and crumble in the yeast and whisk again at medium speed for about 10 minutes. Fold in the softened, diced butter and knead with the dough hook for another 5 minutes until the dough has a supple, even texture. Cover the bowl with a cloth and let the dough rise for 30 minutes at room temperature, then knock it back and put it in the refrigerator to rise overnight.

CAULIFLOWER
Blanch the whole cauliflower for 10 minutes in a large pan of salted boiling water to ensure it is cooked but still firm.

Mix together the butter and mustard and season with fleur de sel.

Let the blanched cauliflower cool, then coat the whole surface of the cauliflower with the soft butter and mustard mixture. Chill in the refrigerator to let the butter coating take effect.

Preheat the oven to 400°F/200°C.

Give the brioche a final extra 30 minutes to rise further, then knock it back again. Transfer the dough to a work counter lightly dusted with flour and roll out roughly in a cross shape. Place the buttered cauliflower in the middle with its head facing down, then wrap the pastry around its stem to enclose it. Turn over the brioche-covered cauliflower, glaze it with the beaten egg, and place on a baking sheet. Bake for 10 minutes, then turn down the oven to 338°F/170°C and cook for another 15 minutes.

Remove from the oven and let stand for about 20 minutes before serving.

TO SERVE
Mix the seeds, berries, capers, and flowers together in a bowl and bind with canola (rapeseed) oil like a sauce vierge.

Cut the cauliflower brioche into thick slices and fry in butter in a pan until well browned. Serve doused in a generous amount of the seeds, berries, and flowers.

2. WILD BLACKBERRY TART WITH GARDEN HONEY AND WALNUT LEAF ICE CREAM

Make the ice cream the day before you want to serve the dessert. We use Savagnin de Voile—*voile* means "veil"—and this particular type of wine is matured in a barrel under a film (veil) of yeast.

SERVES 6
ICE CREAM
– 5 egg yolks
– 80 g brown granulated sugar
– 400 ml whole (full-fat) milk
– 250 ml cold light (single) cream (35%)
– 50 g freshly picked walnut leaves, finely chopped, plus a handful extra to decorate
– 100 ml Savagnin de Voile (Jura yellow wine)
TART PASTRY DOUGH
– 250 g all-purpose (plain) flour
– 100 g very cold unsalted butter, cut into small cubes
– 1 egg
– 100 g brown granulated sugar
"AMANDINE" (ALMOND) CREAM
– 135 g softened unsalted butter
– 165 g confectioners' (icing) sugar
– 2 eggs, beaten
– 200 g almond meal (ground almonds)
– 100 g raw cream

TART TOPPING
– 100 g homemade blackberry jam
– 200 g wild blackberries
– raw honeycomb, to taste

ICE CREAM
Beat the egg yolks and sugar together in a heatproof bowl.

Bring the milk to a boil in a pan, then gradually pour it over the egg mixture. Cook over low heat for 10 minutes and gently stir as though making creme anglaise. Do not let it heat above 183°F/84°C. It is thick enough when the mixture covers the back of a spoon and does not slide off it.

Halt the cooking process by adding the cold light (single) cream and add the finely chopped walnut leaves. Let infuse in the refrigerator overnight.

The next day, pour the Savagnin wine into a pan and reduce it by half. Let cool.

To finish making the ice cream, add the cooled reduced Savagnin wine to the infused custard, pour the mixture into a Pacojet beaker and freeze (with the walnut leaves still in the custard).

TART PASTRY DOUGH
To make the tart dough, put the flour into a bowl, add the butter and rub the flour and butter together until crumbly. Beat the egg and sugar together in a separate bowl.

Combine the 2 mixtures into a ball without over-kneading. Cover with plastic wrap (clingfilm) and put the dough in the refrigerator for about 1 hour.

Unwrap the dough and on a lightly floured work counter, roll it out to a thickness of ⅛ inch/3 mm. Line a 9½-inch/24-cm tart pan with the dough and put the lined pan in the refrigerator while you make the almond cream.

"AMANDINE" (ALMOND) CREAM
Beat the softened butter and sugar together in a bowl until creamy. Add the beaten eggs and fold in the almond meal (ground almonds) with a rubber spatula. Once the mixture is smooth, mix in the raw cream and spread a ½-inch/1-cm-thick layer over the chilled tart shell (case). Put the tart shell back in the refrigerator while you preheat the oven to 320°F/160°C.

Cook the tart in the oven for about 30 minutes, then place it on a cooling rack.

TART TOPPING
While the tart is still warm, spread the blackberry jam over the top, then decorate with the wild blackberries, arranging them closely and evenly across the surface.

TO SERVE
Cut a square out of the honeycomb and micro-blend the frozen ice cream mixture in the Pacojet. Serve the tart with the honeycomb and a quenelle of ice cream on the side.

1

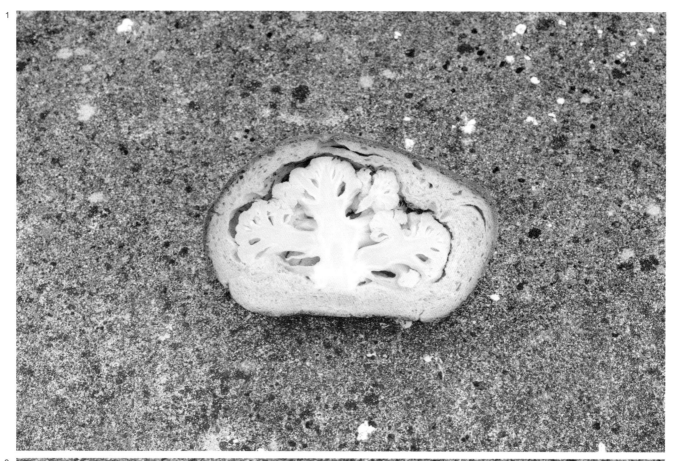

2

Skye Gyngell

MARLE & HEARTH RESTAURANTS AT HECKFIELD PLACE
Heckfield, Hampshire, UK

Set in rural Hampshire, England, Heckfield Place is a hotel, restaurant, and biodynamic farm that plays host to culinary director Skye Gyngell's extraordinary talent for making simple seasonal produce exceptional. The 5-acre (2-hectare) kitchen garden aims to produce 90 percent of the herbs, fruit, and vegetables used in Heckfield's two restaurants, Marle, a showcase of Gyngell's signature style, and Hearth, the hotel's signature restaurant for hotel residents only.

When Heckfield Place was built in the 1760s, the gardens and estate, which were originally planted by William Wildsmith, would have fully supported the house. When I came on board, the dream was to return the market garden, orchards, and farm to organic status. But after working with Jane Scotter, whose Herefordshire farm Fern Verrow grows solely for my restaurant Spring, in London, I fell in love with biodynamic produce, which is just going that little bit further than organic; I look at it as being completely in tune with the rhythms of the earth, and its principles make complete sense to me. So Jane has become a completely integral part of the farm here in Hampshire, too.

Our current vegetable patch covers 5 acres (2 hectares) but will double over the next year, and the adjacent orchard has 500 fruit trees including apples, pears, plums, and quince. The growing areas have been established over the last three years and we have a large glasshouse for propagating and raising young plants, and three polytunnels where we grow vegetables, salad greens, and flowers year-round. The vegetable plot is in an exposed area of the farm so we have also been planting hedges and trees to add protection and shade as well as more visual interest.

The land was stony farmland lacking in organic matter when we started, so we have been slowly reviving it and we are aiming to achieve full biodynamic certification by 2020. It's a big, long job to reenergize the soil and to bring it to a healthy level; it's a living, growing thing and it will only get stronger, healthier, and more fertile. Biodynamic produce has aliveness and energy, and you can see and taste the difference.

For me, growing everything here is an obsession and a passion. As a chef you have to flip how you work on its head; instead of cooks defining what's on the plate, it's the land that tells us what to do. The more I work with really great produce that tastes perfect, that has the most beautiful colors, the more I really just want to showcase that. It's like being given gifts every morning—it's really pleasurable. I always say that we simply "turn the volume up." It's reactive and instinctive cooking—it's not like a set recipe because we can't cook like that, we don't know how a tomato might taste on a certain day, every plate of food that goes out is unique in a way.

I love fish and meat but it's not where my head goes—I'm always more excited by vegetables and fruit. I just find it a richer tapestry to go toward. When I think of a dish I always think vegetables first because I can do so many things with them—amazing soft curd cheese dumplings with fall (autumn) greens, brown butter, and hazelnut dukka; or roasted Jerusalem artichokes with creamed onions, goat curd and winter savory. Winter is heaven and full of delicious and amazing inky, dark, good-for-you vegetables including collard greens, sprout greens, and cavolo nero, as well as gourds, potatoes, and parsnips.

We have a short menu with seven starters, seven mains, and four desserts. And when you are cooking totally seasonally you have to be very creative about gluts—there aren't 400 ingredients to play with—I may only have 10. We have to find clever ways of making the menu feel balanced so that if there's a glut of something like tomatoes, we don't have them on every dish, although we can treat vegetables very differently. We do heirloom tomatoes roasted on a fig leaf with crème fraîche and golden raspberries but at the same time we will serve trout with a tomato *kasundi*—spiced Indian tomato sauce—and they are very, very different dishes. Because of the gluts, pickling and preserving is a major part of the kitchen here.

We aim to use the farm to its full potential and then sprinkle it with all the fairy dust that comes from outside. We'll never grow lots of citrus—it's just not possible—but I couldn't have a season without blood oranges, or pistachios from Sicily, and I don't want to cut myself off from that. We also use as much of a plant as possible—we might use grapes but we will also use the vine leaves, either pickling or brining them. We might use figs but we will also make fig leaf syrup or a liqueur, or we'll use the leaves to wrap fish in. We also make a fig leaf and honey yogurt infused with fig leaves.

Succession planting becomes really important because we also want to spread the growing season as far as we can. The most important thing about working like this is information. For example, we have a WhatsApp group with Jane and the farm so we always know what's available or about to arrive. We use markers—putting beautiful little leeks next to a pencil, for example—so I can see how big things are. And Jane uses a traffic light system. Green means go: it's ready to be harvested and can't stay in the ground. Amber lets us know that something is almost ready, but it can stay in the ground for a week or so. For crops not ready yet but coming up, then it's red.

Every week of the year in the garden presents all this incredible produce for us to use in the kitchen. Sometimes it can be so fleeting—suddenly there are golden raspberries or amazing mulberries. It's really satisfying and exciting for me as a chef. You open up your mind and heart to being completely in tune with nature. It's a beautiful way to work. We are creating a working farm—not a show farm—and as we go on there will be many more layers and it will just get richer and better.

PLANTING BY THE MOON
We use the biodynamic planting calendar to guide us with our work on the vegetable plots, sowing, planting, fertilizing, pruning, and harvesting at the optimum times according to the position of the moon and planets. There are optimum days for each task and everything we grow falls into the following groups: root (potatoes, radishes, carrots, parsnips), flower, leaf (salads, spinach, herbs, greens), fruit (strawberries, raspberries, apples, plums, as well as all fruiting vegetables like tomatoes, zucchini/courgettes, and peas).

MULTIFACETED LEGUMES
We grow so many different varieties of beans, including green and fava (broad) beans as well as cranberry (borlotti) beans—they not only taste delicious but the climbing beans are an elegant visual addition to the garden with their tidy rows of wigwams, pretty flowers, and hanging fruit. Beans are also very good for the soil; their long root systems work their way deep down into the soil, opening it up and bringing life into it. Most of our beans are sown in spring and harvested in mid to late summer; "Hangdown Green" (*Vicia faba*) is a fantastic fava bean producing long pods of fine tasting beans. It can be trained over walls and fences, too.

1. RIVER TEST TROUT WITH HEIRLOOM TOMATOES, TARRAGON, AND HORSERADISH CREAM

SERVES 4
TOMATOES
– 20 ripe, sweet heirloom tomatoes, a
  selection of varieties and sizes, large
  ones cut in half
– 60 ml good-quality extra-virgin olive oil
– 1 tablespoon picked tarragon leaves
– salt
HORSERADISH CREAM
– 100 ml crème fraîche
– 2 tablespoons freshly grated horseradish
– 2 teaspoons red wine vinegar
– salt
TROUT
– 4 x 180-g trout fillets
– ½ tablespoon extra-virgin olive oil
– sea salt and freshly ground black pepper

TOMATOES
Bring a large pot of salted water to a boil, and prepare a bowl of ice water.

Using a small sharp knife make a cross at the bottom of each tomato. Plunge the tomatoes into the boiling water, then immediately remove them using a slotted spoon. Place directly into the ice water to stop them cooking, then remove from the water, peel away the skin from the tomatoes, and set them aside.
HORSERADISH CREAM
Put the crème fraîche into a bowl, add the horseradish, vinegar, and a small pinch of salt and stir well to combine.
TROUT
Preheat the oven to 350°F/180°C.

Place a nonstick ovenproof skillet (frying pan) over medium heat. Season the skin side of the trout fillets generously with salt and pepper.

Once the pan is hot, add the olive oil and place the trout in the pan skin side down. Cook for 3–4 minutes—the skin should be really golden and well colored—then transfer the pan to the middle shelf of the oven and cook for another 2 minutes. The flesh should just be cooked through but still a little translucent. Remove from the oven and set to one side.
TOMATOES
Place the peeled tomatoes in a small pan and add the extra-virgin olive oil along with a pinch of salt. Place over the lowest possible heat and gently and patiently warm them through. You are not looking for the tomatoes to be hot, just evenly warmed through (blood temperature). Once they are warm, add the tarragon and remove the pan from the heat.
TO SERVE
Divide the tomatoes among 4 warm plates. Lay the trout alongside and spoon over the horseradish cream.

2. ELDERFLOWER FRITTERS WITH HONEYCOMB AND SALT

This is a really nice way to end a meal when elderflowers are abundant.

SERVES 6
– about 6 heads elderflower, trimmed to
  make pretty hand-size bunches
– 250 ml buttermilk
– 480 g all-purpose (plain) flour
– 120 g farina (semolina)
– neutral oil, such as peanut (groundnut) or sunflower
  oil, for deep-frying
TO SERVE
– confectioners' (icing) sugar
– sea salt
– hot honeycomb

Check the elderflower heads for bugs—tapping the flowers gently should get rid of them.

Put the buttermilk into a wide, shallow bowl. Combine the flour and farina (semolina), then tip onto a flat plate. Line another flat plate with parchment (baking) paper to rest the coated elderflower heads on before frying them.

Heat the oil in a deep pan or deep-fryer to 320°F/160°C.

Drop the elderflower heads into the buttermilk, one by one, making sure that it coats the stems and blossoms well, then dredge them in the flour and farina mixture. Place the coated elderflower heads on the parchment-lined plate until you are ready to cook.

Deep-fry the elderflowers in batches until just golden brown, then drain on paper towels.
TO SERVE
Arrange the fried elderflower heads on plates, dust with confectioners' (icing) sugar and sprinkle with salt. Spoon a little honeycomb alongside and serve while warm.

2

Gert Jan Hageman

RESTAURANT DE KAS
Watergraafsmeer, Amsterdam, Netherlands

The location of Restaurant De Kas is just one of many quirky details. Set in a series of greenhouses that date back to 1926 and which belong to the Amsterdam Municipal Nursery, the restaurant relies on produce from greenhouses and gardens, where it harvests vegetables, herbs, and flowers. In addition, there is a 10-acre (4-hectare) plot for hardier, organic produce. The founder, Gert Jan Hageman, is also the head gardener.

We have a number of gardens: an orchard with old-style hard and soft fruit, a classic herb and flower garden surrounded by hedges, mainly of box, and a greenhouse that is part of the restaurant. We also have our large production garden at Beemster Polder, which is partly under glass and partly outdoors. When guests come to De Kas, they walk through the orchard and past the greenhouse on the way into the dining room. The herb garden is on the other side of the building, with a terrace where we serve meals when the weather is good.

The idea of the garden predates the restaurant; we were experimenting with and growing vegetables as far back as 1997. I didn't do well at my studies, and I was excluded from school and began working as a cook in a restaurant. By 1993, I was head chef and was awarded a Michelin star. Soon after, on the advice of my friend Jolinde (now my wife), I took a sabbatical and while working in a friend's kitchen garden I had a revelation: I should open my own restaurant, growing my own vegetables that would dominate a menu that changed weekly, while using only local ingredients of the highest quality. Amsterdam Council soon heard of my idea and tipped me off about the old greenhouse at Frankendael, which was scheduled for demolition. After a great deal of to-ing and fro-ing, we managed to rebuild and restore the glasshouse and opened for the first time in January 2001. Luckily for us, the launch was a success, as we had buried ourselves in debt.

The park around De Kas was designed by Buro Sant en Co of The Hague, who added orchards, vegetable gardens, and ponds near the restaurant. We began to grow herbs, edible flowers, and soft fruit, with willow structures as plant supports. In the greenhouse, we grow under LED lamps, with hydroponics and automated ebb and flow cultivations. We grow and cultivate a great variety of strawberries in our greenhouse. We are always excited by the arrival of the first batch of these magnificent berries. We let our homegrown fruit and vegetables be the star of the show and that is exactly what we do with strawberries in our recipe "Strawberries marinated in rose syrup with verbena ice cream and fresh almonds."

Everything grown in one's own garden is wonderful, from humble early potatoes to beautiful ripe tomatoes. But just a few of my favorites are "Korona" strawberries (*Fragaria* x *ananassa*), early potatoes cultivated under glass, fava (broad) beans, the first outdoor lettuce, radicchio, all herbs, tomatoes, and eggplants (aubergines). When our homegrown eggplants arrive in our kitchen it's the first sign of summer. At first glance eggplants look quite strange, but they are so versatile and packed with flavor. At de Kas, we use them in all kinds of dishes: eggplant caviar, steamed mini eggplants with ginger and sesame, and as part of a tasty bowl of caponata.

We grow in a moderate marine climate, with relatively mild winters, mild summers, and rain all year round. The Dutch climate is influenced largely by the North Sea, but our traditional growing season has extended because of climate change. In Beemster, we grow on clay, in Amsterdam on sandy marshland. Root vegetables won't grow on the Beemster clay, at least not without problems.

We're as organic as we can be. Under glass, our pest control includes various parasite wasps and nematodes. We change crops annually, hoeing weeds and tilling the soil very superficially before planting. We use organic fertilizers and minerals like basalt meal and seaweed, to boost the soil and strengthen the plants. We have no fear of modern hybrid crops, which are more likely to succeed, being less vulnerable to disease, and they are usually really tasty. We take soil samples annually, correcting faults and imbalances by adding compost that is specially tailored to our soil, in the spring.

The day starts with picking at around 6.30 a.m. in high season, when we make up orders for the kitchen that have been sent in the night before. Then a quick coffee-and-work meeting, while the Beemster crop is sent to Amsterdam, arriving at the De Kas kitchens at 10.00 a.m. Then it's planting, hoeing, watering, making up delivery lists, mowing the grass paths, cleaning dikes, and carrying out repairs until evening. We do this six days a week during the garden's season, which lasts from about February until December. We adjust our work pace and working hours as crops come and go; in winter, we prepare for the busy times that will come again.

I've learned to follow classic plant and seed calendars and extend the seasons as far forward and back as I can. By pushing the plant calendar to its limits, things go wrong sometimes, with early or late frosts or bolting vegetables (edible flowers can be a happy outcome). Sometimes you get lucky, too: one year, we were able to cultivate and harvest almost all year round. Every day, a cartful of vegetable orders fills us with pride, spurring us on to get back to work. Away from the kitchen, I've learned to be patient, to work with the weather, and look out for, and enjoy, each new season.

Our two brilliant chefs, Jos Timmer and Wim de Beer, make delicious vegetable and herb dishes, and never plan their menus until they've worked out what we can expect to pick the following week. Our menu is driven by the garden and mirrors the cycle of the Dutch seasons; it consists of six dishes, now mostly vegetarian or vegan. The chefs routinely ask us to grow particular things, such as edible flowers, which contribute to the taste of the dishes. We grow many flowers including nasturtiums, violets (for syrups), borage, cucumber, geraniums, and fennel. And the nursery produces vegetables at different stages of growth so the chefs can choose exactly when to use them. In that sense, we inspire each other. Take Kohlrabi, for example. This turnip-like crop often lies around wilting in the vegetable drawer because people don't really know what to do with them. We like using them raw, stuffed, or roasted in a sweet crust.

Growing is in our DNA. We place great importance on where things come from. The inspiration and extreme freshness of our own garden has no price. Smells, colors, the advent of a new season, looking out for the first tomato or strawberry, are things that put a spring in your step and that you eagerly anticipate. Every day outside in the daylight creates a healthier mind and body, not forgetting the physical exercise that working on the land requires. That's what having your own garden does for you. Without a garden there would be no De Kas.

GARDEN TIPS
– Know the soil you cultivate, and whether it is in balance: take samples.
– Buy the Association for Ecological Life and Gardening (Velt) handbook—a real cultivation bible that you will rely on—and take your reading glasses everywhere.
– Make planting and sowing calendars.
– Never hold back on harvesting if you're really keen.

– Have no fear of modern hybrid crops: they are more likely to succeed, less vulnerable to diseases and complaints, and they are usually really tasty.
– Never store potatoes below 46°F/8°C, otherwise they become strangely sweet.
– Explore the limits of the cultivation seasons and you'll be in for some surprises.

MODERN HYBRID CROPS
Butter lettuce is a nice example of a good hybrid crop. There is a variety for every season, ones that work well indoor or outdoor, with or without extra heat or light. And they all come with a beautiful hard, yellow heart with a nice bittersweet aftertaste. Tomatoes are also great, particularly the heirloom hybrids from the United States. They are wonderful: good crop, yield, and taste.

1. BARBECUED EGGPLANT WITH PEANUT VINAIGRETTE, GREEN CURRY, AND HERBS

SERVES 4
HERB OIL
- 1 liter grapeseed or neutral oil
- 75 g parsley
- 75 g Thai basil
- 75 g spinach
- 75 g chervil
PEANUT VINAIGRETTE
- 5 ml sushi vinegar
- 5 ml soy sauce
- Ketjap (a sweet soy sauce), to taste
- 100 g unsalted peanuts, coarsely chopped
- juice of 1 lemon
GREEN CURRY
- 1 cauliflower, broken into florets
- 1 liter coconut milk
- 30 ml water
- 1 lemongrass stalk, chopped and bruised
- 3 lime leaves
- 1 Spanish chile, seeded
- 40 g Siamese ginger (galangal), chopped
- 130 g basmati rice
- 75 g cilantro (coriander)
- 75 g Thai basil
- 75 g lovage
- 75 g spinach
- 300 ml Herb Oil (see above)
TEMPURA SHALLOT RINGS
- 1 liter neutral oil
- 200 g tempura flour
- 100 ml sparkling water
- 1 shallot, sliced into rings
BARBECUED EGGPLANT
- 2 eggplants (aubergines)
- 10 ml good-quality soy sauce
TO SERVE
- 50 g Spanish chile
- 50 g chives
- 4 nasturtium flowers
- 4 chive flowers
- 4 chervil flowers
- 4 cilantro flowers
- 80 g picked cilantro (coriander) leaves
- 40 g micro herbs

HERB OIL
Blend the oil and herbs in a Thermomix for 7 minutes. Strain through cheesecloth (muslin).
PEANUT VINAIGRETTE
Mix the vinegar, soy sauce, and ketjap in a bowl to make a dressing. Add the chopped peanuts and the lemon juice.
GREEN CURRY
Put the cauliflower into a pan with the coconut milk, water, lemongrass, lime leaves, chile, ginger, and rice, bring to a boil and cook until soft. Strain through a strainer (sieve), and let cool. Blend in a food processor with the herbs and herb oil until smooth. Strain again.
TEMPURA SHALLOT RINGS
Heat the oil in a deep pan to 300°F/150°C.
   Mix the tempura flour and sparkling water to a runny batter. Dip the shallot rings into the batter, then deep-fry in the oil until crispy.
BARBECUED EGGPLANT
Wrap the eggplants (aubergines) individually in aluminum foil and barbecue until soft. Let cool slightly, then open the foil and brush with the soy sauce. Barbecue them again, this time with no foil, to get a nice color.

TO SERVE
Put a spoonful each of vinaigrette and herb oil on each plate. Lay an eggplant on top. Drizzle over the green curry, and add the tempura shallot rings, a teaspoon of chile, and a spoonful of chives to each plate and garnish with flowering herbs.

2. KOHLRABI WITH ELDERFLOWER BEURRE BLANC AND CAVIAR

SERVES 4
ELDERFLOWER-INFUSED CREAM
- 6 heads elderflower
- 200 ml heavy (double) cream
PUREED KOHLRABI
- 4 kohlrabi, thickly sliced
- 500 ml whole (full-fat) milk
- salt and freshly ground black pepper
STEWED KOHLRABI
- 3 kohlrabi, thickly sliced
- 50 g farmer's unsalted butter
- 200 ml vegetable bouillon
BEURRE BLANC
- 50 ml shiro dashi
- 50 ml sushi vinegar
- 50 ml white wine
- Elderflower-infused Cream (see above)
- 250 g cold farmer's unsalted butter, cut into pieces
- 50 g caviar
- 1 banana shallot, finely chopped
- 50 g chives, finely chopped
TO SERVE
- 1 handful sea samphire
- 1 handful sea lavender
- 1 kohlrabi, thinly sliced using a mandoline
- 12 oyster leaves

ELDERFLOWER-INFUSED CREAM
Put the elderflower heads into a heatproof bowl. Bring the cream to a boil and pour it over the elderflower, then cover the bowl with aluminum foil. Let infuse for 20 minutes, then strain through a fine-mesh strainer (sieve).
PUREED KOHLRABI
Put the kohlrabi and milk into a pan, bring to a boil, then simmer until very soft. Blend in a blender until smooth. Season to taste.
STEWED KOHLRABI
Stew the kohlrabi slices with the butter in a pan of bouillon until soft.
BEURRE BLANC
Put the dashi, vinegar, and wine into a pan and bring to a boil, then mix with the elderflower-infused cream. Remove from the heat and add the butter, piece by piece, blending with an immersion (stick) blender. The quantity is too much for this dish, so keep half for another time (making less doesn't work as there wouldn't be enough volume to create the perfect sauce). Stir in the caviar, shallot, and chives.
TO SERVE
Cook the samphire and sea lavender briefly in a pan of boiling water, then drain and mix with the stewed kohlrabi.

Divide the pureed kohlrabi among 4 bowls. Add some stewed kohlrabi. Pour over some beurre blanc, then add some slices of raw kohlrabi and raw oyster leaves.

3. STRAWBERRIES MARINATED IN ROSE SYRUP WITH VERBENA ICE CREAM AND FRESH ALMONDS

SERVES 4
PANNACOTTA CREAM
- 1.5 liters heavy (double) cream
- petals from 2 fragrant untreated edible roses
- 10 g gelatin
- 450 g white chocolate
VERBENA ICE CREAM
- 200 g verbena leaves
- 1.5 liters whole (full-fat) milk
- 1.5 liters heavy (double) cream
- 600 g superfine (caster) sugar
- 600 g egg yolks
ROSE-SYRUP-INFUSED STRAWBERRIES
- 200 g gelling (jam) sugar
- 350 ml water
- Petals of 2 fragrant untreated edible roses (we use William Shakespeare)
- 250 g strawberries, hulled
TO SERVE
- 1 good spoon Pannacotta Cream (see above) per person
- zest and juice of ½ lemon
- 4 scoops Verbena Ice Cream (see above)
- 4 fresh almonds, halved and chopped
- 16 edible rose petals
- a few drops olive oil

PANNACOTTA CREAM
Heat the cream and pour it over the rose petals. Let infuse for 20 minutes, then strain.
   Soak the gelatin in cold water. When soft, add to the warm cream, stir well, and add the chocolate. Chill in the refrigerator overnight to set, then blend the cream in a blender until smooth. Transfer to a pastry (piping) bag.
VERBENA ICE CREAM
Infuse the verbena in the milk and cream for 20 minutes, then heat to 185°F/85°C.
   Whisk the sugar and egg yolks in a stand mixer until white and creamy. Mix in the warm milk and cream mixture in 4 batches. Bring it back to 178°F/81°C while continuing to whisk. Place over ice and let cool, then transfer to an ice cream machine and churn.
ROSE-SYRUP-INFUSED STRAWBERRIES
Put the jam sugar, water, and rose petals into a pan and bring to a boil, then remove from the heat. Let stand for 20 minutes, then pass it through a fine-mesh strainer (sieve) into a bowl. Put the strawberries into the cool syrup and crush them a bit. Let infuse.
TO SERVE
Pipe a little pannacotta cream into 4 bowls and lay the strawberries on top. Spoon over a little of the lemon zest, rose syrup, and add a few drops of lemon juice. Add a scoop of ice cream to each bowl and garnish with the almonds, rose petals, and a few drops of olive oil.

1

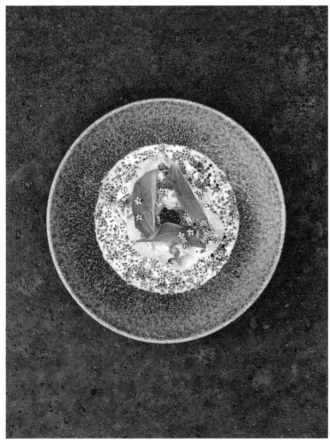

Stephen Harris

THE SPORTSMAN
Seasalter, Kent, UK

Described by chef-patron and self-taught cook Stephen Harris as a "grotty run-down pub by the sea," The Sportsman received its first Michelin star in 2008. Its honest and unpretentious attitude, combined with Harris's belief in using local produce, has led to the restaurant being repeatedly voted as the best in the UK. The menu reflects the pub's surrounding geography, history, and produce. There is a kitchen garden on site, which produces many of the menu's ingredients, the rest being sourced from nearby producers.

The garden at The Sportsman, like the pub itself, has evolved slowly and steadily over time into something we never expected. When we opened, the land at the back was still a caravan site, and had been since the 1950s. Four years later, we decided to grow some stuff in a small plot behind the pub; my girlfriend Emma put in some raised beds, and we grew things for the tasting menu where the produce had to be as fresh as possible—peas, edible flowers, and tomatoes, for example. It wasn't until 2015, though, that the garden started to play a serious role at The Sportsman. My brother Phil had this idea of guests staying among the ingredients, so he built cabins surrounded by a garden.

I wanted to experiment with a polytunnel and one of the local fishermen overheard me talking about it one day and sold me his spare one. For the first year, we used the crop for experimentation, and had no higher aspirations. The next year, we realized that it was evolving into a much bigger project, so decided to hire someone to help. Phil put an advert out—it was pretty vague, saying we needed a gardener who could work 20–40 hours a week, depending. Ronan answered, and he's been with us for the last year and a half. Thanks to him, we now have 2 polytunnels with 50 different fruits, herbs, and vegetables, 16 raised beds, an acre of meadow, and an orchard of apples, plums, and pears.

The soil is alkaline, which basically means it's not great. To improve the quality and bring it back to neutral, in the most natural way possible, we're not planting intensively, and we're being careful with crop rotation. We try to repurpose things in the garden as much as we can, too. For example, the oyster shells in our paths come from the restaurant, but they also put off slugs and snails. We use seaweed from the beach as fertilizer, laying dried seaweed on top of the soil, and then also make a "liquid" seaweed by soaking it in fresh water for six weeks, until it's fermented. And we water everything from the well in the garden.

At the beginning of the year, we plant potatoes, onions, herbs, and peas, with the aim of picking in April. In summer, we have tomatoes, zucchini (courgettes), green beans, eggplants (aubergines), scallions (spring onions), and green bell peppers, among others, and we experiment with between two and five varieties of each. I'm not interested in a purple potato, though—the weird and wonderful has no appeal if the flavour isn't better. A lot of people seem to reject a minimalist approach, but I'm obsessed with the concept of the archetype: a perfect pea or tomato.

The tomatoes always do fantastically well. We grow "Marmande," a French heirloom, and "Sungold," a type of yellow cherry tomato. Marmandes are classic beefsteak tomatoes, and have a superb flavor. They play the role of "the slicer" in a salad, while the Sungolds provide little bursts of sweetness—in fact, it's almost like eating a boiled sweet.

As a chef, your job is to retain the integrity of an ingredient. The nuances of cooking are similar to the nuances of picking; understanding when to pick, I believe, should be a skill every chef has. With every new chef that comes into my kitchen, I try to encourage them to think deeply about ingredients and how to bring out their natural flavor. This is easier to do if they have picked that ingredient.

People's experience of The Sportsman has changed since developing the garden. For example, we serve a chilled zucchini soup in the summer months. When you pick zucchini, your hands will smell of mint and truffle from handling the plant. So the soup is simply very fresh zucchini with a hint of truffle and mint. In that way, the experience of our diners is in line with ours when we step into the garden.

With gardens, you make a decision in October of one year, and see the results in August of the next. A lot of chefs change restaurants in that length of time. To me, this is the real benefit of staying in the same place. I've been back in Whitstable for 18 years, and I couldn't have achieved what I have in the kitchen without the persistence and patience that goes with that. The garden is the same—it's a project that requires both of those things by the spade-full, and it will never be complete.

When people ask why I have a garden, I say it's because my aim has always been to cook food that will blow your mind, but you don't know why. I suppose you could call it the very best version of "normal" food. As the garden develops, I can only see the food getting better and better.

TIPS FOR A SHORELINE ALLOTMENT
- Hardier herbs such as rosemary and fennel and hedgerow shrubs such as hawthorn and sea buckthorn all take very well to salty air.
- Make the most of what you have to hand; our seaweed fertilizer is made using an age-old technique, it's free, and it's very good for all of our plants, but especially "Jersey Royal" and "Pink Fir Apple" potatoes (Solanum tuberosum).
- Think about how the environment will affect crops; we created a kind of windbreak using willow trees to minimize the impact of harsh winds coming in from the sea.

FAVORITE VEGETABLE VARIETIES
We are always trying diferent varieties in the garden and these are some of our favorites:
- "Kelvedon Wonder" pea (Pisium sativum) is an English heritage variety—it's been reliable as an early crop, and the flavor is excellent, bursting with sweetness.
- "Defender" zucchini (courgettes, Cucurbita pepo) are fantastic for two reasons: one, the picking season is quite long, and two, the flowers are reliable. We lightly batter them to serve with our chilled zucchini soup.
- "Firestorm" stick (runner) beans (Phaseolus coccineus) have a tenderness and sweetness that other beans don't quite possess, which means they are fantastic served barely cooked or even raw, dressed in a little lime syrup.

1. STEAMED BASS WITH COCKLES AND SUMMER PISTOU

SERVES 4, AS PART OF A TASTING MENU
- 4 x 125-g fillets wild bass, skin scored (increase the size to 200-g portions for larger main-course size)
- 500 g cockles in their shells, well washed
- 12 thick asparagus spears, trimmed, tips removed, and stems sliced into thin roundels
- 2 tablespoons fresh peas
- 2 tablespoons shelled fava (broad) beans
- Sea salt
SUMMER PISTOU
- handful of basil leaves
- 1 tablespoon grated Parmesan cheese
- 1 tablespoon olive oil
TO SERVE
- squeeze of lemon juice
- drizzle of light Ligurian or Provençal olive oil

Season the fish fillets with salt, wrap them tightly in plastic wrap (clingfilm), and refrigerate for 2 hours to set the shape. Take out of the refrigerator 15 minutes before cooking.

Put a pan onto medium heat and throw in the cockles. Cover and cook for 3 minutes, or until the shells have opened. Shake the pan from time to time to help the process. Let the cockles cool in the pan, then strain the juice and reserve. Remove almost all the cockle meat from the shells (keep a few to decorate) and reserve.

SUMMER PISTOU

Combine the pistou ingredients in a mortar and pound to a paste. Alternatively, use a mini food processor.

Sit the fish fillets on a plate (still in their wrapping) and set in a colander over a pan of simmering water. Cover and steam for around 5 minutes, then check the internal temperature with a probe thermometer. When it reaches 110°F/45°C remove from the heat and let rest in a warm place; it will increase to just under 120°F/50°C with the residual heat.

While the fish is resting, heat the reserved cockle juice in a small pan. Add the asparagus rondels, peas, and fava (broad) beans and cook for 2–3 minutes, adding a tablespoon of water if needed.

Meanwhile, heat a little water in a small frying pan or skillet and simmer the asparagus tips for 2 minutes. Drain and add to the pan with the rest of the vegetables. Stir in the pistou, add the cockles, and warm briefly.

TO SERVE

Divide the vegetables and cockles among 4 warm serving bowls. Dress the fish fillets with a little lemon juice and olive oil. Place on top of the cockle pistou and season. Decorate with the reserved cockles in their shells and serve immediately.

2. CREAM OF VEGETABLE SOUP

I like the idea of understatement and it is used well here as the recipe title slightly downplays the diners' expectations by making them think of canned soup, but then delivers the sweetest, most tender vegetables in a delicate yet flavorful broth. The vegetables you use will depend on what is at its best at the time. In this recipe I give quantities for the ones we use in June. Whatever the season, to achieve the desired result, the most important thing is to pick the vegetables that same morning. The stock can be made ahead of time and keeps well in the refrigerator for up to four days.

SERVES 4, AS PART OF A TASTING MENU
HOMEMADE BUTTER (MAKES ABOUT 600 G)
- 1 liter very good-quality heavy (double) cream or 1 kg crème fraîche
- 6–9 g sea salt
MUSHROOM STOCK
- 2 large onions, finely chopped
- 2 large carrots, finely chopped
- ½ head celery, finely chopped
- 2 large leeks, finely chopped
- 200 g cremini (chestnut) mushrooms, sliced
- parsley stalks
- 1 star anise
- 30 g dried ceps
- filtered water, to cover
- 15 lemon verbena leaves, chopped
SOUP
- 15 g Homemade Butter (see above)
- 1 tablespoon water
- 2 tablespoons freshly shelled peas
- 2 tablespoons shelled fava (broad) beans
- 2 tablespoons chopped fine green beans
- 2 tablespoons chopped scallion (spring onion)
- 2 Sungold tomatoes, halved
- 8 small lemon verbena leaves
- shredded edible rose petals
- 200 ml sour cream
- good squeeze of lime juice
- sea salt and freshly ground black pepper

HOMEMADE BUTTER

Put the bowl of a stand mixer into the refrigerator to chill. Put the cream or crème fraîche into the cold bowl and beat at high speed with the paddle attachment. After about 5 minutes the cream will really stiffen up and you will hear a splashing sound as the butter separates out from the buttermilk. Turn down the speed and cover the bowl loosely to prevent the liquid spraying everywhere. Continue beating until the buttermilk and butterfat separate completely. Be patient as this may take another 5 minutes. Turn off the machine and strain off the buttermilk. Rinse the butter under cold running water and strain again. With the machine on its lowest setting, beat in the salt into the butter until fully incorporated.

Knead the butter between 2 pieces of wax (greaseproof) paper to squeeze out the last of the buttermilk. Shape into a cylinder, wrap in wax paper and store in the refrigerator.

MUSHROOM STOCK

Put all the ingredients, except the lemon verbena leaves, in a large pan and pour over enough filtered water to just cover them. Bring to a boil, then lower the heat and simmer for 15 minutes. Remove from the heat and let infuse for 30 minutes.

Return the stock to a boil, then simmer until the stock has reduced to about 250 ml. Add the lemon verbena leaves and let infuse for 15 minutes. Strain, cool, and chill in the refrigerator until needed.

SOUP

Warm the butter in a nonstick frying pan or skillet. Add 1 tablespoon of water. Shimmy the pan to create an emulsion, then add the peas, beans, and scallion (spring onion) and gently warm them up. It is crucial to note that you don't want to actually cook the vegetables, but merely to warm them—as if they have just been picked on a summer's day.

Once the vegetables are warm, season them with salt and pepper and divide them among 4 small bowls. Add the Sungold tomatoes, lemon verbena leaves, and shredded rose petals.

Heat 500 ml of the mushroom stock in a small pan. Add the cream, then bring to a boil. Add a good squeeze of lime and check the seasoning. Blitz with an immersion (stick) blender until good and frothy, and divide among the 4 bowls.

1

Dan Hunter

BRAE
Birregurra, Victoria, Australia

Chef Dan Hunter transformed a rustic farmhouse into one of
Australia's most exciting dining destinations with a set seasonal
menu. Brae is a place to interact with nature and eat from the land.
Hunter sources fresh and delicious ingredients from local farmers,
and his own 30-acre (12-hectare) organic farm produces a wide
range of ingredients from fruit and vegetables, to olive oil and honey.

Brae sits on a hillside in Birregurra, Victoria, Australia, on a 30-acre (12-hectare) organic farm. When we took over the property in July 2013, there was a small vegetable garden (now an orchard), some 10–12-year-old olive trees, and around 30 fruit trees. Since then, we have expanded: as well as a number of large vegetable beds, we have a citrus grove with more than 60 trees, an orchard with more than 100 fruit trees including stone fruits, apples, quince, and pears, the olive grove has become more productive, plus we have a truffière, a paddock for wheat, nut trees and berries, several spaces dedicated to indigenous Australian food plants and trees, a 100-foot (30-meter) long polytunnel, and chickens. There are also large areas of flowering, indigenous trees and plants that support beneficial insects and birds, as well as the bees we keep for honey and to help with pollination.

We focus on producing uncommon ingredients that have great gastronomic appeal, delicates that do not travel when ripe, expensive ingredients, and any we feel we can't buy at a better quality from a trusted local source. These include white and red fraises des bois (wild) strawberries (Fragaria vesca) that are at their best when harvested warm from the afternoon sun, almonds and pistachios both harvested when green, and asparagus that tastes full of grass, chlorophyll, and nutty notes of popcorn when raw and fresh. These are each true expressions of their season.

Every year, we develop an ever-deepening knowledge of our farm, a clearer idea of our capabilities, and what we want our cuisine to be. When I see food growing, consider plants at different times throughout their growing life, and how the ingredients will be used while observing them, I'm able to see possibilities. Being in nature makes me more creative, inspired, and relaxed, as well as more courageous and spontaneous with dishes for the menu. Often, these dishes are ones that I feel I could never have imagined had I not been in the right place at the right time: a chilled broth of broad (fava) beans and strawberries, fig leaf, and yogurt whey only existed because those plants were growing relatively close to each other in the garden one spring, and so they all suddenly seemed completely logical together. The dishes that result from chance are often the most exciting for us and for the guests who get to experience a very real and raw snapshot of our place on a particular day. These dishes occur because of an interaction with a plant at a particular time of its life, a unique encounter with a seed, a stem, a flower, a tree-ripened fruit, one aroma mixed with another. This can only be experienced by being with the plants on a daily basis. Such opportunities, when captured and distilled into dishes, are the whole point, the absolute pleasure, of having vegetables and fruit growing so close to the kitchen door and dining room. For instance, the greens of

purple cauliflower bolting in the late spring heat would undoubtedly be removed from most commercial market gardens to make way for the next crop: for us, it's an opportunity to toast them in a little oil to serve with salt-baked green garlic and buttermilk left over from lightly churned cultured cream.

I'm really obsessed with letting fruit ripen to the point where it almost falls apart once harvested. The joy found in just-harvested potatoes, asparagus, or mini broad beans, tree-ripened stone fruit, vine-ripened tomatoes, and sun-warmed ripe strawberries is reason enough to grow your own food. These ingredients are transformed with the greatest respect into a daily set menu, served over a period of three to four hours, for both lunch and dinner.

I work with one of our gardeners on a weekly basis to plan quantities, tests and trials, and of course we react to whims. Each day the cooks harvest what they require. They move as one, generally picking or harvesting a single product at a time so that quality and numbers can be monitored while picking at speed. Kitchen waste is added to the compost, eggs are collected, vegetable trimmings and grain are fed to the chickens, their water is topped up and they are let out of their tractors to move freely in a netted area among the fruit and olive trees. Delicate items go straight into containers resting on ice in the warmer months so that they are not heat-affected.

We are lucky to be part of a community of people who are as interested and passionate about their ingredients as we are: pick-your-own berry farms, farm-gate vegetable stalls, and heritage apple orchards are all in our immediate vicinity, plus olives, walnuts, and potatoes are all grown commercially and sold within a 6-mile (10-kilometer) radius. Also, private growers often arrive at the kitchen door with a bucket or car-boot of something in absolutely pristine condition, picked just before making the call. We've met several people that way who now supply us with ingredients—from tree-ripened limes to super-fragrant quinces—and it's usually these guys who have the very best produce.

Everything is within walking distance of the restaurant and kitchen, and our guests are encouraged to spend time around the farm; we hope what we do at the table makes sense when they see the gardens and plants and have the opportunity to walk and be in nature. Usually, lunch guests will take a break from the menu at some stage and go out for a self-guided tour. There are paths that lead them through the orchards, polytunnel, and vegetable garden back to the restaurant. It takes about ten minutes to walk around quickly but most spend about half an hour.

People are starting to understand now that Brae is a farm with a restaurant, not just a restaurant with a garden—a place to be immersed in nature and enjoy the produce from the land.

GARDEN TIPS
– Grow food you like to eat
– Grow food that's applicable to your temperature zone and grow food that is easy, space efficient, and prolific. Tomatoes and basil, zucchinis (courgettes), radishes, a citrus tree, strawberries, potatoes—items that are delicious just after they are harvested and commonly better than when you purchase these items from supermarkets—can all be grown in pots or hanging baskets, or in boxes.
– Don't try and do too much too soon. Get some confidence by growing a few things in the first season and then develop from there.

– Read as much as you can about the "how to," and talk with others about their experiences of growing food.
– Involve children. I think getting your kids involved in growing food is a great and important life skill that also introduces them to new and tasty ingredients—and if your kids can eat from your own garden you know that at mealtimes they've had a good intake of their daily health needs, making mealtimes a little less stressful.

ORGANIC GROWING
Brae farm has been managed on strict organic principles since we took over in 2013. We promote a healthy microbiology, grow beneficial plants and attract insects, build soil through an intensive composting program, rotate crops in a planned and ordered manner, move carefully through the beds so as not to compact them, keep open areas in the beds covered with tarps during resting periods or mulch using Lucerne to reduce weeds and retain moisture. We avoid turning the soil, and we don't use machinery, favoring hand tools instead, employing a fork for aeration only, rather than digging and turning.

1. ASPARAGUS, OLIVE PLANT, AND SEA BUTTER

SERVES 4
SEA LETTUCE POWDER
- 100 g fresh sea lettuce
- salt
SEA BUTTER
- 4 g Sea Lettuce Powder (see above)
- 100 g unsalted butter, colder than room temperature
ASPARAGUS
- 4 fat asparagus spears
- Salt
OLIVE PLANT
- 3–4 small olive plant leaves per piece of asparagus

SEA LETTUCE POWDER
Wash the harvested sea lettuce in salted water, picking through it carefully to ensure all sand, shells, and other debris are removed. It is important to wash the sea lettuce many times, and to give it a good soak in abundant water, as it holds a lot of grit. Once the sea lettuce is completely free of any impurities, taste it to check for salt content. If it is too salty, give it a quick soak in fresh water until the desired salt level is achieved.

To dry the sea lettuce, place it in a dehydrator and dry it at 131°F/55°C for 6–12 hours. Blend the dried sea lettuce in a food processor to a fine powder. It will hydrate readily, so store it in an airtight container.

SEA BUTTER
Combine the 4 g of the sea lettuce powder with the butter in a blender, ensuring there are no lumps and that the mixture is homogenously blended. Reserve the butter, covered and refrigerated, until needed. Reserve the remaining sea lettuce powder in an airtight container for other preparations.

ASPARAGUS
With a sharp turning knife and starting at the tip of the asparagus, peel the first fiber off each piece. It is important to peel in one motion from top to bottom, ensuring you do not peel too deeply or scratch the stems, leaving the chlorophyll intact.

OLIVE PLANT
Remove the olive plant leaves from the plant. Wash them in chilled water and pat dry on paper towels. Store in an airtight container until needed.

TO SERVE
Warm the sea butter in a pan, allowing it to melt but not brown.

Blanch the asparagus in boiling water with a ratio of 10 g salt per liter of water. The asparagus should be just cooked, with a little crunch.

Add the asparagus spears to the sea butter and gently coat them. Remove the spears and transfer to a serving plate. Cover each spear with olive leaves.

2. CHILLED BROTH OF BROAD BEAN, GREEN ALMOND AND STRAWBERRY, FIG LEAF AND YOGURT WHEY

SERVES 4
FIG OIL
- 125 g young fig leaves
- 1 liter olive oil
YOGURT WHEY
- 10 g tender young fig leaves from trees just prior to fruiting
- 200 ml whey extracted from hanging sheep's milk yogurt
FAVA BEANS
- 400 g baby broad (fava) beans
- salt
ALMONDS
- 20 tender or green almonds
- solution of 1 liter water to 1 g ascorbic acid
STRAWBERRIES
- mix of around 40 small Japanese and wild strawberries, both traditional red and fraises des bois white
FLOWERS
- coriander flowers

FIG OIL
Combine the fig leaves and oil in a vacuum pack and heat at 140°F/60°C for 3 hours. Let the resulting oil infuse at room temperature for a minimum of 3 weeks before use.

YOGURT WHEY
Crush and tear the fig leaves and vacuum seal them with the whey. Let infuse in the refrigerator for 12 hours. Strain the fig leaves and transfer the infused whey to the freezer. Freeze until it is icy but not frozen as a solid mass—this will take around 30 minutes, but keep an eye on it.

BROAD BEANS
Remove the broad (fava) beans from their pods and blanch them quickly in salted boiling water. Refresh them in an ice bath and then remove the second skin. Keep the beans covered with a damp cloth to avoid them oxidizing and drying out.

ALMONDS
Peel the almonds to reveal the inner jelly-like tender almonds and place these in the water/ascorbic acid solution. It is best to peel the almonds as close as possible to the time of service.

STRAWBERRIES
Clean any dirt from the strawberries.

FLOWERS
Cut the flowers from the stems using sharp scissors and wash them quickly in chilled water. Store them on a damp cloth in a sealed container until needed.

TO SERVE
Dress the double-podded baby broad beans and the strawberries with a little of the fig oil and season with salt. Make a pile of these in the center of each serving bowl and arrange the tender almonds among them. Pour over a spoonful of the yogurt whey, adding any frozen pieces to the top of the other ingredients. Arrange flowers on top and drizzle with more oil.

2

Christopher Kostow

THE RESTAURANT
AT MEADOWOOD
Napa Valley, California, USA

Christopher Kostow aims to meld the stories of artisans, growers, and foragers to create his restaurant's expression of the bond between landscape, food systems, and communities. He strives to make his cuisine not only delicious, but relevant, singular, and personal. With a 2-acre (8,100 square-meter) organic garden that focuses on new varieties and experimental cultivation methods, Kostow grows fruit, vegetables, and herbs that give a true depiction of the bounty of California's Napa Valley.

After moving to the Napa Valley, California, to open The Restaurant at Meadowood in 2008, I had the good fortune to forge a partnership with the Saint Helena Montessori School. The school was creating a 10-acre (4-hectare) farm campus half a mile from us, and as agriculture is central to the school's curriculum, they offered us some acreage on a former vineyard to use as a restaurant garden, providing us with fresh produce and the students with a professional example of the lessons they were learning in the classroom.

The space was empty and unloved. Our original gardener Gretchen Kimball designed the garden, and together with my cooks and I, trenched the earliest rows, creating a rudimentary infrastructure: a hose, an extension cord to bring power from the nearby barn, and a stolen banquet table on which to work. As we tilled the dirt, there was a palpable sense of giddiness.

Since then, things have moved on considerably. We now cultivate around 3 acres (1.2 hectares), mostly as long rows of vegetables covered with fleece when required, with a polytunnel where we grow micro-greens, seedlings to plant out, and heat-loving varieties. The Restaurant's identity and menu is largely predicated on our garden. The ability to grow fresh, local, and heirloom ingredients is one of the reasons we wanted to work in the Napa Valley. We are very fortunate to have a good year-round growing climate, enabling us to grow a wide variety of seasonal crops: currently, as we move into summer, we are starting to see tomatoes, summer beans, cucumbers, and corn. In time there will be more: our fruit trees—finger citron (Buddha's hand, *Citrus medica* var. *digitata*) and kaffir lime (*Citrus hystrix*)—are not mature enough to produce, so we have developed relationships with local farmers and producers who allow us to have sole access to their trees in the meantime.

Emphasis is placed on experimentation with new crops and varieties, new growing and cultivation methods, and using all edible parts of the plant across the plant's life cycle. This is in constant service of, and aims to cultivate, a broader mission—serving a direct relationship between the natural landscape, food system, and community. It shows a respect for the garden as a part of the ecosystem and is an opportunity for inspiration, health, and education.

We are sustainably focused, with our current gardener Zac Yoder and the team following organic principles, crop rotation, and composting the kitchen waste to fertilize the garden. Zac and the garden team typically arrive very early in the morning. I arrive before 9.00 a.m. to check in on the progress of our produce, and we'll walk through the garden and discuss everything from yields to experimentation with growing methods. Daily harvests are delivered to The Restaurant for cleaning, storing, preparing, and preservation.

We began our gardening efforts thinking that the kitchen's creativity would drive the workings of the garden, that in our drive for creating thoughtful dishes that reflect the Napa Valley, the garden would provide the ingredients we wanted when we wanted them; that has proven to be only partially true. A garden is part of nature, and nature is imperfect. Despite our spreadsheets and best-laid plans, the garden doesn't always give us what we are expecting. Sometimes it provides more than we need; at other times, Zac plants things on the sly and brings them to us without warning. In all cases, the garden informs us more than we inform it. The garden has become the driving force of our menu: we start with what we know will be coming from the garden and then develop the rest of the menu around the ingredients. When brassicas, such as kalettes and flowering broccoli, start appearing in early fall we pair them with grilled local mackerel and light escabeche pickling liquid. Our bar manager responds to what the season and our garden has to offer in much the same way as I do. Each day, he and the team spend time harvesting before service and altering the bar menu to suit. It may result in strawberry-infused gin, or something that takes a little longer to mature: we make our own eau de vie, which may be infused with aromatic Asian pears and quince, as well as spices and other fruits, to create drinks that are a snapshot of our season.

To watch our cooks, veterans of the finest restaurants of the world, work with the kids at the Montessori School has been a revelation. Like growing vegetables, teaching children requires the rarest of kitchen commodities: patience. We learn more about the depths of our knowledge by attempting to distill it into simple lessons for the students. The kids teach us humility. They don't care how many stars we have. Every few months, the Montessori kids—aided by my cooks—prepare lunch for the parents and community members at The Restaurant. That relationship created with the school and the larger community, is, I feel, our greatest success.

Although I'm by no means a farmer myself, and our agricultural efforts are limited to growing produce for our high-end kitchen, working with our growers helps me bind together the various elements that influence my cooking. When I develop a dish based on an old food memory, the fact that we have harvested the vegetables ourselves gives what could otherwise be a conceptual or overly precious dish a sense of gravitas.

I am always open to new ideas. The key to creating a unique style is to find a kernel of something that is wholly mine, that can become my legacy if allowed to flourish and mature. I am an American chef: I am a product of this country's suburbs and all the experiences that have followed. Working with our growers has enabled me to reflect my own identity in the cooking we do at The Restaurant and to immunize myself a little from the popular trends and ideas of others. I endeavor to cook food that is "mine."

Gardens have therapeutic value, and I have always found gardening to be a calming experience. It brings an educational and cultural aspect to our culinary work. The people who work here arrive from all over, having moved to the Napa Valley to cook, like I did. They are often outsiders, far from home, but there is something about our collaboration with the Montessori School that makes us all feel less so. That piece of dirt, which others cultivated before us and which others will likely tend after us, creates a continuum that brings permanence to our efforts. By working with and within the community we are becoming part of it. By opening our doors and offering our labor, The Restaurant has become more than simply a place where food is served. All by planting seeds.

FAVORITE HERITAGE VARIETIES
Heritage varieties make up the bulk of vegetables we grow. Examples include oyster leaf (*Mertensia maritima*), "Oxheart" carrots (*Daucus carota*), "Caraflex" cabbages (*Brassica oleracea*, Capitata Group), Kalettes (a cross between Brussels sprouts and kale, *Brassica oleracea*), "Anne" yellow raspberries (*Rubus idaeus*), and "Mara des Bois" strawberries (*Fragaria* x *ananassa*).

– "Jimmy Red" and "Blue Clarage" corn (*Zea mays* var. *indentata*) have a beautiful color that is great for drying. We dry and mill the corn at the local mill. These varieties require intensive watering and pest control.
– "Dragon Tongue" mustard (*Brassica juncea*) has an amazing spiciness to it. For this variety the soil needs to be well balanced and evenly moist with no overwatering.

1. POTATO COOKED IN BEESWAX

Potatoes fresh from the field are justification enough for the entire farming endeavor—they are simply a different vegetable than those purchased even days later.

Sorrel from the garden is made into a vinegar that cuts through the richness, and the tiny oxalis flowers serve as a garnish.

SERVES 8
BEESWAX CREAM
– 1 liter heavy (double) cream
– 200 g beeswax
FRENCH SORREL VINEGAR
– 30 g French sorrel leaves
– 300 ml white wine vinegar
BEESWAX POTATO PUREE
– 500 g beeswax
– 6 Yukon Gold potatoes per person
– 680 g unsalted butter, cold and cubed
– 600 ml Beeswax Cream (see above)
– 10 g honey
– 200 g crème fraîche
– kosher salt
"BEESWAX" TUILE
– 10 g glycerin
– 100 ml Arbequina olive oil
– 6 g beeswax
– 20g honey
TO SERVE
– 32 wood sorrel flowers
– Maldon sea salt

BEESWAX CREAM
Put the cream and beeswax into a pan and bring to a simmer. Remove from the heat and let steep in the refrigerator overnight. Once chilled, remove the beeswax and pass the cream through a fine-mesh strainer (sieve).

FRENCH SORREL VINEGAR
Combine the sorrel and vinegar in a bag and seal with a vacuum sealer on high. Steep for at least 12 hours. Strain through cheesecloth (muslin). Just before serving, transfer to a squeeze bottle, and put in the refrigerator.

BEESWAX POTATO PUREE
Melt the beeswax in a deep, heavy pot over high heat. Add the potatoes, reduce the heat, and simmer for 5 minutes. Remove from the heat, let cool, then place in the refrigerator for 12 hours. Return the pot to medium heat, bring to a simmer, and cook the potatoes for 15 minutes. Remove from the heat and the potatoes from the beeswax. Let cool slightly, then peel and discard the skins. Pass the potatoes through a tamis into a bowl. Combine the butter and 600 ml of the beeswax cream with the potatoes, mixing gently with a rubber spatula. Do not overwork the mixture. Season with the honey and kosher salt, then push through a chinois strainer (sieve) into a pan, fold in the crème fraîche, and cover with a lid. Keep warm.

"BEESWAX" TUILE
Line a 12 x 17-inch/30 x 43-cm half sheet tray with a Silpat mat. Put the glycerin and olive oil into a pan and place over low heat until the glycerin has dissolved. In a separate pan, melt the beeswax. Put the honey into the blender, then slowly add the warm oil mixture and melted beeswax. Blend on low until just emulsified, then pour onto the tray. Set in the refrigerator for 10–20 minutes or until it hardens. Punch out rounds with a 2-inch/5-cm cutter and cut into 4 uneven quarters, keeping the pieces together.

TO SERVE
Put 1 tablespoon of warm potato puree on each plate. Add a beeswax tuile, 5–6 wild oxalis flowers and 1 teaspoon of sorrel vinegar to each plate. Season with Maldon salt.

2. COD SUNFLOWER

We put abundant sunflower petals to good use here, making a powder out of the dried petals, which we use to gently cook black cod. The fresh sunflower seeds are made into a puree, and sunflower sprouts from the greenhouse finish the dish.

SERVES 8
SUNFLOWER POWDER
– 450 g fresh sunflower petals
CURED COD
– 1 kg boneless, skinless black cod
– kosher salt, to cover
– 300 g clarified butter
SUNFLOWER SEED PUREE
– 500 g sunflower seeds
– 150 g mascarpone
– kosher salt
COD STOCK
– 500 g cod bones
– 50 g kohlrabi, peeled and halved
– 50 g yellow onion, halved
– 8 g wakame
– 4.5 liters chicken stock
COD COLLARS
– black cod collars
– 1 kg salt
– 100 ml light olive oil
WALNUTS
– 100 g red walnuts
RICE
– 100 g Calrose rice
– 95 ml Cod Stock (see above)
– 2 g kosher salt
SUNFLOWER BUTTER
– 100 g cod cooking butter (see method)
– 1 g kaffir lime leaf
TO SERVE
– 24 sunflower sprouts
– 24 dill fronds
– lemon juice, to taste

SUNFLOWER POWDER
Dehydrate the sunflower petals in a dehydrator at 125°F/51.6°C for 12 hours until dry. Blend to a powder in a Vitamix.

CURED COD
Cut the cod into fillets, pack in kosher salt, and cure for 10–15 minutes in the refrigerator, then remove the cod from the salt, rinse, dry thoroughly, and cut into 55 g pieces.

SUNFLOWER SEED PUREE
Put the seeds into a pressure cooker, cover with water, and cook on high for 40 minutes. Transfer the seeds to a blender and blend on high until they form a puree. Put the puree into a bowl, stir in the mascarpone, pass through a chinois strainer into another bowl, and season to taste with salt.

COD STOCK
Grill the cod bones over charcoal until lightly charred on both sides. Transfer to a large pan with the remaining ingredients, bring to a boil, then reduce the heat and simmer for 1 hour. Strain through cheesecloth (muslin).

COD COLLARS
Pack the collars in salt and cure for 1 hour. Rinse and dry with paper towels. Coat in the oil and grill on a charcoal grill at medium heat until cooked through. Remove from the heat, let cool, then pick the collar meat off the bones in large chunks.

WALNUTS
Use a mandoline to shave the walnuts lengthwise as thinly as possible, while still maintaining their natural shape. Reserve.

RICE
Put the rice into a pan with the stock and salt, bring to a simmer, and cook for 3–4 minutes. Once the stock is absorbed, cover, and let steam for 7 minutes. Remove from the heat and rest for 5 minutes.

COOK THE CURED COD
Coat the cured cod pieces in the sunflower powder. Baste the cod in clarified butter, place on a baking sheet, and set under the grill (salamander) for 3–4 minutes. Flake the cod into pieces. Reserve 100 g of the cooking butter from the cod.

SUNFLOWER BUTTER
Warm the reserved cured cod cooking butter in a pan with the kaffir lime leaf. Once the butter has melted, remove from the heat and let steep for 10 minutes.

TO SERVE
Arrange a small quenelle of sunflower seed puree, 3 pieces of cured cod, 3 sunflower sprouts, 3 dill fronds, and 2–3 drops of cod cooking butter on each plate.

Serve alongside individual bowls, each containing 2 large tablespoons cooked rice, 3 pieces grilled cod collar, enough shaved walnut slices to lightly cover, and a spritz of lemon juice.

1

Carlo Mirarchi

ROBERTA'S / BLANCA
Brooklyn, New York, USA

In 2008, bunkered behind a cinder block, a gastro-pizzeria-garden was created. Roberta's has since earned two Michelin stars (for Blanca, its tasting-menu den out back) and is now legendary in Brooklyn's burgeoning restaurant scene. Co-owners Brandon Hoy and Chef Carlo Mirarchi repurposed shipping containers into elevated greenhouses and filled moveable big containers with vegetables and herbs. The restaurant is famous for its pizza, creative modern dishes, and fresh salads, and grows more than 20 percent of what it serves.

When we first opened Roberta's in Bushwick, Brooklyn, in 2008, the garden was very small and inside what is now The Atrium and Tiki Bar. As the restaurant grew, so did the garden. It's now a patchwork garden of around a quarter of an acre in total, with green pockets in the backyard of the restaurant, a container orchard with picnic tables in the middle, a tiki area flanked with palm plants and raised beds on the roof of a shipping container that is also home to the world's pioneer food radio network, Heritage Radio.

Focusing on fresh, seasonal ingredients sourced from on-site gardens and local purveyors, Roberta's and Blanca maintain an innovative, minimalist culinary perspective that maximizes flavor. Most of our produce is grown in food-grade plastic containers that serve as raised beds, with some in front of the restaurant itself, along with rooftop hoop houses, where arching plastic tubes form the polytunnel-like structure for shade netting or clear polytunnel plastic to be attached to alter the growing conditions within. These hoop houses allow us to grow a greater variety through the colder months. We also have a greenhouse on the roof where we grow many varieties from seed.

We've managed to squeeze a lot into the garden, growing over 75 different fruits, vegetables, herbs, cutting and edible flowers, as well as evergreens, perennials, and ornamental plants. We focus on a lot of baby greens in the spring, such as "Scarlet Frills" mustard, "Esmee" arugula (rocket) and "Lacinato" kale (Brassica oleracea), which we use as a garnish on our kitchen dishes as well as for the "White and green pizza." In the summer, we focus on crops such as "Fairy Tale" eggplant (aubergine, Solanum melongena), purple tomatillos, different varieties of basils including Thai, lemon and lime, and holy basil, as well as anise hyssop (Agastache foeniculum), nasturtium, and bronze fennel. In the fall (autumn), we keep our summer crops going, plant baby greens again, as well as crops that can grow in winter, such as purple carrots.

Melissa Metrick, our gardener, grows most things from seed, and educates the chefs, staff, and guests on what is growing and seasonally changing in the garden, as well as what and how to harvest. The garden has specific days for specific tasks, such as a harvest day, a planting day, and a maintenance day. Melissa likes to harvest very early in the morning, before the day gets really hot, with many crops (especially leafy greens) going directly into water in the shade to keep them cool, after which she dries the leaves, and places them in the walk-in refrigerator. We never refrigerate fruit such as tomatoes, as this dulls its flavor.

Melissa meets with the chefs at the beginning of the season to discuss varieties that have worked in the garden in the past, new varieties that she or the chefs are interested in growing, as well as trying to work out why some haven't thrived. We focus on what the chefs actually use, what the garden can grow enough of, what does well in the environment, and of course, what excites everyone.

We garden as sustainably as possible, using natural pest controls. We rotate the crops in our container gardens to avoid a build-up of pests and diseases, use compost, natural fertilizers, and companion planting techniques, as well as integrated pest management. For example, we grow plants such as chives, marigolds, or chamomile with our fruit trees: they all attract pollinators, while the chamomile draws in ladybugs, which then eat the aphids that usually attack our apple trees in the spring. Being observant is crucial to our garden sustainability, allowing us to create an ecosystem and work within it, instead of having to "control" it. Paying close attention means we can identify a problem and deal with it quickly. We can also see which plants work best in each area and which are susceptible to certain pests, and also which plants thrive together.

Since our growing space is limited, we grow varieties that are hard to find, that are potent (like herbs) so that all you need is a small amount to effect a dish, as well as varieties that are best picked fresh and do not travel well, such as edible flowers.

We like to think that both garden and menu influence each other. The garden offers uncommon varieties and parts of plants that we wouldn't usually have access to, for example, with our garlic chives (Allium tuberosum) and "Delfino" cilantro (coriander, Coriandrum sativum), we harvest the leaves, flower buds, flowers, and in the case of cilantro, the seed. Similarly, the chefs at both Roberta's and Blanca influence the garden by experimenting in the kitchen and allowing us to prioritize what they like best, but they also come up with new ideas, for example, a chef requested we grow ice plant (Carpobrotus edulis), which looks like a succulent and develops crystals on its leaves. We had never grown it before and had fun learning about it, while the chefs enjoyed it because they could see how it was grown and harvest it themselves. We may have overwatered it in learning how it grows best, but we did get enough to have a continual harvest for a short time. We used it in a dish with seaweed and honeycomb. The seed structure is similar to a fig. As it grows, the jelly like interior is grassy. When it's fully ripe, the ice plant becomes sweeter and a bit tropical.

As much as it is a working garden, it is also very much part of our guests' experience. People (as well as wildlife) flock to this green space in the middle of the concrete jungle. As part of the garden is in the front of the restaurant and around the seating area of the backyard, it invites guests to look around to see what's in season. It also allows the guests to watch Melissa and chefs harvest ingredients that will go into dishes that same day. We have to be thoughtful about what we grow where, though: our beer garden is usually very busy so we tend to grow mainly hardy crops such as herbs downstairs, keeping the more delicate varieties like baby greens upstairs where the public does not have access.

As well as being a place where we can reconnect with the natural environment, the garden provides a therapeutic, private place where the staff can collect themselves. Working in the service industry can be stressful: the garden, a quiet, green oasis, is where our chefs can take a breather, and where we eat our family meal.

CONTAINER GROWING

The area that is now the Roberta's compound used to be a used car lot, so we didn't trust the soil. Creating a container garden allows you to overcome any soil limitations: we used a mix of bought-in topsoil, potting soil, and compost. The upside of our urban location is that the garden is a little warmer than is typical here in Northeast USA due to the heat island effect of being in a city; the downside is that this, combined with growing in containers, means the plants can dry out faster, are more exposed to temperature fluctuations, and lose nutrients more quickly. We combat this in two ways: firstly, we plant closely, according to the French bio-intensive technique, where you space plants so that when they are three-quarters of the way to full maturity their leaves touch: this blocks out light so weeds can't grow and water is retained, almost creating a living mulch, which helps save water as well as boost crop yield. We also grow green manures in the fall and early spring to enrich the soil and prevent soil erosion and nutrient-leaching that would occur if the soil was left bare.

1. WHITE AND GREEN PIZZA

The green pictured opposite is "Scarlet Frills" mustard, which we have an abundance of in early spring, mixed with other greens. Use a large handful of whatever you can find, such as a mix of arugula (rocket), multiple varieties of mizuna, kale, tatsoi/choi, mustard greens like red, giant, wasabina, as well as broccoli leaf.

MAKES 2 X 12 INCH/30 CM PIZZAS
PIZZA DOUGH
- 306 g fifty/fifty blend of "00" flour and all-purpose (plain) flour, plus extra for dusting
- 8 g fine sea salt
- 4 g fresh yeast or 2 g active dry yeast
- 4 g extra-virgin olive oil
- 202 ml lukewarm water
MUSTARD GREEN AND MOZZARELLA TOPPING
- 2 handfuls fresh buffalo mozzarella
- olive oil, for drizzling
- 2 handfuls mixed greens
- Kosher salt
- Parmesan cheese, for shaving
MUSTARD DRESSING
- 40 g Dijon mustard
- 100 ml lemon juice
- 10 g salt
- 10 g granulated sugar
- 30 ml water
- 230 ml extra-virgin olive oil

PIZZA DOUGH

Thoroughly combine the flour and salt in a bowl and make a well in the center. In a separate bowl, thoroughly combine the yeast, olive oil, and lukewarm water. Pour the wet mixture into the well in the dry mixture and begin mixing the two together with your hands, gradually incorporating the dry into the wet. This process will be more like mixing than kneading. After about 3 minutes, when the wet and dry are well combined, set the mixture aside and let rest, uncovered, for 15 minutes. This allows time for the flour to absorb the moisture.

Dust your hands and a work counter with flour. Gently but firmly knead the mixture on the work counter for about 3 minutes. Re-flour your hands and the counter as needed. The dough will be moist and sticky, but after a few minutes of kneading it should come together into a smooth mass. Divide the dough into 2 pieces, shape them gently into balls, and wrap them tightly in plastic wrap (cling-film). Refrigerate the dough for at least 24 and up to 48 hours before using. This process, called proofing, allows for the fermentation that gives the dough structure—which means a chewy, pliable crust—and flavor.

Preheat the oven to the highest temperature, ideally at least 500°F/260°C. Place a pizza stone or, even better, four 6 x 6-inch/15 x 15-cm unglazed quarry tiles, on the middle rack of the oven. The advan-tage of the tiles is that they're much cheaper than a stone and if they break, they're easily replaced. You can get them at places like Home Depot. Let the oven heat up for 1 hour.

Remove the dough from the refrigerator and let it come to room temperature. Lightly dust your hands and a work counter with flour. Using your fingertips, push down any bubbles in the dough. Then use your fingertips to push down on the round of the dough, from the center out to the perimeter, to encourage it to spread out. Don't push the dough out—any pushing or pulling you do will cause it to toughen, which is something to keep in mind throughout this process: be gentle with the dough. If you push it too hard or overstretch it, you can't just re-form it into a ball and reshape it. It will become stiff and hard to work with and you'll have to toss it out and use a new ball of dough. So, take your time. Spend a minute or two gently flattening the dough ball into a disk shape before you move on to the next step.

Before we explain "slapping out," which is the final step in shaping the dough (and that's really what the process is called, even by Neapolitans), be careful not to spread your dough extremely thin, or you'll end up with a cracker-crisp crust due to baking it at a lower temperature for longer, which gives it time to dry out. At home, too-thin crust is also prone to holes and to getting soggy from toppings. Aim for a round that's no bigger than 12 inches/30 cm across and no less than ⅛ inch/3 mm thick in the center; it should be a little thicker than that at the edges.

"Slapping out" the dough is what you could also call letting the crust form itself. It lets gravity do the stretching and shaping of the dough. There are lots of different ways to do this, and you should experiment to find the way you're comfortable with. This is the way we do it: pick up your disk of dough and hold your hands parallel to the floor. Then squeeze your fingers together and curve them so that your hands are like paddles. Drape the dough over one hand and flip it over to the other hand in a smooth motion. Continue moving the dough slowly back and forth, rotating it 90 degrees every few seconds so that you end up with a circle. It will start to stretch. After 1–2 minutes, you should have a round of dough that's about 12 inches/30 cm in diameter. Transfer it to a floured pizza peel—preferably a metal one—and gently push out any edges that need pushing to make a better-looking circle. Repeat with the second ball of dough.

We don't ever oil the dough before adding toppings—it prevents the sauce from melding with the crust, which is what you want.

Top the dough immediately with the torn mozzarella after transferring it to the peel, so that when it melts it will form a single layer of melted cheese, and then top with a drizzle of olive oil. Pop it in the oven the moment it's topped; it will get soggy otherwise.

Carefully slide the topped pizza onto the stone and bake it for 5–7 minutes, until the crust is bubbling up and beginning to turn golden. The cooking time will vary depending on your oven and other factors (how much you've been opening the oven, for instance). Keep an eye on it. Then turn on the broiler (grill) and broil (grill) the pizza for 1–2 minutes, checking it to make sure the cheese doesn't brown, until the crust is golden and just starting to char in a few places. If your oven doesn't have a broiler, just cook the pizza a minute or two longer, until the crust is nice and golden. Serve it hot.

MUSTARD DRESSING

Blend the dressing ingredients in a Vitamix, adding the olive oil last and gradually to create a stable emulsification.

TO SERVE

Dress a bowl, not the greens, then toss the greens in the dressed bowl, adding a pinch of kosher salt, then place them on the cooked pies. Top the finished pizzas with freshly shaved Parmesan cheese.

1

John Mooney

BELL BOOK & CANDLE
Manhattan, New York, USA

Chef John Mooney and his co-owner Mick O'Sullivan opened Bell
Book & Candle in a converted launderette in New York's West
Village in 2010. It was the first restaurant in the city to have its own
aeroponic rooftop garden, and subsequently won awards for its
sustainable approach. At least 60 percent of the ingredients used
in the restaurant's casual, seasonal dishes are from the on-site garden. Since opening Bell Book & Candle, the team have gone on to
launch a similar project, Bidwell, in Washington DC.

I first came up with the idea for creating a rooftop garden when I visited a farmers' market in Winter Garden, Florida, and met Tim Blank who had invented the Tower Garden, a soil-free growing system. At the time I'd opened Highland Manor, a restaurant and plantation nearby, and we were experiencing lots of issues with pests and disease and there was also a lot of work required to maintain the garden. In a soil-free, aeroponic system pests are less of an issue and the garden needs a lot less maintenance.

So when we opened the Bell Book & Candle in New York it was a natural evolution to try to get my food as close to my restaurant as possible by growing on the roof using this aeroponic system. The empty 2,400 square-feet (223-square-meter) roof space, with great views of the Empire State Building, was going to waste, so the landlord let us have it for free and it is now home to 60 vertical growing towers. There is no soil so the whole garden is light enough to sit six storys up on the 100-year-old building. The restaurant covers the same area down in the basement and we winch the daily harvests down in a bucket using an old-fashioned pulley system.

The plants we grow get everything they need from the nutrient solution that is held in an elevated reservoir—every 12 minutes the water runs through the towers drenching the plants roots. The reservoir gravity feeds the whole garden using no energy other than the pump, which uses the equivalent power of Christmas tree lights. It also uses less than 10 percent of the water required to grow the same quantity conventionally, and we have rapid growth because the plant food is more easily obtained—we can harvest a lettuce in four weeks, tomatoes in less than three months. We don't use fertilizer or pesticides and if we do have a pest issue we control it naturally. For example, if we have an attack of aphids we release predatory mites to remove them.

The garden is the nucleus of the restaurant and there are so many advantages gained from our "rooftop-to-table" system. Firstly, the freshness and quality of the produce is amazing—we cut herbs as we need them; tomatoes are picked ripe from the vine and are never even refrigerated; and lettuces remain living with roots attached until we prepare them in the kitchen. Our living salads are one of the most popular things on our menu. They are my take on American food: domestic ingredients, some common, others a little more exotic. Most of my entrées have just five ingredients. I try not to get too crazy.

I grow a large variety of salad greens (lettuces) and other greens including mustard, collard (spring greens), kale, and a large quantity of cucumber (enough so that we never have to purchase a pickle). We have up to 20 varieties of tomato, a few varieties of summer squash, and more than a dozen herbs including basil and mint. There's also pumpkin, tomatillo (*Physalis philadelphica*), okra, watermelon, and cantaloupe as well as four varieties of nasturtium and four varieties of chiles. Strawberries grow perfectly with no soft spots because they never rest on the ground in our vertical system.

The growing season for our garden varies with the weather. The growing climate mid-season can be very hot and humid with cooler temperatures in the beginning and end of the summer months. We typically plant in March and finish the last harvest of non-flowering plants in November. We grow more than 50 varieties of vegetables excluding roots and tubers (which are among the few things we can't grow with an aeroponic system).

The garden requires about four hours of work a day, which covers system maintenance, seeding, harvesting, and plant upkeep, and I have one full-time gardener who is also a chef, but all the staff and some local students help to maintain the plants too. Growing produce so close by gives the staff a greater sense of pride for what we do and it influences the menu—we all brainstorm new and interesting ways to use our amazing products; edible flowers such as squash blossoms are stuffed with mushrooms and goat cheese, then lightly roasted to showcase their quality and delicate beauty. We make salads from our heirloom tomatoes and plates of roasted vegetables. Multicolored nasturtiums are placed atop rooftop greens to add vibrant color and a subtle peppery finish to the taste of a dish. We actually list what we grow on the menu so customers can see what we grow, which sets us apart from other restaurants in the area too. My philosophy is to keep produce close to its natural form and try not to manipulate ingredients that are already perfect.

The garden can produce about 60 percent of the produce used in the restaurant and we waste nothing. Any surplus is either pickled, dried, or canned. Any inedible plant is bagged and dropped to the local farmers' market for compost. We also have a small stand out front of the restaurant where we give herbs for free to the tenants in our building and nearby. We wanted to create the kind of casual neighborhood place we like to visit when we're not working but we're also pioneering a food movement that's growing across the whole country.

GROWING HERBS

Herbs are the easiest plants to start with and I love adding herbs to everything. There's not one herb I don't like and most have medicinal qualities too. Always prune your flowering plants like basil or mint, cutting the top 2 inches/5 cm frequently so that the plant bushes out; this will help the plant to produce more leaves and will also make it stronger.

TOMATOES

My key plants are tomatoes (*Solanum lycopersicum*)—there isn't a tomato I don't love. Nothing says summer like heirloom varieties with their different flavors, textures, colors, and uses. They also need to be pruned to increase yield; remove the side shoots from the middle of the flowering stalks to help the plant focus on fruiting. Use very sharp shears when doing any clipping to reduce the chance of damage or infection.

FAVORITE TOMATO VARIETIES

- My favorite tomato is "Green Zebra," which has green striped skin and green flesh. It's a medium size and has the best texture. In my opinion it's the perfect tomato.
- "Supersweet 100," which is also known as "Sunburst," is smaller than a cherry tomato so I always serve it whole. They are sweet but also acidic and they pack a punch.
- I really enjoy "Cherokee Purple," a large tomato. Although they are larger, they are not too watery and have a nice firmness. They are big, beautiful, and irregular in shape, and are great in a sandwich or a Caprese salad.

1. ROOFTOP HEIRLOOM TOMATO AND BASIL SALAD

SERVES 4
VINAIGRETTE
– best-quality extra-virgin olive oil
– best-quality Spanish sherry vinegar
SALAD
– 900 g assorted heirloom tomatoes
– red onion, shaved, to taste
– 1 handful Opal basil leaves
– 1 handful Genovese basil leaves
– 50 g domestic blue cheese crumbles
  (Point Reyes or Maytag)
– sea salt and cracked black pepper

VINAIGRETTE

Put the oil and vinegar into a squeeze bottle and shake it vigorously.

SALAD

Cut any small tomatoes in half and big ones into wedges (removing the core).

TO SERVE

Arrange the tomatoes on 4 plates or a large platter. Sprinkle with shaved red onion. Next, place both types of basil on top, tearing large leaves but leaving small leaves whole. Dress the salad with the vinaigrette, season with salt and pepper, and sprinkle over the blue cheese crumbles.

2. STUFFED ZUCCHINI FLOWERS

SERVES 10–12 AS AN APPETIZER
ROMESCO SAUCE
– grapeseed oil, for brushing
– 3 large beefsteak tomatoes, cores removed
– 120 ml extra-virgin olive oil
– 10 cloves garlic
– 50 g whole hazelnuts
– 50 g whole almonds
– 10 pimento chiles (from the can)
– salt
STUFFED ZUCCHINI FLOWERS
– vegetable oil, for frying and greasing
– 2 kg cremini (chestnut) mushrooms, sliced
– 6 shallots, sliced
– 3 cloves garlic, sliced
– 240 g fresh goat cheese (chevre)
– 20 g thyme, leaves picked
– 50 zucchini (courgette) flowers, stamens removed
  with forceps or tweezers
– salt and freshly ground black pepper

ROMESCO SAUCE

Lightly oil the tomatoes and cook under a broiler (grill) until wilted and charred. Set aside. Put the extra-virgin olive oil and garlic into a medium pan over medium heat. Once the garlic begins to lightly brown, add the nuts and toast for 3–4 minutes, being careful not to overcook the garlic. Once the nuts are starting to brown, add the charred tomatoes and pimento chiles. Cook for 5 minutes, then transfer to a blender and blend until smooth. Season with salt, to taste.

STUFFED ZUCCHINI FLOWERS

Heat a little vegetable oil in a large sauté pan over high heat, add the mushrooms, and sauté for 8–10 minutes. Add the shallots and garlic and sweat them until all liquid is gone. Remove the pan from the heat and let the mixture cool slightly, then transfer to a food processor or blender and blend to a mince. Put the mixture into a mixing bowl and fold in the goat cheese and thyme, then season with salt and pepper. Chill the stuffing mix in the refrigerator.

TO SERVE

Place the chilled mushroom mix in a pastry (piping) bag and fill the zucchini (courgette) flowers. Heat on a lightly oiled baking sheet for 4–5 minutes or until hot throughout. Place 8–10 tablespoons of romesco sauce on serving platters and top each spoonful with a stuffed zucchini flower.

3. WATERMELON GAZPACHO

SERVES 6–8
– 1 whole medium watermelon,
  flesh only
– 2 seedless cucumbers
– 500 g jicama (Mexican tubers,
  Pachyrhizus erosus)
– ½ red onion
– 1 red bell pepper, stem removed
  and seeded
– ½ jalapeno chile, seeded
– 120 g cilantro (coriander)
– 200 g parsley
– 500 g "Supersweet 100" cherry tomatoes
– juice of ½ lime or 30 ml sherry vinegar
– 2 cloves garlic
– ground cumin, to taste
– ground coriander, to taste
– salt
BASIL OIL
– 800 g basil, plus extra to serve
– 240 ml extra-virgin olive oil

Chop the watermelon and vegetables and put into a large container with the herbs, cherry tomatoes, lime juice or vinegar, garlic, and spices and let marinate overnight.

BASIL OIL

Blanch the basil leaves briefly in a pan of boiling water, then transfer to a bowl of ice water. Drain the blanched basil leaves and blend them with the oil in a blender until smooth, then transfer to a squeeze bottle.

Grind the marinated watermelon and vegetables through a meat grinder (mincer) and season to taste. Serve the gazpacho chilled, topped with basil leaves, and drizzled with basil oil.

1

2

Magnus Nilsson

FÄVIKEN MAGASINET
Järpen, Jämtland, Sweden

Sustainable practice is at the heart of chef Magnus Nilsson's philosophy, with food at Fäviken following seasonal variations and existing traditions at the heart of the Jämtland community. A forager, hunter, and gardener, Nilsson cultivates half of the produce for Fäviken from its garden. A set menu for a limited 24 guests is expertly designed to present ingredients and evoke experiences of his home territory. The gardens provide seeds, herbs, and vegetables and the rest is hunted, fished for, or foraged in the surrounding area.

Gardening is my passion and has become a part of my job, too. At home, it's what I do when I don't work; in the morning before heading to the restaurant, in the light summer evening when I come home, and on my days off. I think that it is actually what I spend most of my time thinking about, aside from cooking.

At Fäviken, the gardens are run by a team of gardeners but we plan them together; those who cook what is grown and those who know how to grow it. Most of the gardening that I do myself happens outside my home, where I grow vegetables for myself and for my family. I don't have a small garden, but it's not a huge one either. It consists of a 322 square foot (30 square meter) greenhouse and a few hundred square meters of permanent beds, some in the ground and some further raised with the aid of wooden sides. At home I grow about 1500 kg of vegetables every summer. At Fäviken we grow much more, about a third of what we use throughout the year in our kitchen. The number of kilograms depends a lot on the specific vegetable we choose to grow in any given year, which in turn depends a lot on what we want to cook.

For me, the pleasure of gardening is divided into many parts: from the act of tending to my plants, to cooking and eating what I have grown and seen develop over many months.

The most important reason I garden, though, is my fascination with the seemingly magical process of growing something from a seed. This is a process that never ceases to amaze me. It all starts with a tiny little grain, sometimes no larger than a speck of dust, a brown thing that doesn't look like it can contain anything of interest. When you put that seed into the ground, humidity from the dark loam permeates into the seed coat itself and further, softening the protective skin of what's inside. The embryo starts to swell, cracks its protective barrier, and out comes the sprout. Feeling, poking, and stretching its way up through the layers of soil, guided by gravity and the promise of sunlight. The first pair of leaves soon emerges as the plant consumes the last of the stored energy it was provided by its parents, and photosynthesis is about to start. An explosion of growth is to come, a period where leaves, stem, and root are produced at rapid pace to build the framework for the plant to breath and to absorb water, sun, carbon dioxide, and minerals from the earth. Flowers emerge. All of them uniquely suited to fill the space of their particular biological niche. Some loud, colorful, and visually appealing; others gifted with the most marvelous scent or the sweetest nectar. Most of them adapted to attract some specific bird or insect to help the plant carry its genetic imprint onwards to further generations; some preferring the help of wind or water to do the same job. Grains of pollen land on the stigma and the heritage of mother and father fuse. Formation of a new seed begins and later ends with the fall of summer.

To be allowed to follow and be part of this natural process gives me an almost indescribable pleasure and is something ever present when I garden. I think that every gardener has reached a new level in their craft the day they understand that the only thing a plant wants to do is to grow and set seed. To always keep this fact in mind helps us to understand why most things taking place in our garden happen—both the good and the bad. I don't believe (as some do) that the plants I grow are aware, but I don't think that they are inanimate objects either. We are allowed to be part of their lifecycle because it benefits them, and in the end also us.

1. VEGETABLES COOKED WITH AUTUMN LEAVES

This dish started as an attempt to recreate the feeling you get when harvesting and cooking new potatoes, bringing to the diner the experience of the chef cooking them or the gardener picking them. The idea is that you pick a perfect little potato from your garden, and cook it a couple of minutes later to get that extraordinarily delicious earthy-waxy fragrant experience of really fresh potatoes. We cook the potatoes with plenty of fall (autumn) leaves that have been lying outside for almost a year since last fall, and are already starting to decompose into humus-rich soil. This further enhances that desirable aroma.

The leaves can be collected from the floor of a forest where trees such as birch grow. When collecting them, be sure to pick over the leaves very carefully before cooking them, because you are very likely to find the odd creature among the decaying plant material you collect. While these are not necessarily dangerous, they will not add to the pleasure of the diner or the reputation of the chef.

After cooking, the potatoes are plated with the hot leaves on top and the diner is then asked to dig them out of the dark, earthy-smelling mound, crush them between their fingers and dip them into some good butter before eating them straight from the hand. After using this recipe successfully for potatoes, we later applied the same principle to a wide selection of other vegetables: carrots, beets (beetroots), turnips, radishes, or whatever we had.

SERVES 6
- 18 very good new potatoes, picked and rinsed well no more than 15 minutes before cooking them
- 6 handfuls fall (autumn) leaves from last year
- 100 g butter

Place the potatoes and leaves in a pot, cover with water, and put a lid on. Bring to a boil and cook until done, but do not overcook.

Plate the potatoes on a hot stone and cover them completely with the leaves. Serve some good butter on the side and explain to your diners how to unearth them from the leaves with their hands, crush them in their fingers, and dip them in butter in order to enjoy the experience to the full.

2. LAMB SWEETBREADS AND CHARD

This dish consists of a delicate, milky, super-fresh lamb's sweetbread, fried very lightly in a nonstick frying pan or skillet. It is finished with the lightest brushing of mild thyme butter as its only flavoring and placed on a raw leaf of just-picked chard to lift it up with, like a little edible casing around a sausage. It is dipped in a very light juice or sauce made from the same plant, just slightly thicker than a pure juice and almost raw in flavor.

SERVES 6
- 6 very fresh lambs' sweetbreads
- bunch of very good-quality chard, with the full length of the stalk still attached to the leaf
- 200 g flavorless cooking oil
- melted butter, for brushing
- thyme butter
- 250 ml water
- salt

Take the sweetbreads out of the refrigerator at least 1 hour before cooking them, and remove any membranes or blood vessels that look unappetizing. Salt them very lightly, allowing the salt to dissolve on the surface.

Reserve 6 perfect chard leaves for later and keep them at room temperature under a damp cloth.

Prepare an aromatic oil using about 3 handfuls of chard leaves.

Brush a cold nonstick frying pan or skillet very lightly with butter, place the sweetbreads in it and place over maximum heat on the stove. When lightly amber in color, turn them and fry the other side, then brush liberally with thyme butter. Transfer somewhere warm but not hot to rest.

Bring the water to a boil. Meanwhile, take the Thermomix used previously to make the oil and fill it to the brim with more chard. Pour 2 tablespoons of the chard oil into the beaker of the Thermomix, add a little salt and pour the boiling water over the green leaves, then mix on maximum speed for about 1 minute. During this time the small amount of oil will emulsify, making the result a little pastel in color and giving the chard a rounder feel in the mouth. The chard that had the hot water poured over it will cook, while the leaves further down will be mixed in raw.

Push the chard mixture through a fine-mesh strainer (sieve). Most of the pulp should stay in the strainer and the result should be an emerald green liquid slightly thicker than water. Pour some of this liquid into a hot bowl with a brim, add a spoonful of chard oil, place a fresh chard leaf on the brim, and place a sweetbread on the leaf. Repeat with the remaining ingredients.

2

Nicolai Nørregaard

KADEAU
Vester Sømarken, Bornholm, Denmark

Bornholm, a tiny island in the Baltic Sea, just off the coast of Denmark, provides the culinary inspiration for Kadeau. Describing his only neighbors as the forest, the beach, and the sea, the focus of co-owner and head chef Nicolai Nørregaard's menu is his love for his native island. Ingredients come from the herb and vegetable garden, and wild foods are foraged from the surrounding landscape; the nature of Bornholm, Nørregaard says, is the backbone of the restaurant.

I was born and bred on Bornholm and I consider it to be my backyard; I know it as well as anyone. The food at the restaurant is what I call "Bornholm *terroir* cuisine." Everything is based on what we forage and grow here throughout the year. If I can't get an ingredient from the island itself, I try to make sure it has come from within Denmark, although I do get a few ingredients from Sweden and Norway. I also try to make the dishes as plant-based as possible, rather than protein-based. These boundaries have compelled me to focus and have really helped me develop as a chef. What we cook now is not merely Nordic cuisine, it is Bornholm cuisine.

The restaurant opened in 2007 and at first I relied on the island's wild places as my "hunting grounds." Foraged foods were the point of departure for my cooking, and remained so for several years, but I started to long for a proper kitchen garden as well. I realized I might be able to find similar inspiration in a cultivated environment that would give me more control over what I could harvest. So, in 2014, we started the garden in a field of 540 square feet (50 square meters), about a mile from the restaurant.

Initially, we filled the garden with berry bushes, kales and cabbages, herbs, pumpkins, potatoes, root vegetables, and asparagus. Over the next three years, we expanded the plot to about 2½ acres (1 hectare) and added more crops such as tomatoes, mustard greens, horseradish, celery root (celeriac), alliums, salsify, rhubarb, lettuce, hops, and herbs such as nasturtium, and lovage. We also increased the number of different varieties. At the moment, for example, we grow 10–12 different cabbages and kales. The garden is now also home to a dozen fruit trees—apples, pears, plums, and quince—and 4 hives that house about 150,000 bees. Harvesting honey from bees that have gathered nectar from our own flowers is as beautiful and complete as it gets. In fall (autumn), the bees also delve into the fermenting windfall fruit lying underneath our trees and then produce the most amazing, aromatic, dark amber honey. This alone is a great reason for having fruit trees but of course they also supply us with fruit for the kitchen.

Bornholm has a unique climate, due to its location in the middle of the Baltic. One side of the island is hilly and rocky, with caves and dramatic scenery. The other half is much flatter, with meadows, white sandy beaches, and deep forests. The cold rock and the proximity of the sea mean that spring comes late but, once heated by the sun, the rocky ground stays warm and the island actually has a longer, warmer summer than the rest of southern Scandinavia. This makes it possible for us to grow quite tender crops such as figs, and we find that fruits like apples and plums seem to get particularly ripe and tasty.

In addition to the large kitchen garden, there is a small plot right next to the restaurant itself with six raised beds where we grow herbs and edible flowers to go into juices and herbal teas. We cultivate 10 varieties of thyme, 20 different mints, and a range of lemon-scented herbs, such as lemon catnip (*Nepeta cataria* "Lemony"), as well as other aromatic plants like woodruff. This little garden is also where we experiment with herb and flower varieties before we decide whether to grow them on a larger scale in the main garden.

The restaurant is open from early May until late September but we rely on produce from the garden, and from the wild parts of the island, throughout the year. Twice a week we send a pallet from the island to our sister restaurant in Copenhagen (also called Kadeau), laden with vegetables, preserves, and herbs, as well as meat and dairy products from the island. The word "cadeau" is used in Danish to mean a tribute. At both restaurants, we are paying tribute and respect to Bornholm, the sea, the farmers, the forest.

Kadeau food is multilayered, delicate and complex, full of fresh produce and peppered with unusual ingredients such as spruce needles and lyme grass, lichen, and wood ants. Our cooking is rooted in this land and what it gives us, and we are always trying to evolve and develop new ways using these ingredients. The fact that I don't have formal training as a chef is a real advantage because I am not held back by preconceived ideas of what will and won't work.

Preserving is an enormously important part of what we do here. In the more abundant months, we pickle, cure, ferment, dry, and smoke like mad, as well as making spirits, syrups, oils, and vinegars. For example, we infuse oils with rhubarb root and black currant twigs; we ferment rosehips, nasturtium pods, crushed peas, and unripe crab apples; we pickle Noble fir cones (*Abies procera*), Scots pine pollen, and elm seeds. Green strawberries and white currants we turn into wine, and our homemade vinegars are produced from quince, pears, gooseberries, or spruce. Raw honey from our hives is poured over herbs, leaves, or flowers, then diluted with water (which allows the natural yeasts in the honey to ferment), producing fragrant flavored syrups. Last year, we pickled and preserved nine to ten tons of wild and cultivated food. Winter is my favorite season because it's when I get to use this huge library of preserves the most.

In my mind, the Kadeau story is just getting started. I have a dream of making the Bornholm garden an independent and self-supporting unit, supplying both our restaurants, our preservation kitchen, and even our butchery. There will be sheep, pigs, and chickens browsing the outskirts of the garden, and we will grow a much wider array of berries and fruits. All things will happen in due time; as we say on Bornholm, "the sea wasn't charted in a day."

GROWING ON SANDY SOIL
Being close to the beach, the soil of our kitchen garden is very sandy. Experienced farmers have looked at our soil here and shaken their heads. But in fact the sandy surface allows for optimal drainage, letting the water sink down to the next layer, which in contrast is dense and heavy, retaining the water really well. This creates good conditions for growth. As with any sandy soil, we do have to build up richness with manure and compost, as well as add chalk to reduce the natural acidity. Plants have to work their way down through the top 4 inches/10 cm before they can start taking up nutrients, and not every plant likes this struggle. The more the plants are challenged, the more intense the fruit tastes. We don't know why, but the soil has something special about it—it provides fantastic produce.

FAVORITE VARIETIES
– Currant family—This is one of my favorite plant groups. The flowering currant, or blood currant (*Ribes sanguineum*) is a wonder. It doesn't provide any berries but the leaves and flowers have a fantastic aroma and we use them in our preserves. It is one of the first plants to put out shoots each year, and to me the smell encapsulates early spring. The more widely known black currant is another essential, with its deep, complex fragrance. We pickle and ferment the flowers, leaves, and berries (ripe and unripe), and also infuse the branches in oil. The juice from gooseberries (also a member of the currant family) is one of our most important ingredients too, used in every corner of the kitchen to add acidity to both sweet and savory dishes.

– Pine family—I've been exploring this wonderful plant family for years in my quest to find new ingredients. We use Scots pine cones, shoots, pollen, and needles, as well as silver fir cones and needles, which have a sharp taste not unlike yuzu. Douglas and Sitka spruce provide other citrus notes, while Norway spruce cones and shoots remind me of wine gums and lemonade.
– Figs are not common in the Nordic kitchen because the fruit doesn't usually mature well in Scandinavia. But due to the long, warm summers on Bornholm, there are fig trees all over the island. We use the leaves for tea, in spirits, and in oil. The unripe figs are pickled and served raw, and the semi mature and mature fruits are made into pickles, semi dried, or lacto-fermented.

1. PALTHÄSTA—SAVORY BORNHOLMSK PANCAKES

SERVES 6–8
HEMP OIL
– 500 g fresh hemp leaves (*Cannabis sativa*)
– 500 g canola (rapeseed) oil
FIG LEAF OIL
– 250 g fig leaves
– 400 g canola (rapeseed) oil
HEMP SALT
– 200 g picked fresh hemp leaves
– 350 g coarse salt
– 1 x packet food-safe silica gel
PALTHASTA PANCAKE BATTER
– 200 g barley koji
– 50 g very active sourdough starter
– 1 extra-large (UK large) egg
– 150 ml whole (full-fat) milk
– 100 g Øland flour
– 2 g salt
MARINATED FIGS
– 3 semi-ripe figs, cut lengthwise into thin strips
– 50 ml Fig Leaf Oil (see above)
GRILLED HEMP
– 4 hemp leaves and stalks, 20 inches/50 cm long
– 50 ml Hemp Oil (see above)
TO SERVE
– aged beef fat, for frying
– browned butter, for brushing
– gammel Havgus cheese, aged for 3 years, finely grated
– 20 g chopped wild flowers, such as cornflower, fireweed, or Jerusalem artichoke
– hemp salt, to taste

HEMP OIL
Put the hemp leaves and oil in vacuum bag and seal. Steam overnight at 138°F/70°C. Strain through a fine-mesh strainer (sieve).

FIG LEAF OIL
Put the fig leaves and oil into a Thermomix and blend at high speed for 6 minutes. Strain through a fine-mesh strainer.

HEMP SALT
Blend the hemp leaves and coarse salt in a Thermomix at high speed. Pass through a fine-mesh strainer into a container and let dry under a fan for 20 minutes. Mix and store in an airtight glass jar with the silica gel.

PALTHÄSTA PANCAKE BATTER
Combine all the ingredients in a bowl. Cover and let rest at room temperature for 3 hours.

MARINATED FIGS
Marinate the sliced figs in the fig leaf oil for 1 hour at room temperature.

GRILLED HEMP
Heat a charcoal grill. Lightly brush the hemp leaves and stalks with the hemp oil and grill until lightly charred, with crisp leaves.

TO COOK THE PANCAKES
Brush a 6-inch/16-cm cast-iron skillet with aged beef fat. Cook 200 ml batter per pancake over the hot coals for 3 minutes, then flip and cook for another 2 minutes until crunchy on each side and soft in the middle.

TO SERVE
Brush the palthästa lightly with butter and top with cheese, grilled hemp, the fig slices, and wild flowers. Season with hemp salt.

2. OUR GARDEN TOMATOES WITH NOBLE PINE, HAZELNUTS, AND WHITE CURRANTS

SERVES 6–8
DRIED AND ROASTED KOMBU OIL
– 200 g fresh kombu
– 400 g canola (rapeseed) oil
TOMATOES
– 1 kg small cherry tomatoes from the garden
– 50 ml Dried and Roasted Kombu Oil (see above), plus extra to serve
– 1 "German Red" garlic clove, charred and grated
WHITE CURRANT SAUCE
– 500 g white currants
– 100 g gooseberries, juiced (50 ml)
– 50 g black currant wood oil
TO SERVE
– Noble pine cones, pickled
– a few sliced fresh green hazelnuts

DRIED AND ROASTED KOMBU OIL
Dry the fresh kombu 3 feet/1 m above a fireplace in a lightly smoky area for 24 hours.

Put the dried, smoked kombu into a vacuum bag with the oil and steam overnight in a combination oven set to 170°F/75°C, then strain and reserve the oil.

TOMATOES
Score the tomatoes, blanch briefly in a pan of boiling water, remove with a slotted spoon, and peel off the skins. Place in a bowl with the kombu oil and marinate for 1 hour at room temperature.

Preheat the oven to 122°F/50°C. Place the tomatoes on a baking sheet and bake for 4 hours, brushing with the kombu oil every 30 minutes until they are semi-dry.

WHITE CURRANT SAUCE
Blast-freeze the white currants, then juice in a cold press juicer while semi-thawed. Mix the juice with the gooseberry juice and black currant wood oil and keep chilled.

TO SERVE
Lightly marinate the tomatoes and garlic in 75 ml fresh kombu oil for 30 minutes.

Place the tomatoes on plates with the pine and 3–4 hazelnuts slices per plate, and 3 tablespoons of white currant sauce.

3. NEW POTATOES WITH WILD BLUEBERRY KOMBUCHA, FRIED LOVAGE, AND WHEY CHEESE SAUCE

SERVES 6–8
WILD BLUEBERRY KOMBUCHA (MAKES 1 LITER)
– 10 g black tea leaves
– 50 g dried blueberry leaves
– 500 g wild blueberries
– 100 g white sugar
– 500 g water
– 100 g kombucha from previous batch
– 1 Scoby
WHEY CHEESE SAUCE
– 5 liters buttermilk whey
– 500 g cold unsalted butter, cut into ¾ inch/ 2 cm cubes
– 250 g Havgus cheese, finely grated
– salt
– apple cider vinegar, to taste
KOMBUCHA AND BERRY GLAZE
– 1 liter Wild Blueberry Kombucha (see above)
– 600 g mulberries, juiced (300 ml)
– 750 g blackberries, juiced (300 ml)
– 500 g black currants, juiced (200 ml)
FRIED LOVAGE
– 800 g grapeseed oil
– 200 g lovage leaves
POTATOES
– 1 kg very good new potatoes, just dug up from the garden
– coarse sea salt
– 1 large handful lovage (stems and leaves)
– 50 g salted butter, melted, for brushing
TO SERVE
– 20 g pickled elderflower buds
– 20 g elderberry capers
– reduced blueberry kombucha and berry glaze
– woodruff oil, for drizzling

WILD BLUEBERRY KOMBUCHA
Steep the tea leaves and dried blueberry leaves in cool water for 24 hours. Strain, add the blueberry juice, sugar, water, and kombucha. Stir to dissolve the sugar. Add the Scoby, then transfer to a glass jar and cover with cheesecloth (muslin) pulled tight. Leave at 68°F/20°C for 10–14 days.

WHEY CHEESE SAUCE
Reduce the buttermilk whey in a pan over medium–low heat until you have 500 ml. Remove from the heat and while hot, gradually blend in the butter with an immersion (stick) blender. Blend in the grated Havgus cheese. Season with salt and cider vinegar.

KOMBUCHA AND BERRY GLAZE
Put the kombucha into a dehydrator at 122°F/ 50°C until it has reduced by an eighth.

Combine the berry juices in a pan and reduce slowly over very low heat until it reaches 34 brix. Combine the reduced juices with the reduced kombucha to make a glaze. Let cool and store in an airtight container.

FRIED LOVAGE
Heat the oil in a pan to 284°F/140°C. Line a baking sheet with paper towels. Fry the lovage leaves in the oil for 2–3 minutes. Transfer to the lined sheet and let cool. Store in airtight container lined with paper towels.

POTATOES
Lightly scrub the new potatoes with coarse salt. Place in a pan with cold water and the lovage stems and leaves, bring to a boil, then simmer until cooked but still slightly firm in the middle. Drain, peel while hot, then cut in half and lightly brush with salted butter.

TO SERVE
Glaze the cut edges of the potatoes with the kombucha glaze. Garnish with the fried lovage, elderflower pickles, elderflower capers, and drizzle with woodruff oil.

Lightly foam the whey cheese sauce with an immersion (stick) blender and finish each dish with 2 tablespoons of this foam.

Matt Orlando

AMASS
Refshaleøen, Copenhagen, Denmark

Located on the outskirts of Copenhagen, Amass's surroundings directly reflect the holistic approach to food and sustainable agriculture initiatives at the restaurant. Every table has a direct view of the kitchen garden, and guests and locals alike are encouraged to treat the space as an urban oasis. With more than 80 varieties of leafy vegetables, berries, herbs, and flowers, the garden is more than just a source of ingredients for Californian chef Matt Orlando, it's the soul of the restaurant and the inspiration for future dishes.

We decided to locate Amass outside of the city of Copenhagen, as we wanted space to grow our own ingredients, to allow us the freedom to do what we wanted to do. We found what we were looking for in Refshaleøen, a previously lesser known part of the harbor area, where we could make productive a piece of land that had long been unloved.

We created a garden of knee-high, square raised beds right in front of the restaurant in 2013, and since then our original 54 beds have steadily grown to 137, and been joined by an 60-foot (18-meter) long polytunnel, home to an aquaponic system of growing in mini-hanging gardens. Inside and out, our focus is on flavor rather than volume—I'm more interested in how delicious our harvest is than how much we produce. Diversity of flavors is paramount: we now grow 80 different edible plants—multiple-harvest crops like kale and chard, along with mustards, berries, chives, radishes, a whole range of cilantro (coriander) and basil, as well as incredible figs. Orpin (*Sedum telephium*), a leafy northern plant with a gently bitter flavor, is another of my favorites. It goes really well with meat dishes, giving them a lighter "summery" touch.

Although it's around an acre or so in total, the garden can't produce everything we need—it provides five to ten percent of our ingredients—so we augment it with our foraging and using local suppliers. For example, deep-rooting crops, such as parsnips, take up space for a long time, and we are lucky enough to be supplied by excellent growers, including a biodynamic farm in the south-west of Zealand.

Edible flowers are one of our key ingredients—cornflowers, borage, and violets among them—and I get super-excited about the marigolds flowering every year. As well as being a great companion plant, I love the gentle medicinal flavor of its leaves and flowers. I dry the leaves and blend them with oil, which releases this incredible, tangerine skin flavor. I mostly use the flowers in sauces—savory and sweet—because it gives them some of the color and flavor of saffron.

The polytunnel is quite a different experience to the outdoor garden. You step through the door and onto a bridge, below which carp swim: we collect the solids they produce and use them to feed 80 Zipgrows—a vertical system of "hanging gardens" in the tunnel. In my experience, food grown using aquaponics can taste fishy, so we have devised a way to avoid that: instead of using the solids to feed the plants directly, we add worms to the bags ensuring the solids are broken down, with the worm casts providing a more bio-available range of nutrients for the growing plants. It has worked incredibly well. The ingredients of fish food are often mind boggling—pork for heaven's sake—so we make our own using the waste from our kitchen along with canola (rapeseed) oil pressings, all ground together, which allows us to feed both the fish and in turn the plants. We experiment with different feeds to ensure that the fish have what they need but also that the plants—tomatoes, mustards, baby cabbages, watercress—receive the specific nutrients they need to flourish, which is obviously different for tomatoes and, say, kale. It's a fantastic way of closing the only open loop in our system, using our "waste" to create flavor.

Our gardener, Jacquie, and I created the garden together. We met while at Noma—she's a trained chef, so of course understands the kitchen side so well, but having worked on organic farms worldwide she brings a global perspective to our garden. For the first three years, it was just us tending the space, so we feel very connected to it. It was a time of experimentation, of finding out what grows here, which plants like our sandy and salty soil, and what worked well for the restaurant. The temperature swings over a day can be considerable—80°F/27°C in the day and perhaps 50°F/9°C at night—so we had to discover what could handle that. Fennel, chard, cabbage, sorrel do; certain types of squash and leafy herbs native to warmer climates don't like it.

As well as being a beautiful and productive space, the garden has quietly, naturally, become the hub around which the restaurant and everyone connected to it spins. The waiters and waitresses do a shift out there every week and the chefs can spend an hour out in the garden at the start of the day not only picking herbs and harvesting but also watering, weeding, and turning the compost. Of course, Jacquie takes the lead in the garden and she's assisted by interns that join us for anything up to four months, working in the kitchen as well as the garden.

Even when work ends, you are likely to find us in the garden. We congregate on a Saturday night after clear-down; everyone migrates outside, there's usually a bonfire and drinks. It has added another dimension both to the garden and the sense that this is still the place to be when work is done, to be together. Even on a Sunday, when the restaurant is closed, it's perfectly likely that we'll be in the garden cooking and relaxing together. People bring friends, so it is continually building our community. We also use the garden as the basis for the Amass Green Kids Program, our farm-to-table initiative for local schoolchildren.

The garden is very much part of the visitor experience—it's not only that guests are allowed into the garden; we also actively encourage it. The first thing we tell them is that they are welcome to walk around the garden with a drink. I'm very keen that everyone who comes here gets as much pleasure as possible from every part of the experience, and of course they might well see us harvest something from the garden for their plate once they have ordered.

The garden isn't just a source of ingredients for the kitchen—it also influences what and how we cook. It forces us to be hypersensitive to the seasons and to change frequently and adapt to the weather. What we do is often described as "New Nordic" but it's not about moving past "Nordic" cuisine, but rather evolution, where we can take it. The rise of the Danish food scene, largely driven by Noma (where I used to cook), has attracted plenty of culinary incomers with their experiences and influences. I'm from California, via the kitchens of Le Bernardin, Aureole and Per Se in New York, and the Fat Duck and Le Manoir aux Quat'Saisons in England, so here at Amass we can approach Nordic cuisine in a different way. The garden helps us do this. We grow what we like, and then our menu responds to what's ready, when it's ready.

Somehow, without planning for it to be, our garden has become something that nourishes us all in so many ways—it is a luxury we never take for granted.

FAVORITE EDIBLE FLOWERS
- Borage flowers—they taste like cucumber.
- Calendula flowers—for their subtle sweetness.
- Cornflowers—for their sweetness.
- Marigolds—they taste like tangerine skin.
- Nasturtiums—they are spicy.
- Violets—they are juicy and sweet.

COMPANION PLANTING
We are very mindful of gardening with a light touch. We grow without chemical pest control—we've found lemon and chile water, along with copper bands around containers, to be very effective in limiting slug and snail damage. Companion planting—a system of interplanting that works to the benefit of at least one of the plants involved—is a key part of our approach. We pair plants with the aim of repelling pests, attracting pollinators, to offer support or shade, to cool roots, retain water, or feed the soil and in turn neighboring plants. It works well for us—for example, planting marigolds with raspberries draws in pollinators, which ensures we get a higher yield from our raspberry plants; growing cornflowers with fennel means they offer each other mutual support as they grow.

1. SALTED MACKEREL, MARINATED CABBAGE FLOWERS, BURNT WOOD OIL

SERVES 4
BURNT WOOD OIL
- 100 g sunflower oil
- 10 g burnt wood chips
MACKEREL
- 1 x 500-g fresh mackerel
- 1 liter water
- 100 g sea salt
- 40 g burnt wood chips
MARINATED CABBAGE FLOWERS
- 75 g carrots, thinly sliced
- 25 g shallots, thinly sliced
- 250 g cold-pressed canola (rapeseed) oil
- 125 ml white wine
- 125 ml apple cider vinegar
- 8 lemon cucumbers
- 240 cabbage flowers
- 24 small purple basil leaves, to serve

BURNT WOOD OIL
We use pine wood chips. Place the wood chips in a metal container, light with a kitchen blowtorch, and let them burn for 30 seconds. Cover with a lid to put out the flames.

Put the oil and wood chips into a small pan and heat until it reaches 194°F/90°C on a thermometer. Remove from the heat and let stand overnight at room temperature.

The next day, strain the oil through a fine strainer (sieve) and reserve at room temperature. It will keep for 6 months.
MACKEREL
Fillet the mackerel and place the 2 fillets in the refrigerator.

Combine the water, salt, and wood chips in a medium pan and heat until it reaches 194°F/90°C on a thermometer. Remove from the heat, let cool, and store in the refrigerator. When the brine is cold, strain through a fine strainer to remove the wood chips.

Place the mackerel fillets in the burnt wood brine for 6 minutes, then remove and dry with paper towels. Place them in the refrigerator, skin side down, overnight to let the flesh dry slightly and the salt to penetrate the flesh.

Split the fillets of mackerel lengthwise down the middle, along the bloodline, cutting along both sides of the bloodline on the thicker end of each fillet. This will not only remove the bloodline, but will also remove the pin bones at the top of the fillet. Turn the 4 half fillets over so they are skin side up. Gently score the skin with a sharp knife, taking care not to cut the flesh under the skin. Set to one side at room temperature.
MARINATED CABBAGE FLOWERS
Put the carrots and shallots into a medium pan over low-medium heat with 25 ml of the canola (rapeseed) oil. Cook until just tender. Add the white wine, increase the heat to medium and cook for 2 minutes, then remove from the heat and add the remaining canola oil and the apple vinegar. Let the mixture sit until it cools to room temperature.

While the mixture is cooling, peel the cucumbers and cut into ½-inch/1-cm dice. Set aside at room temperature.

When you are ready to serve, pass the cooled carrot and shallot mixture through a fine strainer, add the cabbage flowers and diced cucumbers, and season with salt to taste. Let marinate for no longer than 5 minutes.
TO SERVE
Lay the 4 mackerel half fillets flesh side down and run a kitchen blowtorch on a medium flame up and down the skin of each one for 10 seconds. Place a half fillet flesh side down just off center on each plate. Spoon a healthy portion of the cabbage flower mix alongside the mackerel for the whole length of the fillet. Drizzle 1 teaspoon of burnt wood oil over each piece of mackerel and garnish with 6 basil leaves per plate.

2. GARDEN SHOOTS, LEMON SKIN, ALE YEAST, AND DRIED BERRIES

Ale beer yeast is a wet by-product from brewing beer. Ask your local brewery for some.

SERVES 4
SALTED KALE STEM OIL
- 200 g kale stems
- 4 g salt
- 175 ml sunflower oil
LEMON SKIN AND ALE YEAST PURÉE
- 50 g lemon skin
- 37.5 g ale beer yeast
- 5 g salt
- 3 g shishito pepper
- 10 g dried plum
LEMON AND ALE YEAST EMULSION
- 63 g Lemon Skin and Ale Yeast Purée (see above)
- 1 egg yolk
- 250 ml sunflower oil
DRIED BERRY POWDER
- 10 g freeze-dried raspberries
- 10 g freeze-dried strawberries
- 10 g freeze-dried red currants
HERBS AND SHOOTS
- 32 small Swiss chard leaves
- 16 medium mizuna leaves
- 32 wild watercress shoots
- 32 mustard leaves
- 32 curly mustard leaves
- 32 borage flowers
- 32 kale flowers
- 32 carnation flowers
- petals from 2 calendula flowers
- salt

SALTED KALE STEM OIL
Place the kale stems and salt in a vacuum food bag, vacuum seal, and let stand for 4 days at room temperature.

After 4 days, preheat the oven to 140°F/60°C. Remove the stems from the bag and dry until crispy. Place the stems in a medium pan and cover with the sunflower oil. Heat the oil until it reaches 185°F/85°C on a thermometer, remove from the heat, and let stand at room temperature overnight. Strain the oil, then store in a sterilized bottle at room temperature. It will keep for 3 months.
LEMON SKIN AND ALE YEAST PURÉE
Put all the ingredients into a blender and blend to a thick paste. Transfer to a bowl, cover, and put in the refrigerator for at least 3 days (and up to 1 month) before using.
LEMON AND ALE YEAST EMULSION
Combine the lemon skin and ale yeast purée with the egg yolk in a blender and blend on medium speed until smooth, then slowly drizzle in the oil (with the motor running) to form a thick emulsion. Season with salt to taste. Keep in the refrigerator, covered, until required.
DRIED BERRY POWDER
Put the freeze-dried berries into a blender and blend on high speed until the berries are completely pulverized. Pass through a fine sifter (sieve) into a clean container, cover, and store at room temperature until required.
TO SERVE
Spread the lemon skin and ale yeast emulsion on 2 flat plates in an even layer so it covers the entire plate. Divide the herbs and flowers evenly between the 2 plates, arranging them so they are evenly spread out and not piled up. Drizzle 2 tablespoons of the salted kale stem oil evenly over each plate. Put the berry powder into a fine sifter and sift it evenly over each plate. Season each plate with salt to taste. Each plate is meant to be shared between 2 people and enjoyed with your fingers. Don't be afraid to get dirty.

1

Matthew
& Iain Pennington

THE ETHICUREAN
Wrington, Somerset, UK

Set within a stunning walled garden, The Ethicurean is founded on
a sense of place. Matthew and Iain Pennington's menu is updated
twice-daily, depending on what the gardeners bring to the kitchen.
With a passion for historic recipes and exploring new combinations of
harmonious flavors, the chefs are driven by what they call "the taste
of nature." Their passion for produce extends to guests who want to
take a little piece of The Ethicurean home, with pickles, fermenta-
tions, and vegetable boxes, all bounty from the garden, on offer.

In many ways, we walked into a dream when we first came to Barley Wood Walled Garden, where we set up The Ethicurean in the cold winter of 2010. I was selling produce at farmers' markets that I'd made from local ingredients, not even vaguely contemplating starting a restaurant, when another producer told me about the walled garden, so I paid a visit. And now, somehow, here we are, running a restaurant in the converted Victorian glasshouse that I hope is not only making the best of the produce on our doorstep, but also playing a part in the wider development of our food culture.

The walled garden is quite spectacular, leaning gently toward the south with views across Wrington Vale and the Mendip Hills. The beds are dominated by heritage vegetables, herbs, and flowers that draw in pollinators, along with fruit trees, including pears and plums, trained as fans and espaliers against the walls. Sun-lovers including tomatoes are grown in polytunnels, which also provide the extra warmth and shelter for many seedlings. As you'd expect with a Victorian walled garden, everything has been planned and built well, especially drainage, which takes excess water down the slope to replenish a borehole that we in turn pump up water from to nourish the crops when needed.

Mark Cox has been gardening within the walled garden since 2003. He's a self-taught, inquisitive gardener, someone who parallels our approach to food in the way he grows. I imagine it is unusual when a restaurant and a garden inhabit the same patch of land that the garden and gardener came first, but that's how it is here.

A couple of years ago, Mark converted to a no-dig approach and the results have been remarkable. Rather than unsettle a healthy soil ecology by digging and upturning the soil, layers of compost are added to the surface (this mirrors the natural process of soil accumulation by leaf fall). This feeds the soil, builds greater depth of topsoil and helps retain moisture. Even in this hottest, driest of years, the plants are thriving. In a very real, tangible way, our interest and passion for fermented foods and the wider topic of our own internal gut flora is mirrored perfectly by Mark's development of the soil's microbiome; we are both striving to maximize the bacterial health of ourselves and our customers, as he is that of the soil, and in turn the plants that are nurtured by it.

The relationship between garden and kitchen is far more than one of supply and demand. Iain and I are out in the garden most days talking with Mark, discussing what's thriving in the garden, working well in the kitchen, and what we might grow in future. We aren't just taking vegetables, herbs, and fruit at their classic "peak": having a flourishing garden adjoining the restaurant means we can harvest at any point in a plant's life cycle. At the moment, for example, we have pale cream-colored arugula (rocket) flowers—beautiful and as intense in flavor as the leaves—and crunchy, peppery, mustard- flavored turnip seeds, that we can add to a dish. Our relationship is very much a collaborative, creative one.

Of course, a walled garden can't supply us with everything we need—we would require considerable acreage just for potatoes—so we concentrate on high-value, multiple-harvest crops like salad greens, where no food miles, plastics, or processing mean we get the best there is with no "footprint." We never buy salad greens: it is perfectly common for us to take 88 lb (40 kg) of salad greens from the garden in a week. As well as familiar lettuce varieties and arugula (rocket), Mark grows a wealth of other greens including the spicy red and green mustards, tatsoi, and bitter chicories, many through the winter as well as the warmer months. Mark and I are very keen on heritage vegetable varieties: what you might gain with new varieties in disease resistance, uniformity, and yield, you lose in flavor, aroma, and texture. Of course, some hybrid varieties are exceptions—"Gardener's Delight" tomato (*Solanum lycopersicum*), for one—though we grow them separately from others, should we be saving any for seed.

As well as salad greens, we are particularly fond of ingredients that are their best within moments of being picked: *agretti* (*Salsola soda*), also known as monk's beard, is a salty land vegetable that we use in many ways in the restaurant. As well as having a fabulous "green" and salty flavor, it is a great cropper that takes well to being cooked over charcoal or in water, is surprisingly substantial, almost meaty, as well as noodle-like when used in place of them. We also have a great fondness for winter greens, such as cavolo nero and "red Russian" kale, that are robust and adaptable. In summer, I guess we get 80 percent of our ingredients from the garden.

Having a restaurant was never the point; it still isn't. We want to be part of something bigger, in taking the idea of food and what it can be in a different direction. We want to encourage people into nature, to embrace foraging and develop a deeper understanding of the processes of the wider natural world, and Mark is very much in tune with that. He enables us to bring more of that essence into our recipes, not only by growing ingredients that fit, but in mirroring our ethos. The garden and restaurant are just part of our approach to encouraging people to interact with food, especially how young people taste, experience, and enjoy food. It is part of an inquisitive mindset that we hope comes across in our food. Of course, with the restaurant being inside the walled garden, the garden is very much part of the guest's experience, and we actively encourage them to be curious about and inspired by the garden.

Fermentation is a big part of what we do at the restaurant. It extends the life of ingredients, helps us deal positively with gluts, the process enriches the raw ingredients, and in turn those who eat it. There are flavors—often sour and/or savory/umami—that result from fermentation that broaden what we do, too. We have a good number of guests from Japan, a culture rich in preserving and fermentation, and it is a frequent occurrence to be told by them that our food tastes "alive." To my mind, that is the perfect coming together of Mark's work in the garden and ours in the kitchen.

GROWING MUSHROOMS

Mark and I are fascinated with fungi, and we are working with the mycologist from Kew Gardens & Forever Fungi to encourage edible varieties to flourish in the garden: different species thrive on wood chips, straw, or logs, and among the species of mushroom we are hoping to grow are shiitakes, wine caps, and oyster mushrooms. Each offers great flavor and texture, but they also play an important part in our fermented dishes, including making our own "soy" sauce from spent coffee grounds. It's a highly efficient use of materials: 1 kg of waste wood chips or logs will typically yield 1.5 kg of mushrooms. Growing mushrooms also allows us to sidestep arguments or con-

siderations about foraging mushrooms in any quantity. It also means we can have a dish on the menu for days and weeks rather than one-offs.

We are also keen on exploring how fungi operate in enriching the processes in the garden, hence we are introducing mycorrhizal fungi to the garden. These fungi create a subterranean network that acts as a secondary root system for plants they come into contact with, taking a few carbohydrates in exchange for a greater wealth of nutrients for the plant. In combination with the no-dig regime, this has brought a greater resilience and integrity to the garden.

FAVORITE VEGETABLE VARIETIES

- Agretti (saltwort, *Salsola soda*)—This vegetable is unique and very productive once summer arrives. It has sea-samphire-like qualities, salty and crisp, and has a flavor akin to a chop suey noodle. We griddle, ferment, and blanch kilos of this through July.
- Lovage (*Levisticum officinale*)—What an outstanding herb. Celery-like, curry-flavor, vegetal, prolific in growth, and perfect in so many dishes and drinks.
- Miner's lettuce (winter purslane, *Claytonia perfoliata*)—A succulent salad leaf, it grows well under cover and is the main reason we've managed 100 percent salad crop self-sufficiency in all our time at this garden.

1. PAN-ROASTED HAKE, FENNEL AND PINE PUREE, BRAISED SAVOY, SHIITAKE SOIL, CLAMS, AND HAZELNUTS

The edible soil on this dish always takes our guests by surprise. It really does bear a striking resemblance to real soil, yet has beautiful and rich, mushroom umami and sweet notes that are most welcome when matched with the best fish available that day. Scots pine, which is abundant around the Mendips, may also seem an unusual source for flavor but it offers a delicate taste similar to cream soda. We are glad to live near those majestic trees.

SERVES 2
HAKE
- 30 g sea salt
- 500 ml ice-cold water
- 240 g hake, skin on and cut into 2 portions
- a little canola (rapeseed) oil
- neutral oil, for frying
- piece of salted butter
- 100 g young purple sprouting
- fine sea salt
SHIITAKE SOIL
- 40 g raisins
- 10 g walnuts
- 15 g dried shiitake
- salt
FENNEL AND PINE PUREE
- 50 g salted butter
- 1 fennel bulb, thinly sliced
- 30 g Scots pine needles
- 100 ml heavy (double) cream
- salt and white pepper
BRAISED SAVOY CABBAGE
- 2–4 Savoy cabbage segments (sliced through its center, the stem holding it together)
- 1 tablespoon dark brown muscovado sugar
- 1 teaspoon truffle oil
DRESSING
- 40 g roasted hazelnuts
- 20 g capers
- 25 ml apple cider vinegar
CLAMS
- 10 clams
- 100 ml cider
- 1 tablespoon honey
TO SERVE
- small selection of edible flowers: radish, mizuna, rocket (arugula), or mustard flowers

HAKE
Dissolve the sea salt in the ice-cold water in a pitcher (jug) to make a brine of approximately 6%. Submerge the hake in the brine and place in the refrigerator for no longer than 1 hour.

SHIITAKE SOIL
Preheat the oven to 350°F/180°C. Put the raisins into a roasting pan and roast in the oven for 30 minutes, then remove and let cool. Roast the walnuts for 6 minutes or until lightly brown.

Put the cooled raisins into a blender with the roasted walnuts and dried shiitake and blend to a soil consistency. Add salt to taste and let come to room temperature.

FENNEL AND PINE PUREE
Heat the butter in a pan over medium heat until past the point of foaming and let the separated milk solids come to a light hazel brown, then remove from the heat.

Add the fennel, pine needles, and cream to the butter and simmer until the fennel is very soft. Remove from the heat, pick out and discard the pine needles, and blend with an immersion (stick) blender to a silky-smooth consistency. Season to taste, pass through a fine-mesh strainer (sieve), and keep warm.

BRAISED SAVOY CABBAGE
Preheat the oven to 410°F/210°C.

Coat the Savoy cabbage segments in the muscovado sugar and cover in the truffle oil. Roast until the sugar is well caramelized, then reduce the heat to 320°F/160°C and cook until the cabbage is cooked through. Remove from the oven and keep warm.

DRESSING
Combine the hazelnuts, capers, and cider vinegar in a bowl and mix well.

COOK THE HAKE
Preheat the oven to 400°F/200°C.

After 1 hour, remove the hake from the brine and dry very well with a clean dish towel. Take special care to dry the hake skin well and season lightly with fine sea salt and a little canola (rapeseed) oil. Heat a lightly oiled ovenproof frying pan or skillet over medium heat, add the fish skin side down and cook for 2 minutes, then increase the heat to high and cook for another minute before transferring to the oven, with the butter and purple sprouting, and roast for 3 minutes for a beautifully golden skin. Remove from the oven, turn the fish over, and let rest in the butter for 2 minutes.

CLAMS
While the fish is resting, place the clams, cider, and honey in a lidded pan over full heat and bring to a vigorous boil. The clams are cooked once opened. Remove from the heat; the clams can rest in the cider and honey liquid until serving.

TO SERVE
Base each plate with the fennel puree, then the braised cabbage and purple sprouting with the hake resting on top. Drain the clams and place around the plate in their shells. Dress with the dressing and garnish with the shiitake soil and edible flowers.

2. SEA BUCKTHORN, RE-MILLED BREAD, HONEY, AND THYME CAKE

This cake is unusual. Sea buckthorn, which grows wild and is a low-carbon alternative to typical citrus fruits, gives it a lovely tang. This is balanced by the sweetness of honey from our hives. The lemon thyme adds further floral complexity. The use of re-milled bread in place of flour is another way to repurpose our leftover bread and reduce food waste.

SERVES 12
CAKE
- 400 g crustless leftover white bread, sliced
- 275 g salted butter (preferably grass fed/organic), plus extra for greasing
- 200 g golden superfine (caster) sugar
- 6 tablespoons honey (preferably local)
- 4 free-range/organic eggs, at room temperature
- 100 g roasted ground hazelnuts
- 2 teaspoons baking powder
- 4 teaspoons chopped lemon thyme
- 2 tablespoons sea buckthorn juice
SYRUP
- 6 tablespoons honey
- 6 tablespoons sea buckthorn juice
- 3 sprigs lemon thyme
TO SERVE
- organic clotted cream
- a few yarrow leaves, to garnish

CAKE
Place the leftover sliced bread in a dehydrator at 104°F/40°C or an oven at its lowest setting overnight. The following day it should have completely dried out. Blitz it in a food processor until as finely ground as possible. Measure out 200 g.

Preheat the oven to 350°F/180°C. Grease an 7-inch/18-cm springform cake pan and line with parchment (baking) paper.

Beat the butter in a large mixing bowl with an electric beater until creamy. Add the sugar and honey and beat until light and fluffy. Add the eggs one at a time, along with a spoonful of bread flour with each, and beat thoroughly after each addition.

Combine the remaining bread flour in a bowl with the ground hazelnuts and baking powder and carefully fold this into the butter, sugar, and egg mixture. Stir through the lemon thyme and sea buckthorn juice.

Carefully pour the mixture into the prepared cake pan and spread it out evenly with the back of a spoon. Bake for 45–50 minutes until the cake is golden brown and springs back when pressed gently. Remove from the oven and leave the cake in the pan.

SYRUP
Put the honey and sea buckthorn juice into a pan, bring to a boil, then simmer until reduced by half. Remove from the heat and add the sprigs of lemon thyme.

While it's still in the pan, prick the cake all over with a toothpick, about three-quarters of the way through. Drizzle with the warm syrup and let the cake cool before removing it from the pan.

TO SERVE
The cake is delicious with organic clotted cream and garnished with yarrow leaves.

1

Simon Rogan

L'ENCLUME
Cartmel, Cumbria, UK

Simon Rogan is renowned for his innovative style and passion for "forgotten" vegetables, fruits, herbs, and foraged wild foods. It's an approach that has helped him gain two Michelin stars for L'Enclume, his restaurant in the Lake District, northwest England. After initially working with a local grower to produce the unusual varieties he wanted for his menu, in 2011 Rogan set up "Our Farm," his own dedicated smallholding that now produces more than 200 different types of edible plant. The farm also has a crucial part to play in utilizing waste, making the whole operation as sustainable as possible.

The site of Our Farm, not far from L'Enclume in the Cartmel valley, was initially just a huge field with rocks rising from the ground, but it had some promising natural features, being flanked on either side by woodland and hedgerow. Lake District winters are long and hard, and there is a lot of wind and rain, so natural protection is very desirable.

I worked with Dan Cox—a talented chef and grower and my right-hand man at the time—to build the farm from scratch. Our vision was to create a harmonious relationship between cooking and growing.

The native soil here is a slightly acidic clay-loam. It's great for growing but, once wet with rain, very difficult to work, so we opted for a system of permanent raised beds in which we could build up the soil with green waste, improving the structure and reducing the clay content. The beds still sit on the bare earth, maintaining contact with the local soil and boosting microbial activity. We also have six polytunnels: two smaller ones for propagation, and four larger ones for crops such as tomatoes, cucumbers, peas, and edible flowers that could easily be overwatered in the Cumbrian climate.

Dan and I wanted to create the most sustainable growing operation possible. We were strongly influenced by the American organic grower Eliot Coleman and the Quebecois farmer Jean-Martin Fortier. From them we learned that the best way to achieve amazing flavor in produce is to nourish and respect the soil. That remains at the heart of our system.

We feed the soil with compost, manure, nettle, and comfrey preparations, and liquid seaweed feeds. We are also careful about preserving soil structure. Heavy digging and rotavating can disrupt the delicate ecosystem in the topsoil, as well as bringing weed seeds up to the surface where they can germinate, so we use a broadfork instead, a simple tool that allows us to loosen the soil without mixing up the layers, improving aeration and drainage. We attack weeds at surface level when they are very small with hoeing and also flame-weeding. It all seems to be working! Since we began, the farm has tripled in size, now covering 12 acres (5 hectares), supplying all the fresh produce for our restaurants, and supporting poultry and livestock too. We offer farm tours to diners (by prior arrangement) who want to see all this at first-hand.

The farm is an extension of our kitchens—our menu and our cooking would be quite different without it. It gives us the freedom to study each variety at every stage of its growth, which has allowed us to discover some incredible new flavors. With "Red Russian" kale (Brassica napus), for instance, we start off using the young shoots in early summer, then we move on to using the whole young plant, followed by the larger leaves and stems of the mature plant. As the kale matures further, it produces spicy yellow flowers and then, finally, sweet and tender seed pods.

Rare herbs or vegetables from elsewhere in the world can also be cultivated here. Apple marigold (chinchilla, Tagetes minuta) is a favorite example. Native to South America, it has delicate feather-shaped leaves with an intense mint-apple flavor. We sow it from early spring to late summer, and use the small, tender leaves raw. After the last frost we let it grow into huge plants (up to 8 inches/20 cm tall) from which we can harvest larger leaves to flavor oil, syrup, and sorbet. Our aim is to grow produce that is almost perfect, so that we barely have to do anything to it. Our dish "Aynesome offerings," for example, features 15 different vegetables and herbs, along with lobster tail, but they are prepared simply, or even left raw, so they can speak for themselves.

We use various organic methods to maintain productivity throughout the colder months. Double-walled crop cover tunnels protect outdoor plants from the cold, and we use fleece on all crops inside the polytunnels. We also utilize the heat generated by compost: piles of it are built up against the outside of the polytunnels, covered over, then left to do their thing. When the piles are nice and hot, they not only insulate but also radiate heat into the tunnel. "Hot beds" help us grow through the winter too—constructed by putting soil over a layer of fresh manure that generates heat as it breaks down.

Good old-fashioned "clamping" can extend the season for root vegetables: this means storing harvested vegetables in boxes of compost and sand, which keeps them fresh and firm. We also "clamp" veg still growing in outdoor beds by blanketing them with hay and fleece so they can survive the cold. We can then "force" clamped carrots, beets (beetroots), parsnips, and chard roots by bringing them indoors but keeping them in the dark. This produces tender new leaf growth, with vivid yellows and pinks.

At L'Enclume, we use as much as we can from our immediate environment and no imported ingredients—not even lemons. We are committed to sustainability and moving toward zero waste, and the farm is helping us achieve this. We have a hot compost system for meat and fish waste, which produces a coarse compost full of beneficial bacteria and fungi. Shellfish shells are smashed up and used as gravel. We even repurpose polystyrene trays by spraying them with metal oxide to make them food-safe, then using them as planters—they are great for carrot-growing as they can be easily raised to a level above 24 inches (60 cm), which the dreaded carrot fly cannot reach.

The daily running of Our Farm is handled by a team of four growers but I make sure all my chefs spend time working there too. It's vital that they engage with the growing of ingredients. Each day on the farm starts with the whole team harvesting the day's produce, ready to be delivered to L'Enclume and Rogan & Co., our sister restaurant, also in the village of Cartmel. Harvest to plate can take less than an hour, and all our shoots and young plants are delivered to the kitchens still growing, in soil-filled trays, so they're as fresh as possible and retain that link with the earth.

FAVORITE GARDEN VARIETIES

- "Ceresa" pea (Pisum sativum). This dwarf petits pois variety is practically self-supporting and great for growing in the open field. We pick it very young to get intensely sweet, tiny raw peas.
- "Kalibos" cabbage (Brassica oleracea) is a beautiful red pointed cabbage with a sweet flavor that makes it delicious to eat raw. We harvest it in the fall (autumn).
- "Red Ruble" kale (Brassica napus) is very tasty, with serrated, blood-red leaves. We sow this successionally so we can harvest the young leaves for eating raw from June to February. The iron content is typically ten times higher than other kale varieties.
- Chinese artichoke (Stachys affinis) is a member of the mint family and produces lots of small, grub-like tubers that have a nutty flavor and firm texture.
- Black mulberry (Morus nigra) is a classic example of a "forgotten" fruit, and is not available commercially as it is too delicate to transport. But it has an exceptional, wine-rich flavor.
- Shiso (Perilla frutescens). Also known as perilla, this herb is often used in Chinese and Japanese cooking. We use the bi-colored variety, which has a distinct floral flavor reminiscent of bubble gum.

1. TURNIPS WITH HAM FAT CREAM AND SALTED PLUMS

SERVES 4
SALTED PLUMS
– 2 kg red plums, cut in half and pitted
– 20 g sea salt
HAM FAT CREAM
– 200 ml ham stock
– 170 g guanciale, chopped and rind removed
– 1 g xanthan gum
– salt
SALTED PLUM SAUCE
– 300 ml turnip juice
– 50 g anise hyssop stems
  (*Agastache foeniculum*)
– 5 g white miso paste
– 150 g unsalted butter
– 20 ml Salted Plum Juice (see above)
– 60 g Salted Plum Flesh (see above)
– 100 ml light (single) cream
– salt
TURNIPS
– 200 g greens from the baby Tokyo turnips
– 200 g whey
– 20 g unsalted butter
– 24 baby Tokyo turnips, washed and skin on
– salt
TO SERVE
– 30 g crisp pancetta
– 10 small anise hyssop flowers
– 5 radish flowers

SALTED PLUMS
Season the plums with the salt. Put them into a vacuum bag, seal, and leave at room temperature. They will ferment after about 1 month. When the plums have fermented (they should have a sparkling flavor), strain and reserve the juice for the salted plum sauce. Blend the strained plums in a food processor, then pass through a strainer (sieve).

HAM FAT CREAM
Put all the ingredients into a blender and blend to a smooth paste, then season. Chill until ready to serve, then transfer to a squeeze bottle.

SALTED PLUM SAUCE
Bring the turnip juice to a boil in a pan and skim off any scum. Remove from the heat, add the anise hyssop stems, and let infuse for about 30 minutes.

Pass the infused turnip juice through cheesecloth (muslin) into a clean pan and bring to a boil. Add the miso paste, butter, plum juice, and plum flesh, transfer to a blender, and blend until smooth. Pass through a fine-mesh strainer (sieve). Season with salt and stir in the cream.

Use an immersion (stick) blender to make it frothy just before serving.

TURNIPS
Put the turnip greens and whey into a Thermomix and blend at 140°F/60°C for 4 minutes. Pass it through a fine-mesh strainer into a pan and add the butter and some salt. Bring to a boil, add the turnips, and cook for 30 seconds. Drain and keep warm.

TO SERVE
Divide the turnips among 4 bowls and add some dots of the ham fat cream. Garnish with the crisp pancetta, anise hyssop leaves, and radish flowers. Pour in some hot frothy salted plum sauce at the last moment and serve.

2. AYNESOME OFFERINGS

For this recipe, choose small, juicy, and firm red and golden beets (beetroots). We use fresh new scallions (spring onions)—the "White Lisbon" variety are good. Locoto chiles have black seeds and are sweet and juicy.

SERVES 4
CRISP HAM THREADS
– 1 x pork side (belly)
– vegetable oil, for frying
– salt
BEETS
– 200 g all-purpose (plain) flour
– 100 ml water
– 100 g salt
– 4 young red beets (beetroots), unpeeled
– 4 young golden beets (beetroots), unpeeled
CANOLA EMULSION
– 3 soft-boiled eggs, cooled and peeled
– splash of apple cider vinegar
– 150 ml canola (rapeseed) oil
– salt
FLAVORED OIL
– 50 g garlic, chopped
– 1 small locoto chile, chopped and half the seeds
  reserved
– 215 ml grapeseed oil, plus extra as required
– 40 g picked parsley leaves
– 3 g salt
FROM THE FARM
– 4 whole Moon Red gem lettuces
– 8 young scallions (spring onions), cut in half
  and grilled
– 8 young "Cherry Belle" radishes
– 8 bunches fava (broad) bean tips
– 4 bunches brassica flowers
– 8 micro pea pods
– 8 bronze fennel fronds
– 8 red orache tips
– 4 chervil tops with flowers
– 4 horseradish greens with flowers
– 8 allium flowers
– flowers from 3 thyme sprigs
– 32 micro fava (broad) beans
TO SERVE
– 1 native Cumbrian lobster tail, cooked and cut into
  10-g slices
– Crisp Ham Threads (see above)

CRISP HAM THREADS
Put the pork side (belly) into a vacuum bag and slow cook. Remove and let cool, then pick the meat—it will look like threads.

Preheat the oven to 150°F/65°C. Place the pork threads on a baking sheet and put in the oven. Once dry, pan-fry the threads in a little vegetable oil and season to taste with salt. Store in an airtight container.

BEETS
Preheat the oven to 347°F/175°C.

In a large bowl, mix together the flour, water, and salt to form a dough. Transfer the dough to a work counter and flatten so it is the size of your roasting pan.

Place the unpeeled red and golden beets (beetroots) in a roasting pan and cover with the flattened dough. Salt-bake in the oven for 30–45 minutes, then remove, let cool slightly, and peel.

CANOLA EMULSION
Put the soft-boiled eggs into a blender with the vinegar and blend, gradually drizzling in the canola (rapeseed) oil, to form an emulsion. Season to taste with salt and transfer to a squeeze bottle.

FLAVORED OIL
Put the garlic, chile, and grapeseed oil into a pan and cook until the garlic is golden. Strain through a fine-mesh strainer (sieve), then add more grapeseed oil to bring it back to 200 g.

Blanch the parsley in a pan of boiling water, refresh in a bowl of ice water, and squeeze dry. Put the chile oil, parsley, and salt into a blender and blend until you have a bright green oil. Place a bowl in a larger bowl of ice, strain the oil through a fine-mesh strainer into the bowl and whisk until slightly thickened.

TO SERVE
Divide all the farm ingredients, the beets, and sliced lobster tail among 4 bowls, arranging them attractively. Pipe on dots of canola emulsion and sprinkle over some crisp ham threads. Serve the flavored oil separately and drizzle over a little at the last moment.

1

2

Niko Romito

REALE
Castel di Sangro, Abruzzo, Italy

In 2011, chef Niko Romito renovated a sixteenth-century monastery, Casadonna, in Abruzzo, Italy, to create a new site for his three-Michelin-starred restaurant, Reale. Along with opening his own cookery school and a small boutique hotel, he has spent the last few years developing the terraced kitchen gardens and native fruit trees that form the basis for much of his experimental, highly complex cooking.

Reale is in Abruzzo which is in the center of Italy, a couple of hours east from Rome, and we are perched on the hills of the Val di Sangro, 2,600 feet (800 meters) above sea level, in an unblemished national park—it's the greenest Italian region and it's a breathtaking setting.

The restaurant is part of the Casadonna estate, which is 15 acres (6 hectares). Within that the gardens, which are right in front of the kitchen, occupy a third of an acre arranged in large terraces with grass embankments and dry-stone walls cutting across the slope, to help to control water run-off and minimize soil erosion. Around that we have orchards with apple, pear, cherry, plum, and peach, as well as walnut, hazelnut, and almond trees and an apiary for honey production. There's also an experimental vineyard where we grow native grapes like Pecorino as well as Riesling and Pinot noir. In the herb garden we grow aromatic plants including rosemary, sage, thyme, lemon balm, and lemongrass, and wild herbs such as dandelion, burnet, wild fennel, potentilla, and wild carrot.

We started developing the kitchen garden in 2012 and it is constantly being improved and refined. We have a yearly average temperature of 52°F/11°C with high rainfall so along with our agronomist, Maurizio Facchini, we choose vegetable varieties that benefit from our microclimate. From the beginning, the main focus has been to grow old, local varieties—varieties absolutely particular to the place that have a long relationship with the *terroir*—including "San Giovanni" pears (*Pyrus*), red garlic (*Allium sativum*) from near Sulmona, "Pera D'Abruzzo" and "Saraceno" tomatoes (*Solanum lycopersicum*), and some plants like hawthorn and wild plum trees that are typical of the area.

The kitchen garden guarantees absolute freshness and it's central to everything we do at Reale; we describe the food as "apparently simple" yet it hides a significant complexity: it is the result of endless research into raw materials, and we then focus on a few selected ingredients that in each and every dish express their full power.

Because of this simplicity, plants that are harvested at the perfect moment are the main inspiration for the kitchen; for example, one of our signature dishes, "Alcoholic mixed wild greens with almond" is made of almost 20 different species of edible plants growing around Casadonna; or the fruit jam that is made with no added sugars and pressed fruit and vegetable juices, which are part of breakfast for guests.

We grow garlic, celery, onions, eggplants (aubergines), zucchinis (courgettes), tomatoes, bell peppers, cauliflowers, radishes, beets (beetroots), spinach, and salads. We work with a lot of legumes and leafy vegetables, achieving surprising gastronomic results thanks to cooking techniques and processes applied to transform them, such as our "Roasted Savoy cabbage" in which Savoy cabbage is roasted, seasoned, ripened, and steamed before being served with a sauce made from the outer leaves and on top of a silky potato emulsion.

The research that we do for many of the dishes has been born from fermentation, extraction, infusion, and cold contamination. Signature dishes on our menu that really embody these processes are "Spaghetti and tomato," "Eggplant, tomato and peach caramel," and "Gratinèe cauliflower." For the last one, cauliflower is steamed and the bottom part is blended to a cream, which is then distilled and reduced until it eventually forms a glaze. Raw cauliflower is then cut very thinly and toasted in a pan and then it is blended to resemble bread crumbs. The cauliflower tops are roasted until slightly brown. We serve it with the "bread crumbs" on the plate, then the cauliflower on top and the glaze, and finally some garlic-infused oil.

We are passionate about the vegetable world here and the amazing versatility of raw materials and I don't want the ingredient to get lost, but rather explode on the palate with all its vitality. We aim to maximize the quality and vitality of each plant—we don't use any plant protection or mechanical system (like netting or greenhouses). Every day we do a manual check on all the plants and vegetables in the gardens, removing insects by hand from each plant, removing any diseased leaves or plants affected by fungi or other pathogens.

We work on prevention and timeliness as well as on constant observation to limit disease. Crop rotation is the foundation of our garden routine and deep processes, such as digging, that alter the structure of the soil and bring to the surface the deep asphyxiated and non-fertile layers, are completely avoided. We invest space, time, and resources for making compost. We avoid using any synthetic products.

The garden is an integral part of the dining experience and it arouses deep emotions in our diners and guests. The great scenic and aesthetic charm of the place, the vegetation and its aromas, the dishes created with the fresh fruits and vegetables farmed on site, and the architectural project, make Casadonna a unique system in which beauty and taste are linked to wellness and health, offering guests an exceptional experience.

AN ORGANIC APPROACH
We interfere with nature as little as possible. We avoid any kind of deep digging that can alter the fertility of the soil and instead we tend to use green manures in the periods when the soil is being rested. Once those herbaceous plants have matured we chop the plants and leave them on the soil to enhance the health of the soil, improving its structure and fertility and also preventing the growth of weeds.

HEALTHY JAMS
We continually experiment with healthier approaches, whether it's how we grow or how we prepare produce. We grow apples, pears, cherries, and plums, as well as local varieties of peaches and medlars, and the jams we make for our breakfasts are made with very small percentages of sugar (up to 7 percent, depending on the sweetness of the fruit) and lemon juice to help them set. We don't use any other additives or preservatives so the jams only have a shelf life of six months.

1. ROASTED SAVOY CABBAGE

In this dish, the cabbage, a very common and humble ingredient, acquires great gastronomic importance and a strong identity of its own. Both cabbages and rosemary are farmed at Casadonna's gardens. The cooking process aims to respect the texture and strong fibers of the cabbage. First, the cabbage is smoked over charcoal, then it is marinated with salt, wine, and vinegar, wrapped in foil and left to age for 30 days. The core is then steamed and eventually roasted in the oven. The outer cabbage leaves are emulsified with extra-virgin olive oil and spread over slices of the steamed core of the vegetable. The star anise distillate conveys elegance to the dish, while the rosemary extract enhances the flavor of the cabbage, and is perfectly counterbalanced by the potato emulsion.

SERVES 4
ROASTED CABBAGE
– 1 whole Savoy cabbage
– extra-virgin olive oil, for roasting
– white wine
– white wine vinegar
– salt
STAR ANISE DISTILLATE
– 30 g star anise
– 200 ml pure alcohol
– 200 ml water
ROSEMARY EXTRACT
– 200 g rosemary leaves
POTATO EMULSION
– 200 g Agata potatoes, peeled
– 130 ml extra-virgin olive oil
– 200 ml water
TO SERVE
– 16 drops Rosemary Extract (see above)
– a few drops extra-virgin olive oil
– a few drops Star Anise Distillate (see above)

ROASTED CABBAGE

Wash the cabbage, then roast it whole on a charcoal barbecue for 10 minutes. Weigh the cabbage, lay it on a sheet of parchment (baking) paper, and slather with olive oil. Season with salt, white wine (10% of the cabbage weight), and white wine vinegar (2% of the cabbage weight). Wrap tightly in the parchment paper and aluminum foil and age for 30 days in the refrigerator at 39.2°F/4°C.

After 30 days, unwrap the cabbage, remove the outer leaves and set them aside. Cut the core in half, wrap tightly in more parchment paper and aluminum foil, and steam in a steam oven at 225°F/110°C for 2 hours.

Put a few drops of oil in a nonstick skillet (frying pan) and braise the outer leaves for 20 minutes. Remove from the heat and when cool, freeze them in a foodbag. Once frozen, put into a blender and blend until the texture is that of a thick emulsion.

STAR ANISE DISTILLATE

Put the star anise and alcohol into a distillator, pour in the water and vacuum distill at 77°F/25°C. It will take about 2 hours. Remove, transfer to a foodbag, and store in the refrigerator.

ROSEMARY EXTRACT

Wash the rosemary leaves and put into a juice extractor. Once juiced, transfer to a foodbag and store in the refrigerator.

POTATO EMULSION

Boil the potatoes in a pan of boiling water. When they are cooked, let cool, then add the oil and water and whip until smooth. Once blended push through a strainer (sieve) to make the emulsion totally smooth.

TO SERVE

Preheat the oven to 325°F/160°C and line a baking sheet with nonstick parchment (baking) paper.

Cut the steamed cabbage core into ¾-in/2-cm thick slices, then place on the lined sheet. Bake for 6 minutes. Divide the potato emulsion among 4 plates and add 4 drops of rosemary extract to each. Season each cabbage core "fillet" with salt and place on the potato emulsion. Top with about 10 g of cabbage leaf emulsion per serving, add a few drops of star anise distillate and extra-virgin olive oil.

2. ALCOHOLIC MIXED WILD GREENS WITH ALMOND

Twenty different types of wild greens are harvested around Casadonna and represent the unique identity of the place. These include: purslane, goosegrass, lamb's quarters (goosefoot), chickweed, sow thistle, bristly oxtongue, bull thistle, coltsfoot, field scabious, salad burnet, amaranth, buckhorn plantain (ribwort plantain), wild carrot, potentilla, lucerne (alfalfa), common hogweed, sorrel, dandelion, and wild radish. The base is made purely of almonds, which are pureed cold to make a smooth cream. On top are wild local greens drizzled with Monkey 47 gin, which enhances the freshness and gives strength to the natural aromas of the leaves. The flavor therefore has a prolonged herbal note and a notable alcoholic kick. The sage extract complements all the different flavors, giving them strength as a combination but also to each single type of leaf. This is probably the dish that most represents the natural ecosystem of Casadonna, an authentic "herbaceous fingerprint."

SERVES 4
ALMOND CREAM
– 1 kg whole peeled almonds
– water, to cover
SAGE EXTRACT
– 200 g sage leaves
WILD GREENS
– 200 g wild greens (see intro)
– 20 ml Sage Extract (see above)
– 30 g extra-virgin olive oil
– 8 ml white vinegar (aged for 7 years)
– a few drops of Monkey 47 gin

ALMOND CREAM

Put the almonds into a blender with enough water to just cover them and blend until they form a cream. Pass the cream through a strainer (sieve) into a bowl to make it smooth and soft.

SAGE EXTRACT

Wash the sage leaves and put into a juice extractor. Once juiced, transfer to a foodbag and store in the refrigerator.

WILD GREENS

Toss the wild greens in a bowl with the sage extract, olive oil, white vinegar, and gin.

TO SERVE

Spoon the almond cream onto 4 plates, then top with the seasoned wild greens.

2

Ana Roš

HIŠA FRANKO
Kobarid, Slovene Littoral, Slovenia

On a charming Slovenian countryside house and estate, three generations live and run world-renowned restaurant Hiša Franko. Inspired by the fertile Soča Valley, chef Ana Roš creates a new tasting menu each evening, inspired by what she has been able to source from her surroundings and local producers that day. Dishes vary by season; behind the house there is a creek brimming with trout and a large vegetable, herb, and flower garden.

My mother-in-law lived in a mountain village, part of a big family in very poor surroundings: surviving with what nature was giving in that particular moment and place is part of her. Their daily food was based on the garden, foraging, and dairy products. When she and my father-in-law dreamed about buying the old countryside house that became Hiša Franko today, it was important for them that the house had some land belonging to the building. On the left side of the house they created trout pools, nourished with fresh spring water; at the back are some garden terraces as the ground is sloping. Maybe they were dreamers but the only way of life they knew was the one connected to the land. The gardens were not big enough to feed all the needs of the restaurant but the family would never buy a single vegetable for their personal use. My husband has been raised with this philosophy, which underpins everything we do today.

When my husband Walter and I took over Hiša Franko in 2000, I wanted to retain the close connection to the land that my parents-in-law Joži and Franko had created before us. They bought the house in 1970 and opened the restaurant three years later, having created a garden right next to the restaurant to provide some of the produce. We also took inspiration from a friend of my husband's, who also has a garden at his restaurant. He supplied us, too, in the early days, and we slowly started to grow more for ourselves.

Hiša Franko is a beautiful countryside house with three generations living on different floors. Behind the house, there is the herb, flower, and vegetable garden; beside it you can hear our lively creek, home to the trout that appears so often on our menu.

We built a wine and cheese cellar and instead of a simple roof, we covered it with the herb garden: you step out from the terrace straight onto it. Here, we grow a lot of aromatic plants, such as chamomile and tarragon. I'm in love with tarragon—not the French tarragon (*Artemisia dracunculus*) that most people know, but a central European variety that has a strong balsamic flavor. It plays a defining role in Slovenian cooking, and I use it in many dishes, especially with game. Perhaps my favorite dish I used it in is the dessert "Potita," where it infuses its flavor into sour cream, which is then baked in a brioche-like pastry.

We also grow a wide range of beans, peas, chicory, potatoes, cucumbers, and zucchini (courgettes), as well as sun-lovers including ten kinds of tomatoes, eggplant (aubergines), and bell peppers. Fruit is a big thing for me too: we have so many berries, as well as rhubarb and an orchard with apple, plum, and pear trees that were here when my parents-in-law first came. We have the luxury of picking them just before service to show them at their best. I'm particularly grateful for the black currants—most recently I used them in a recipe with bear and trout. We made a salad of red currants and black currants dressed with green juniper powder, green juniper oil, honey, and trout roe and it gave the fish sour and sweet notes which are so common for Viennese and Central European cuisine.

We cannot hope to be self-sufficient, but in Slovenia, everyone has a garden, everyone forages. It is not a question of trends; we are peasants by culture and people have always lived very close to nature. Even in the cities, you can see a lot of green spots where people spend their time growing their own salads and vegetables. It is natural that so much is available from others throughout the year; only the other day, I bought four varieties of peach and some chicory from a neighboring grower.

In Slovenia, we garden in a different way to many other cultures. It is less formal; wilder than most. Spontaneous plants—weeds and other natural occurrences—are welcome, being part of what we do. I couldn't be without purslane in salads, for example, but it is not something we grow intentionally.

The gardens and wider countryside are not only used for food, but for healing purposes too. Some of the guests staying in our rooms can look out on the garden: it is very much part of what and who we are, and we encourage everyone to walk around. If we have time, we take them round ourselves, so we can explain what is growing and how we like to use it.

Our climate is pure rock and roll: half Alpine and half Mediterranean, with a lot of rain, much humidity, and big swings in temperature. Our winters may freeze the ground deeply and for a long time, so that even rhubarb gives up sometimes. But then there are some easy, mild winters, when we're taking our jackets off in February and March. Even in this quite unpredictable climate we gain an understanding of what works well and less so. Sadly, rosemary, which does so well nearer the Mediterranean, grows well enough here but the flavor and scent lacks intensity, so we grow other plants that suit the climate better, such as our local tarragon.

The garden is still mostly run by my parents-in-law, with some involvement from me, my son helps with watering in summer, and the whole kitchen team joins in once every two weeks to help. I did not grow up in the mountains, depending on nature for every meal, but I still learn little tricks on how our garden can be even more rooted in traditions and in nature.

USING TRADITIONAL METHODS
To plant the gardens, my parents-in-law followed old-fashioned rules and beliefs; they used a moon calendar. My mother-in-law still has a deep knowledge regarding the eating and use of long-forgotten plants, flowers, and weeds. When they plant they still look to the sky, they follow the moon calendar, they plant flowers and vegetables together, as companions, helping each other. There is a huge compost area and coffee grounds are used as fertilizer; egg shells are used to keep away snails; they cover the garden with onion and garlic peels—I still do not understand precisely how this works, but it does. I am keen for this old knowledge, handed down through generations, to transfer to my generation and those that follow too. A garden is a symbiosis of old and new. We have to learn how to listen before we start thinking of having one.

1. RABBIT THAT WANTS TO BE MEXICAN CHICKEN

SERVES 8
RABBIT ROLLS
- 2 whole chicken skins (ask your butcher for these)
- 1 x 2-kg whole rabbit (including the liver, if possible, or buy rabbit liver separately)
- 1 egg white
- 100 ml heavy (double) cream
- 2 sprigs tarragon
- 2 nori sheets
- peanut oil, for frying
RABBIT SAUCE
- neutral oil, for frying
- 3 large orange carrots, tops intact
- 2 large yellow onions, coarsely chopped
- 4 celery stalks, coarsely chopped
- 200 ml red wine
- 2 star anise
- 3 cloves
- 1 long pepper
- 1 small dried chile pepper
- 1 cinnamon stick
- 50 g semisweet (dark) chocolate (70% cocoa solids)
ROASTED CARROTS
- 1 large orange carrot, top intact
- 1 large purple carrot, top intact
- 1 large white carrot, top intact
- 1 large yellow carrot, top intact
- 100 g olive oil
- 30 g sage
- 100 g butter
APRICOT GEL
- 4 sheets leaf gelatin
- 500 ml fresh apricot juice
- 3 g agar agar
CARROT-TOP PESTO
- 4 carrot tops (see above)
- 300 g shelled, salted almonds
TO SERVE
- Maldon salt
- hibiscus flowers, to serve (optional)

RABBIT ROLLS
Lay the chicken skins flat on a cutting board so the feather side is face down. Scrape all the excess fat away from the skin. Carefully lay the skins out and set aside.

Carefully remove the liver (if it hasn't already been removed) and the inner loins from the rabbit and reserve for the stuffing. Cut away the belly flaps from the saddle, being careful to keep them in as large pieces as possible. Place the belly flaps between sheets of wax paper and pound with a meat mallet until thin.

Cut the loins and liver and freeze just until they are hard on the outside but not frozen all the way through. Put them in a food processor with the egg white, cream, sprigs of tarragon, and salt and blend to a paste. Divide the stuffing paste between the pounded belly flaps and wrap the flaps around the meat to make two roulades. Roll a sheet of nori around each roulade then roll them up in the pieces of chicken skin you've laid out. Wrap each roulade tightly in plastic, then two separate layers of aluminum foil. Put aside for later.

RABBIT SAUCE
Heat a little oil in a roasting pan, add the rest of the rabbit meat, and roast over medium heat until it starts to color.

Meanwhile, wash and roughly chop two of the large orange carrots (setting the tops aside). Add to the pan with the onion and celery and roast for a further 5 minutes with the bones. Deglaze the pan with the red wine, scraping up any little brown bits from the bottom of the pan. Cover with water, bring to the boil, reduce the heat, and simmer for 6–8 hours.

Strain the stock into another pan, add the star anise, cloves, long pepper, chile pepper, and cinnamon stick. Reduce the stock by half then strain it again. Blend in the dark chocolate using a immersion (stick) blender, then let cool and set aside.

ROASTED CARROTS
Preheat the oven to 335°F/170°C. Carefully wash the carrots. Remove the tops and reserve them for the pesto. Lightly coat the carrots in olive oil in a roasting pan and add the sage. Bake for 15–20 minutes or until tender. Remove from the oven and cut each carrot into quarters lengthwise. Set aside.

APRICOT GEL
Soak the gelatin sheets in a bowl of cold water until softened.

Bring the apricot juice to a boil in a pan. Add the agar agar and boil for 30 seconds, then remove from the heat and add the softened gelatin. Pour the mixture into trays and set aside to cool and solidify. Take a small ring cutter and cut out circles of the gel. Set them aside for later.

CARROT-TOP PESTO
Put the washed tops from the carrots you roasted into a blender with the almonds and blend until it forms a crumbly pesto.

TO SERVE
Cook the wrapped rabbit rolls in a pan of boiling water for 10 minutes. Meanwhile heat the roasted carrots in a pan with the butter. Heat the rabbit sauce in a separate pan, taking care not to burn it (it's more difficult to heat with the chocolate in it). Remove the rolls from the water and carefully remove the foil and plastic wrap (clingfilm). Place the rolls in a hot nonstick pan with a little bit of peanut oil and fry, turning them every so often to ensure the chicken skin gets crispy all over. Remove the rolls and cut them in half. Season the portions of rabbit with Maldon salt.

Place the apricot gel circles on plates and cover with the carrot-top pesto. Place one of each color of carrot and the roulade on top and cover in the rabbit sauce. We add some of the hibiscus flowers that grow in our garden (they're edible) because that's what we imagine a rabbit who wants to be a Mexican chicken would wear.

2. WILD PLANTS

SERVES 8
GREEN ASPARAGUS CREAM
- 30 g olive oil
- 60 g butter
- 40 g shallot, chopped
- 500 g green asparagus spears, tips trimmed off and reserved and remaining spears cut into small pieces
- 20 g white wine
- 50 g spinach clorofila
- 45 g pumpkin seed oil
- salt
PORK SAUSAGE CREAM
- 1 kg local pork sausage (unsmoked and semi-dry)
- 300 g whole (full-fat) milk
- 300 g heavy (double) cream
- 150 g homemade cream cheese
PORK CRACKLING
- 250 g local unsmoked and semi-dry pork sausage, cut into small pieces
WILD PLANTS
- 100 g wild asparagus, trimmed to 2 inch/5 cm tips
- 50 g asparagus tips (see above)
- 200 g mixed wild and garden plants, such as, yarrow, wild garlic flowers, garden chicory, borage leaves, garden radish leaves, wild sorrel, garden sorrel, young linden leaves, wild and garden violets

GREEN ASPARAGUS CREAM
Heat the olive oil and butter in a pan, add the shallots, and sauté until the shallots are transparent, then add the chopped asparagus spears and sauté until cooked. Add the white wine and simmer to reduce. Place the mixture in a bowl and make an inverted bain marie to keep the vibrant color.

Put the mixture into a Thermomix and blend until it forms a smooth puree. Add the spinach clorofila to keep the puree's green color. Add the pumpkin seed oil to emulsify the mixture. Once it is creamy, transfer to a container and season with salt.

PORK SAUSAGE CREAM
Place all the ingredients into the Thermomix and blend at 120°F/50°C for 10 minutes.

PORK CRACKLING
Place the pieces of sausage in a pan over medium heat, and fry until all the fat has melted, stirring so the sausage doesn't stick to the pan. Reduce the heat to low and cook the sausage pieces until crispy. Strain and reserve the fat to sauté the wild plants.

WILD PLANTS
Blanch the wild asparagus in boiling water for 3 minutes, then transfer to a bowl of ice water. Drain and pat dry. Put 1 tablespoon of the pork fat into a hot pan and, once smoky, add the blanched wild asparagus. Sauté, then add the asparagus tips and mixed wild and garden plants. Sauté for just 5 seconds. Remove from the heat and season with salt.

TO SERVE
Pipe the asparagus cream and the sausage cream onto plates. With a small and flat plate, press the purees carefully to create an effect. Finish the dish with the sautéed wild plants and the pork crackling.

1

Ben Shewry

ATTICA
Ripponlea, Victoria, Australia

Chef Ben Shewry grew up in rural New Zealand, surrounded by nature, influenced by the traditions of the Maori people, and inspired by his family's bucolic self-sufficiency. At his acclaimed restaurant Attica in Melbourne, Shewry has been the author of a new chapter for indigenous Australian produce, and a true champion of modern Australian cuisine. In 2011, he established an on-site kitchen garden to further explore his fascination with native ingredients and also now grows produce at the nearby Rippon Lea Estate.

Attica is located in the small suburb of Ripponlea in the southeast of Melbourne, Australia. The restaurant relies on a small raised herb garden on site at Attica and a series of garden plots at the nearby Rippon Lea Estate, a heritage-listed property built in 1868 that covers almost 14 acres (5.5 hectares) in neighboring Elsternwick.

We established our first garden at Attica in 2008, in what used to be a parking lot at the back of the restaurant. We built four large rectangular raised beds, poured in the soil, and just tried our hand at growing. The idea to plant the garden was born out of my frustration with the variable quality of the herbs and greens and edible flowers, and the sheer lack of diversity in what was available from suppliers. We started out with tomatoes and they were a dismal failure. We now have two separate garden sites (Attica and Rippon Lea Estate) with a total space of around 27,000 square feet (2,500 square meters).

My exposure to gardening started in my childhood. My mother Kaye kept a big kitchen garden at the farm that I grew up on in rural Awakino, New Zealand. That garden provided most of what we needed to eat when I was growing up. When I started the garden at Attica, I realized just how much I had learned from my mother as a child and I continue to learn from her to this day.

About a year after we started our garden at Attica, I met Justin Buckley, the head of horticulture for the National Trust. I casually asked if he thought there might be any chance of us starting a garden at Rippon Lea Estate—the National Trust-listed estate that is a two-minute walk from the back of the restaurant. He replied immediately, saying, "We always wanted you to have a garden over at Rippon Lea; we just didn't know how to approach you." It was odd that we were both thinking the same thing at the same time but were reluctant to approach one another.

Over the past few years we have gradually taken on several plots at Rippon Lea and that's where we now do the bulk of our growing. We also have access to its orchard with about 100 old varieties of apples and pears. In 2010 we took on a large area of about 1,300 square feet (400 square meters). It wasn't a proper raised bed, just a patch of lawn that we dug up. Rippon Lea Estate is less than 1¼ miles (2 kilometers) from Port Phillip Bay, so the soil here tends to be quite sandy. We had to work hard to establish good soil condition (with compost, mulch, and manure), but it paid off. We only grow hardy plants in the poor soil, plants like garlic or thyme, wormwood, and pineapple sage (*Salvia elegans*). In the better soil we grow things that are fussier, like fava (broad) beans and mustards.

Ten years after we first tried to grow tomatoes, I can say that we very confidently grow them now. That first crop failed due to the soil. We didn't understand anything back then; you can't just dump soil on a raised bed, then plant tomatoes and expect them to grow.

Tomatoes are high-maintenance, greedy plants; they require much more attention than I gave them at the time. We've since had two very successful seasons with tomatoes and recently supplied the restaurant with tomatoes solely from our beds for three months.

For the first nine years, our chefs and staff all pitched in and worked in the garden. Now it's too big to manage so we have two full-time gardeners who take care of all the composting, maintenance, and planting. The kitchen staff still go to harvest every day.

More than anything, my real interest lies with indigenous Australian edible plants, quite a few of which—macadamia nut trees (*Macadamia integrifolia*), plum pines (*Podocarpus elatus*), lilly pilly (*Syzygium paniculatum*)—have been happily growing in the garden at Rippon Lea for almost 100 years. My interest in indigenous plants comes from my heritage in New Zealand: growing up with Maori culture and Maori food, Maori practices, and that history all around us as children. Justin knew a lot about indigenous plants growing at Rippon Lea, so he was a wonderful resource. I later spent time researching traditional Aboriginal uses for these plants so that we could use them in the kitchen at Attica.

Bruce Pascoe, an Indigenous Australian writer from the Bunurong clan, is someone who has inspired my exploration of these plants. Bruce gave me the first murnong (yam daisy, *Microceris lanceolata*) seeds that I had ever seen. Murnong was a very important food source for the Bunurong people in this area. Before white settlement it was cultivated everywhere around here. When we planted our own murnong seeds a few years ago, it was the first time it had been on these soils since the estate was established 140 years ago. To grow such a culturally significant plant and serve it to our guests is something very special. It's delicious, with little yam-like tubers; you can eat the stems, leaves, and flowers, too. We serve the whole murnong so that our guests can appreciate the magnificence of the whole plant.

We've made our on-site garden at Attica a lot smaller because we now have guests dine out there every night. It has become more of a show garden, with just a few raised beds and different herbs growing. You can tell customers that you grow produce and you pick it each day, but unless they actually see it they don't always make that connection psychologically. When we take guests outside, they realize that we are indeed sincere about it.

It's incredibly healthy to spend time in the fresh air every day, in the sun or the rain. It's also really important for cooks to understand how difficult it is for growers to grow things. If you've had a hand in growing something you just have a different level of respect for it. That can be the hardest thing for a chef to teach young cooks but when they're involved in the process themselves, it opens their eyes to a much bigger picture.

SOIL QUALITY
Establishing good soil quality is one of the most crucial steps in the entire gardening process. It doesn't work to just plant things and expect them to grow; the condition of the soil will dictate the success of everything that you plant. It will take time and effort to get soil right, but with the help of good compost, mulch, and manure the benefits will more than repay your efforts.

If you look after the soil, first and foremost, the plants will grow. Don't try to look after the plant, look after the soil. Make compost, add the compost, and rotate your crops. If you repeatedly grow the same thing in the same area you'll have disastrous results—especially after the second or third go. The plants will be weak, they will have low productivity, and they'll be more susceptible to disease.

FAVORITE INDIGENOUS EDIBLE PLANT VARIETIES
Herbs:
– Indigenous oregano: highly aromatic, with a robust, slightly medicinal flavor yet soft texture. We pair it with other indigenous ingredients like kangaroo and wattle seeds. It is a perennial so can be used all year round.
– Lemon myrtle (*Backhousia citriodora*): versatile herb with refreshing citrus aroma. Best used as a flavoring, although uses are limited only by one's creativity. Lovely with shellfish, incredible in sweet preparations.
– River mint (*Mentha australis*): native herb with an aroma and flavor similar to spearmint. Grows in the summer and thrives in wet and moist soils. Can be used anywhere that you require a spicy mint.

Fruits and berries:
– Magenta lilly pilly (*Syzygium paniculatum*): firm-fleshed pink berry that tastes a little like apple or pear.
– Tasmanian pepper berry (*Tasmannia lanceolata*): small black berries with a sharp, spicy herbal-tinged pepper flavor. Leaves, stems, and berries can all be used. Suited to cool and alpine climates.
– Plum pines (*Podocarpus elatus*): fleshy purple-black berries with a grape-like texture and semi-sweet, mildly resinous flavor.

1. CHEWY CARROTS

SERVES 6
CHEWY CARROTS
- 2 liters water
- 40 g fine salt, plus extra for sprinkling
- 40 g superfine (caster) sugar, plus extra for sprinkling
- 3 pieces orange carrot
- canola (rapeseed) oil
- fresh pepper leaves
CARROT OIL
- 20 carrots
- 40 g grapeseed oil
- pinch of fine salt
SMOKED EGG PASTE
- 3 extra-large (UK large) eggs
- 6 g canola (rapeseed) oil
- 15 g garlic, thinly sliced
- 15 g shallot, thinly sliced
- 4.5 g coconut sugar
- 5.5 g tamarind paste
- 2½ teaspoons sweet apple vinegar
- ½ bunch tarragon
- lemon juice, to taste
- 1–2 tablespoons fish sauce
- fine salt
TO SERVE
- Sweet Chardonnay vinegar
- flaked sea salt
- fresh pepper leaves

CHEWY CARROTS

Bring the water to a boil with the salt and sugar in a large pan. Add the carrots and boil until they are tender, but still have texture. Drain and put the carrots into a big tray. Rub the carrots with a good amount of canola (rapeseed) oil, then sprinkle with a little more salt and sugar.

Fill a smoker with wood pellets and heat to 265°F/129°C. Cover the rack with pepper leaves, place the carrots on the leaves, and cook them for 17–20 hours. Keep turning the carrots every hour as you go, so they are caramelized all over.

CARROT OIL

Slice the carrots thinly on a mandoline and dehydrate them overnight in a dehydrator or oven at 158°F/70°C. Blend 30 g of the dried carrots to a fine powder in a Thermomix. Add the grapeseed oil to the carrot powder and blend on speed 2 for 25 minutes. Add the salt to the finished carrot oil. Keep at room temperature until ready to serve. Only 10% of the quantity made is required, save the rest for another time.

SMOKED EGG PASTE

Cook the eggs in a pan of boiling water for 8 minutes, then put them immediately into a bowl of ice water. Crack all sides of the eggs, but don't break the shell. Place them on a smoking tray and smoke them over wood chips for 16 minutes—8 minutes on each side. Peel the eggs while they are still hot, then set aside.

Heat the canola oil in a pan, add the sliced garlic and shallot and cook until very soft but not colored. Add the coconut sugar to the pan and cook for a couple of minutes, then add the tamarind paste and mix well before deglazing the pan with the sweet apple vinegar. Cook for another couple of minutes, then remove from the heat and set aside.

Put the smoked eggs in an upright blender with the shallot and garlic paste and blend until smooth, then pass through a chinois strainer (sieve). Let cool.

Pick the tarragon leaves off the stems and blend them with the cooled egg paste in a Thermomix set to full speed, until the mix turns light green in color. Season the paste with fine salt, a good amount of lemon juice, and the fish sauce.

TO SERVE

Place the smoked egg paste in a ramekin and make a swirl through the paste with the carrot oil. Cut the carrots in half lengthwise. Dress the carrots with Sweet Chardonnay vinegar and flaked salt. Place them on top of fresh pepper leaves and light up some of the leaves.

1

Takayoshi Shiozawa   CAINOYA 1931
                         Kagoshima, Kyushu, Japan

Located in Kagoshima, Japan, cainoya 1931 is one of the country's
most highly regarded Italian restaurants. With space for only eight
tables, the restaurant's supply of organic produce comes from the
kitchen garden, which is managed by Chef Takayoshi Shiozawa's
father and located in the mountains outside the city. Shiozawa's
modern dishes use traditional Italian ingredients and evolve gradually according to how the garden is changing. The menu changes
daily and the dishes the guests eat are left to his discretion.

Both the garden and the restaurant have belonged to my family for three generations. My grandparents moved here to Kagoshima in 1931 and opened an eatery called Kai no ya Shokudo. Two generations later, when I wanted to establish my restaurant serving Italian-influenced cuisine, I decided to keep the name, but change the "K" in Kainoya to a "C" (because the letter K is not part of the traditional Italian alphabet). The restaurant moved to its current location in 2005. It's a small place—only about 1,076 square feet (100 square meters)—and we usually seat just six people for lunch and eight for dinner. I am the only chef, though my daughter works with me as an assistant.

The garden, situated in the mountains outside the city, about 20 minutes' drive from the restaurant, has also been in our family since my grandparents' time. My father is in charge of it now—he manages the garden with the help of my mother. The garden is so important to my family, and to me as a chef. The whole identity of my restaurant is rooted in the fresh vegetables that we grow there.

This relationship between my restaurant and garden came about by necessity. I have long had a passion for Italian food and I launched cainoya 1931 in 2005 as essentially an Italian restaurant. At that point, I had not established my own style. I taught myself to cook Italian food by studying cookbooks from Italian chefs and I imported lots of foreign ingredients, such as arugula (rocket), Italian parsley, fennel, endive, radicchio, romanesco, puntarelle (a type of chicory), and cime di rapa (turnip greens). But this was expensive, and the vegetables weren't very fresh. What's more, I was struggling financially: it is difficult to make money running a high-end restaurant in rural Kagoshima. I worked hard at developing my culinary skill, but even so, I got to a point where cash-flow was bad and I couldn't buy the ingredients I wanted. So I started thinking about the vegetables in my father's field. I asked myself what kind of dishes I could make with these ingredients right in front of me. It changed my way of thinking.

I began to look for a way of re-interpreting the Italian dishes I loved, using our fresh, homegrown ingredients. Some of these were traditional Japanese vegetables such as turnip and radish, but we also began planting some of my favorite European varieties, too. Crops like arugula and zucchini (courgette) were very successful. I have now developed a kind of Italian cuisine interpreted and adapted from a Japanese point of view. For example, I make a savory panna cotta, flavored with scallions (spring onions) from the garden, and my focaccia bread has sweet potato kneaded into the dough. I frequently make dashi—a traditional Japanese soup stock flavored with dried bonito and kelp seaweed—but I add pancetta

fat, too. Another key dish on the menu is my vichyssoise, made with our new potatoes. We also have four types of fresh pasta, two of which change depending on the season. The menu changes gradually, according to how the garden is changing.

My father feels strongly that we should garden organically. I did once suggest that we could employ just a small amount of agrichemicals, but he asked me "would you drink chemicals?" so we don't use them. Though I wish we could find another good way to keep insects off the vegetables! Organic gardening is challenging. My father spends a great deal of time weeding. We tried sheet-mulching in the spring, to stop the weeds growing, but the soil became too hot and the plants grew too quickly.

We leave things to nature as much as possible. Rather than irrigating, for example, we rely on rainfall. The climate in Kagoshima is quite extreme. It's very hot and humid and we're often hit by typhoons. What's more, we get volcanic ash falling because the nearby volcano, Sakurajima, is still active. This environment doesn't suit all crops, so it's a constant process of trial and error for us, trying new plants and seeing what will grow well. Really successful crops include arugula, which we allow to flower so that it self-seeds. We can harvest lots of this from fall (autumn) through to early summer. Beets (beetroots) are another reliable crop, as well as eggplants (aubergines) in the summer, and sweet potatoes in fall. I love the Jerusalem artichokes and tasty sweet turnips we harvest in winter, and we grow various types of cabbage. We also have plenty of herbs, including basil, lemongrass, and several kinds of mint, which I make into fresh herb tea for our guests.

A lot of things don't grow well here. We've tried many varieties of seed over the years that didn't even sprout. Celery root (celeriac) was a notable failure. I managed to raise a grape seedling from Italy once, but I could not harvest any fruit from it, and I had to abandon that. In a way, we're still amateurs—but we are learning all the time. My father works very hard. He's in the garden almost every day, often from morning until evening, and he does a lot of research on cultivation methods. Unlike many farms, where the growers don't know who's eating their vegetables, my father knows his son will be using his crops. I think he puts more care into growing them because of this.

Despite all the hard work and the unpredictability, for me the garden is a place of inspiration, and rejuvenation too. When I drive there in my car, I have my favorite rock music playing at full volume. But I don't play music on the way back. I feel peaceful then. The garden relaxes me and helps me press the "reset" button. That is one of the many wonderful things about it.

A NEW WAY TO COOK VEGETABLES

Technically, my food blends the modern and the traditional. One of my favorite devices is the Gastrovac, which allows me to cook food in a vacuum, at much lower temperatures than normal. It is a fantastic way to maintain the delicate structure in fresh produce—even really fragile ingredients like lettuce. Another key feature is that the release of the vacuum creates pressure that forces the cooking liquid into the food, infusing it with moisture and flavor. This "impregnation" effect is behind one of my signature dishes, the "crystal salad." I cook garden vegetables in the Gastrovac, then release the vacuum so the cooking liquid (mineral water) penetrates the ingredients. When cooked in this way, greens and broccoli become shiny and translucent, like beautiful jewels, with the deepest flavor, and a texture that's both crunchy and juicy. I also use the Gastrovac to cook our winter turnips, impregnating them with a broth that I make from the turnip tops and peel.

1. SWEETCORN SOUP

SERVES 10
– 10 corn cobs, harvested in the morning, husks still intact, and kept cool in ice water
– milk (4–5% fat), to cover
– extra-virgin olive oil, for drizzling
– salt

Immerse the corn, husks still intact, in slightly acidic electrolyzed water to sterilize.

Bake half the corn cobs, with husks on, in a combination steamer oven at a temperature setting of 338°F/170°C and a humidity of 15 percent.

Steam the remaining cobs at 185°F/85°C, then immediately cool all the cobs (baked and steamed) in a blast chiller. Peel and discard the husks and scrape off the corn kernels.

After scraping off the kernels, simmer the cobs with enough milk to cover them in the combination steamer oven to extract their flavor. (Using the combination steamer oven avoids exposing the milk to an open flame which can cause it to burn.) Remove the cobs from the milk and discard. Add the kernels to the milk, simmer gently for 30 minutes, then immediately cool in the blast chiller.

Process the chilled soup in a food processor and strain it first through a strainer (sieve), then through a fine-mesh strainer. Season with salt.

TO SERVE
Pour the strained soup into bowls and finish with a few drops of olive oil.

2. VICHYSSOISE

Cooking the potatoes in their skins retains a stronger potato flavor. We pair this dish with our *maewari shoch*, created in collaboration with local Kagoshima distillery, Komasa Jyozo. *Maewari* is a Japanese distilled spirit. When served it is premixed with water.

SERVES 10
VICHYSSOISE
– 1 kg potatoes, washed
– extra-virgin olive oil, for sautéing
– 1 garlic clove, halved
– 1 onion, chopped
– 1 celery stalk, chopped
– 350 ml chicken stock
– 100 ml milk (4–5% fat)
– salt and freshly ground black pepper
BUTTER GELATO
– 440 ml whole (full-fat) milk
– 150 g unsalted butter
– 100 g superfine (caster) sugar
– 15 g glucose
– 30 ml skim milk
– 15 g malt syrup
– 15 g Parmesan cheese
– 7 g pectin
PEPPER FOAM
– 3 peppercorns
– 100 ml whole (full-fat) milk
– 2 g soy lecithin

VICCHYSSOISE
Immerse the potatoes in slightly acidic electrolyzed water for 30–60 minutes to sterilize them.

Bake half the potatoes in a combination steamer oven. Steam the remaining potatoes in the combination steamer oven. Quickly cool them in a blast chiller, then peel both the steamed and baked potatoes.

Put a little olive oil, the garlic, onions, and celery into a large pan and sauté in the combination steamer oven until softened but not browned. Add the peeled potatoes, some salt and pepper, and just enough chicken stock to cover. Simmer until the potatoes have softened.

Transfer to a food processor while still warm and process until smooth, then strain through a strainer (sieve). Add a little more chicken broth and the milk to the vichyssoise base and heat until it reaches 185°F/85°C, then cool it quickly and completely in the blast chiller.

BUTTER GELATO
Put all the ingredients into an ice-cream machine and follow the manufacturer's instructions to churn.

PEPPER FOAM
Combine the peppercorns with the milk, place in a Gastrovac for 15 minutes and heat to 185°F/85°C. Remove and strain the milk with a fine-mesh strainer and discard the peppercorns.

Add the soy lecithin to the milk, mix well, and heat to 138°F/70°C. Turn the mix into a foam using an immersion (stick) blender.

TO SERVE
Pour the thoroughly chilled vichyssoise into chilled bowls. Add a quenelle of butter gelato and top that with some pepper foam.

3. CRYSTAL SALAD

The Gastrovac machine enables the umami from animal products to enhance the flavor of vegetables, in a dish consisting solely of vegetables. We pair this salad with a Spumante and serve it towards the end of the meal, before the meat course. According to Cainoya tradition, this is when we serve our first sparkling wine pairing.

SERVES 5
– mixed greens: 5 leaves each of lettuce, red leaf lettuce, frill lettuce, chicory, endive, mustard greens, wasabi leaves, violet cabbage, washed
– 5 slices beet (beetroot)
BONITO DASHI
– 500 ml water
– 1 x 4 inch/10 cm square konbu
– 50g dried bonito
SEASONAL ROOT VEGETABLES

– mixed root vegetables: 5 bite-size pieces of wax gourd, pumpkin, turnip, and taro
– 1.5 litres chicken broth
– Ayu fish sauce, to taste
– 30 g trehalose
– 70 g salt
– 50 g grilled bacon
– neutral oil, for deep-frying (optional)
– 30 g all-purpose (plain) flour
– 2 g salt
– 2g sugar
– 50 ml carbonated water
TO SERVE
– salad dressing of your choice

Put the mixed greens, beet (beetroot) slices, and some water into the Gastrovac for 20 minutes. Repeat three times, then immerse the leaves in water and store in the refrigerator.

BONITO DASHI
Put the water and konbu into a pot and leave for 20 minutes. Heat the pot and remove the konbu just before the water boils, then add the dried bonito to the water. Wait 3 minutes, then strain the bonito with a strainer (sieve) lined with cheesecloth (muslin). Reserve the dashi liquid.

SEASONAL ROOT VEGETABLES
Immerse the root vegetables in slightly acidic electrolyzed water to sterilize them.

In a pot, mix the chicken broth, Ayu fish sauce, trehalose and salt, and grilled bacon with the dashi and bring to a boil. Add all the root vegetables except the taro and cook for 5 minutes, then cool in a blast chiller.

Once cool, transfer the root vegetables to a Gastrovac with the cooking liquid and cook for 15 minutes. Remove the vegetables from the Gastrovac and grill them over hot embers. Finally cool again in the blast chiller.

Cook the pieces of taro in a combination oven steamer set to 185°F/85°C for 20 minutes, then cool in the blast chiller.

Peel the cooled taro pieces and boil in the chicken broth cooking liquid for 8 minutes, then cool again in the blast chiller. Transfer the pieces and cooking liquid to a Gastrovac and cook for 5 minutes. Remove from the Gastrovac and pat dry.

Mix together the flour, salt, sugar, and carbonated water in a bowl. Dip the taro pieces in the batter to coat, then deep-fry the coated taro in a deep pan of neutral oil heated to 350°F/180°C until golden.

To serve
Arrange the fried or grilled root vegetables on plates, then add the leafy vegetables on top. Lightly dress the vegetables—the dressing should be no more than a whisper; we want diners to enjoy the flavor of the vegetables.

1

2

César Troisgros

TROISGROS
Ouches, Loire, France

Sustained through three generations of exceptional chefs, and holding three Michelin stars for 30 years, the Loire Valley's Troisgros is one of France's most celebrated restaurants. Chefs Michel and César—father and son respectively—have always focused their attention on a handful of seasonal ingredients, with the aim of turning something simple into something exceptional. Having relocated to a renovated farmhouse in Ouches, the dining room is built around an imposing oak tree, with the extensive garden providing daily inspiration for the kitchen.

In 2015 we bought a manor in Ouches, a small village 6 miles (10 kilometers) away from Roanne, where we opened our very first restaurant. Our new hotel-restaurant, Le Bois Sans Feuilles, is right in the middle of the countryside, set within pastureland, ponds, and woods. Our kitchen garden is a natural extension of the landscape around us: it lies not far from the restaurant, nestled in the heart of wooded grounds that span 42 acres (17 hectares), with views of the Roannais hillsides in the background. It is a 300-square-meter (3,230-square-foot) walled garden, and when we took over the property we kept the original layout created by the previous gardener, which divided the garden into raised beds, and there were even still the roots of some of his aromatic herbs. We realized very quickly that keeping the garden in the same place was the most obvious thing to do. It is in the ideal spot: south-facing, closed in by a wall along the northern edge, and therefore sheltered from the wind. We also now have a strip of land just nearby dedicated to growing ornamental plants, which attract pollinating insects to our rows of vegetables, as well as an old orchard, where we have replanted most of the fruit trees.

We have a gardener to help us manage the whole area. The soil is our biggest issue: we have very heavy clay soil, and it will take a long time to be able to lighten it. Rather than resorting to bringing in sand as a solution, we have opted to use raised beds, so as to keep the soil enriched while making the most of the space available. The beds are made up of several layers of organic matter, to which we add compost and mulch. We don't use any other extra fertilizer and our approach is based on techniques inspired by agroecology, permaculture, and natural soil fertilization. We draw up a cropping plan in the winter and then start planting the first seedlings in February. Planting is staggered throughout the year at different periods, depending on each variety: most of what we grow comes from old, regional seed varieties, whose seeds we keep very carefully to ensure they live on. As a result, we have a wide array of tomatoes plus snow peas (mangetout), candelabra aloe, Auvergne beans, and "Vert Petit de Paris" (*Cucumis sativus*) pickling cucumber, and we have also brought in seeds from other parts of the world to grow plants such as shiso (*Perilla frutescens*)—a type of Japanese basil— and habanero chile. The sky is the limit and when we go away traveling it not only opens up our horizons in terms of both knowledge and cuisine, but also leaves its mark in our kitchen garden.

We have a continental climate, namely cold in winter and hot in the summer. So we aim to grow vegetables that thrive in these conditions, whether they are local or exotic varieties. We have chosen to grow only rare plant varieties, and in small quantities, as we are constrained by the size of the garden. Obviously that doesn't produce enough to cater for all the restaurant's needs. But then we are not fixated on productivity. When you run a restaurant that seats 65 people and a hotel with 15 bedrooms, and you multiply that by 10 services per week, that means quite a large volume of food going through our kitchens. It is an immense joy to plant your own vegetables, let them grow, then pick and eat them. Yet at the same time, we have been working closely for many years now with local market gardeners based here in the area who specialize in organic and biodynamic farming, and we will always remain loyal to them.

This local economy needs our support, and so we try to focus on growing rare and old plant varieties that you can't find at the market or from market gardeners, who offer more common varieties. We want to keep them working, so we try to grow the vegetables they do not. That is why we have decided to ban the use of hybrid seedlings that produce sterile seeds. All the different plants we grow come from old seed varieties—what we call "population" varieties. They are very rarely grown, and many of them are threatened with extinction. We try to multiply them by keeping back a part of what we grow every year to replant the seeds the following year.

The garden is our daily source of inspiration, firstly because it is right on the kitchen doorstep, but also because there is an irresistible urge to cook with ingredients we have grown ourselves. The chefs dip in and out every day to pick their ingredients, and the seasons also help lead the changes in our menu. The colors and light also have an influence on us, sometimes even unconsciously: in the spring we are naturally inclined to put more greenery on the plate, whereas in the fall (autumn), as the surrounding landscape here becomes tinged with ocher, yellow, and red, warmth enters the kitchen. Obviously, the first buds in spring spark more excitement than the tuber and root vegetables in winter, but life in the garden itself has many surprises in store. This year, for example, slugs were our biggest disaster. They destroyed a large part of our seedlings in the spring. However, that unfortunate episode also inspired us to create a cabbage and snail dish—because snails, as much as slugs, are attracted to cabbage. Usually we use oysters for that particular recipe, and when we returned to the kitchen, we couldn't understand why we hadn't thought of using snails sooner.

When you have a kitchen garden, you have to constantly take your cue from nature and fashion your menu based on what it provides. At Le Bois Sans Feuilles we are still at the learning stage. As for our vegetables, in the long term we'd like to stretch beyond the garden walls and grow them throughout the surrounding grounds as well, mixed in among other ornamental plants and wooded areas. It would be wonderful to be an edible forest where we could pick elderberries, raspberries, and black currants.

FAVORITE VARIETIES
– Auvergne bean (*Phaseolus vulgaris*)—This is a very old variety that is local to the region, and particularly robust. Two years ago there were only 22 lb (10 kg) of it left on the planet. We have a few of its seeds, and we have eaten little of the beans so far so we can multiply it. It has a floral, subtle taste, similar to orange blossom.
– Sorrel—This is a must-have plant for your garden as it is so easy to grow. It has a herby, acidic quality to it that tickles the palate. It is a clever, though not immediately obvious, way of bringing a touch of acidity to a dish.
– Habanero chile—This is the hottest chile you'll find: it needs a lot of sunlight, but it thrives on our land. What we like about it is its unique character, as well as its lightly smoky flavor. Use it to season pastas and vegetable mash, but be careful how much you use.

TIPS FOR GARDENING WITH RAISED BEDS
– Grow vegetables that are adapted to your soil and climate, and avoid sterile hybrid seeds.
– Mulch liberally to preserve the microbiological life on the soil substrate and keep watering to a minimum.
– Ban all chemical fertilizers and avoid tilling the soil.

1. PEEK-A-BOO, I AM UNDER THE CABBAGE

SERVES 4
- 16 live and preferably wild garden snails
- 1 liter chicken stock
- 1 head of green cabbage
- 2 purple-top turnips
- 250 ml Orleans white wine vinegar
- 30 g fine salt
- 150 g superfine (caster) sugar
- 100 g fresh butter
- handful of cilantros (coriander) leaves
- 100 g tamarind paste

Prepare the snails: let them purge in the refrigerator for 1 week. Sprinkle them with flour every morning and rinse them with water every night. The last morning, sprinkle them with salt, let them purge for 1 hour, then rinse again and put into a pot with the chicken stock. Cook until they are tender. Remove from their shells and clean. Discard the shells and set the snails to one side.

Remove the leaves from the cabbage, put the outside leaves on the compost. Cook the inner leaves in salted boiling water until tender, then drain on paper towels. Reshape them back into leaves.

Cut the turnips into thin strips and marinate them in vinegar, salt, and sugar for 1 hour.

Toast the cabbage leaves in a nonstick skillet (frying pan) over medium heat until golden brown.

In another pan, sauté the snails in the fresh butter over medium heat, until hot.

Drain the turnips and arrange them on a serving plate. Put the snails on top of it. Place a dot of tamarind paste on each snail, add a few leaves of cilantro, and finish with the cabbage leaf. Drizzle with the butter that was used to sauté the snails.

2. CRAYFISH FLOWER WITH RASPBERRIES AND SWEET PEPPERS

SERVES 4
- 12 large crayfish
- 2 green bull's horn peppers
- olive oil, for drizzling
- 100 g raspberries
- 10 ml sherry vinegar
- 5 g Habanero chili powder
- 2 slices of pancetta, cut into very thin strips
- 5 g red Phu Quoc peppercorns
- salt

Cook the crayfish in boiling water for 5–8 minutes, depending on their size, then drain, reserving the water, and set aside.

Preheat the oven to 350F/180°C.

Place the peppers on a baking sheet with a dash of olive oil and roast in the oven. Once cooked, remove them from the oven, let cool slightly, then peel, remove the seeds, and cut into thick strips.

In a bowl, crush the raspberries with a fork and season with salt, sherry vinegar, and chili powder.

Re-heat the crayfish in the reserved cooking water. Place some of the crushed raspberries on each plate, arrange the crayfish into a flower shape (3 on each plate), then place a piece of pancetta on top of each one. Finish with the bull's horn pepper strips, a drizzle of olive oil, and grind a little red Phu Quoc pepper over the top.

2

Jorge Vallejo

QUINTONIL
Polanco, Mexico City, Mexico

Chef Jorge Vallejo is considered one of Mexico's finest innovators, rediscovering and showcasing local gastronomy, while also exploring channels of sustainability. Vallejo established his restaurant, Quintonil, in leafy Polanco in 2012, with his wife, Alejandra Flores, who he met while working at Pujol in Mexico City. Quintonil's menu is uncompromising in its adherence to seasonality, with the rooftop garden functioning as a testing ground for ingredient potential.

Vegetables have always been essential to our offering at Quintonil. Beyond the restaurant's name (referring to one of the edible plants that has sustained the people of Mexico since pre-Hispanic times), many of our recipes feature vegetables as central elements. Cactus paddles (*Opuntia*), huauzontles (hairy amaranth blossom, *Chenopodium nuttalliae*), *quelites* (indigenous greens), and fig-leaf gourd (*Cucurbita ficifolia*) all appear on the menu and are perpetual favorites among diners.

Two years after opening the restaurant, the idea of tending our own vegetable garden seemed quite logical. We thought about where to develop it and considered the restaurant roof to be the perfect spot. We sought expert advice, got hold of the planters, the right soil, the seeds and—with enormous enthusiasm and not a little naïveté—we jumped straight into an urban agriculture adventure.

Immediately, fantasy was overtaken by reality. A garden of 129 square feet (12 square meters) is insufficient for covering the needs of a restaurant like Quintonil. Over time we began to look at the plant varieties we were growing and the uses to which we were putting them. We used to grow fruits and vegetables but they required hard mantainance. The garden now focuses on growing edible flowers and aromatic plants, which we use to make tisanes and for enhancing recipe flavors. For instance, *pitiona* (in the verbena family, *Lippia alba*) is added to fish, its leaves used in making *cuitlacoche* (a type of black culinary paste which uses corn infected with fungus). We favor perennials in the garden since we can harvest from them intensively and they give a higher yield in such a small space.

In general, herbs such as *quelites* give identity to Mexican cuisine. We apply aromatic profiles to dishes according to the leaves we have available, whether they are Mexican pepperleaf (*Piper auritum*), oregano, or epazote (a pungent herb, *Dysphania ambrosioides*). Examples of dishes that use such herbs are "Charred avocado tartare with 'escamoles' and Mexican herb chips" and "Fish 'barbacoa' in a grasshopper 'adobo' with nixtamalized 'ayocotes' and 'vaquita' beans." The garden also provides seeds for crops that particularly interest us, which we send to ranches and farms, or share with other chefs. Sometimes we'll allocate a few feet of the garden for plant experiments. We were successful with chilhuacle chiles (*Capsicum annuum*) from Cañada Chica in Oaxaca, which we wanted to grow for ourselves. This has also been achieved with kohlrabi, sorrel, nettles, and snake plant (*Sanseviera trifasciata*, traditionally used in treat-ing snake bites). However, perhaps the most important thing is the symbolic value the garden has taken on for us.

A combination of cooks and gardeners tend the garden but I am the most involved with it, as the chef. From the beginning, the hard work involved in planting and maintaining it has made us aware of the value of field labor and what it means to produce our food. The whole process of growing, from sowing to ripening, has changed our relationship with the ingredients we use, and has helped us to see their authentic value. It makes us think again about what it means to acquire food in a place like Mexico City.

According to statistics from Mexico's Census Bureau, the city was home to 8,918,654 inhabitants in 2015, making it one of the most densely populated places on the planet. A little known fact is that more than half of the city's territory is protected from urban development. These areas include wetlands, forests, and grasslands, as well as 115 square miles (300 square kilometers) of agricultural land. This is where cactus paddle is cultivated (Mexico City is the country's number-one producer), alongside amaranth and other crops, herbs, and ornamental plants.

Mexico City's age-old connection to its surrounding lakes—sadly now all but lost—has a final stronghold in the Xochimilco district. There, growers still cultivate crops grown on *chinampas*, floating gardens that are constructed using ancient, pre-Hispanic techniques. Regeneration projects in our locality are currently underway to reestablish the value of *chinampas* as a viable and sustainable farming method. New and ancient food-production techniques are being analyzed in an attempt to arrive at the best solutions that might ensure our own survival, as well as the ecosystems that make up our planet.

It strikes us that Mexico City has a lot to contribute to these efforts, provided we understand, respect, and rehabilitate city lands and the wide-ranging livelihoods they support. Xochimilco and its *chinampas* are one example, as well as the cactus paddle harvests of Milpa Alta and further farming traditions in Tláhuac and Cuajimalpa, not to mention forest and grassland preservation in the south of the city. Our 129 square feet (12 square meters) of rooftop has led us to appreciate that there's still a lot to do in Mexico City in support of high-quality local food for local people. We have reached an understanding that our relationship to the land can improve, despite the fact that we live in one of the world's most complicated cities. We sincerely desire to be part of that change.

ORGANIC ROOFTOP GARDENING
We apply organic principles, using our own compost made with green waste from vegetable leftovers, peelings, and leaves. We mainly use soft material to speed up the composting process, given that we are gardening in a small space.

Maintaining an urban garden along organic lines is a challenge. Birds and squirrels from the nearby forest visit the garden; they have eaten crops, along with insects. We are dependent on nature and need to look after it but we also need to protect the garden. We try to use methods that do not attack the surrounding fauna and we've had to learn how to do this ourselves and by talking to other gardeners. For ants we use sugar traps; for snails we use containers buried in the raised beds that are filled with beer. We eliminate plagues of aphids from leaves and stems by washing them with neutral soap. We are always on the lookout for alternatives to insecticide that will not damage the fauna that surrounds us and therefore the health of the garden.

1. FROM THE "CHINAMPAS" SALAD

Chinampa is an Aztec harvesting method that involves artificially built small field plots (islands) floating on shallow lake beds. They are located in Xochimilco, in Mexico City, and we were inspired by them to create this salad.

SERVES 8
CLAM PUREE
- 500 g clam meat
- 500 ml whole (full-fat) milk
- 2 egg yolks
- 1 egg
- 20 g granulated sugar
- 8 g coarse salt
- 5 x 20-g leaf gelatin sheets
GREENS VINAIGRETTE
- 150 g cilantro (coriander) stems
- 190 ml vegetable oil
- 120 ml olive oil
- 35 ml pumpkin seed oil
- 35 g cotija cheese
- 40 ml champagne vinegar
- 225 ml water
- 3 g xanthan gum
KOHLRABI PUREE
- 4 kg trimmed kohlrabi
- 4 g coarse salt
- 1.2 kg unsalted butter
ARUGULA PUREE
- 200 g arugula (rocket)
- 100 g spinach
- 5 g coarse salt
- 320 g Kohlrabi Puree (see above)
- 80 ml water
SALAD
- 96 g diced beets (beetroots)
- 96 g diced broccoli
- 50 g salted butter
- 80 g mixed types of carrot
- 120 g mixed types of lettuce
- 120 g Greens Vinaigrette (see above)
- 16 g sliced white onion
- 8 g kombu
- 96 g mizuna greens
TO SERVE
- 120 g Clam Puree (see above)
- 80 g Arugula Puree (see above)
- 160 g cotija cheese
- 15 g salt
- untreated edible rose petals
- edible flower petals, such as primrose
- radish, thinly sliced
- bora-king radish, thinly sliced

CLAM PUREE
Smoke the clam meat with a smoking gun for 30 minutes at a cold temperature.

Bring the milk to a boil in a pan, add the smoked clam meat, then remove from the heat and let cool. Let infuse in the refrigerator for 8 hours.

After 8 hours, strain the milk into a clean pan and discard the clams. Heat the milk. Mix the eggs, sugar, and salt together in a bowl. Temper and add to the preparation. Soak the gelatin sheets in a bowl of cold water for 5 minutes, then squeeze out excess water before adding to the warm milk mixture and stirring until they dissolve.

GREENS VINAIGRETTE
Blanch the cilantro (coriander) stems for a few seconds, then transfer them to a bowl of ice water. Drain and put into a blender with the oils and blend until emulsified. Add the cheese and champagne vinegar, and finally the water and xanthan gum, and blend.

KOHLRABI PUREE
Cook the kohlrabi in a large pan of salted boiling water until soft. Drain and blend in a blender with the butter until smooth.

ARUGULA PUREE
Blanch the arugula (rocket) and spinach in a large pan of salted boiling water for a few seconds. Transfer to a blender with 200 ml of the cooking water. Add the rest of the puree ingredients and blend until smooth.

SALAD
Preheat the oven to 430°C/220°C.

Roast the beets (beetroots) and broccoli with a little of the butter in the oven for 40 minutes. Roast the carrots with the remaining butter.

Mix the roasted beets and broccoli with the roasted carrots, lettuce mix, and the greens vinaigrette. Add the onion, kombu, and mizuna.

TO SERVE
Put 15 g clam puree and 10 g arugula puree on each plate. Top with the salad and grate over the cotija cheese. Season with the salt, garnish with the rose and flower petals and slices of radish, and serve.

2. SARDINES ON TOMATO WITH VERDOLAGA HERB AND GREEN DRESSING

SERVES 8
OLIVE-OIL-CURED SARDINES
- 8 Portuguese sardines
- 300 g sea salt
- 1 liter white vinegar
- 50 ml olive oil
SMOKED SARDINES
- 500 g ice cubes
- 16 Olive-Oil-Cured Sardine fillets (see above)
- 15 g charcoal
- 50 g mesquite wood chips
GREEN DRESSING
- 180 g parsley stems
- 120 g cilantro (coriander) stems
- 300 ml water
- 600 ml vegetable oil
- 10 ml lime juice
- 5 g fine salt
SEARED TOMATOES
- 3 kidney tomatoes—similar to heirloom tomatoes
- 1 teaspoon fine salt
- 8 Crimea cherry tomatoes
- 1 teaspoon vegetable oil
TO SERVE
- 400 g verdolaga herb leaves (purslane, *Portulaca oleracea*), cleaned
- 80 g fennel bulb, julienned in ⅛-inch/ 2-mm-thick slices (fronds reserved)
- 80 g purple onion, julienned in ⅛-inch/ 2-mm-thick slices
- 800 g Green Dressing (see above)

OLIVE-OIL-CURED SARDINES
Fillet the sardines, then remove the pin bones. Place the fillets on a flat tray, skin side down, cover with the salt, and let cure for 8 minutes. Rinse off the salt under cold running water, then soak them in the vinegar for 8 minutes. Remove the fillets from the vinegar and place them into vacuum bags with a splash of the olive oil, seal using a vacuum machine, and refrigerate.

SMOKED SARDINES
Use one deep (6-inch/15-cm) and one medium-depth (4-inch/10-cm) Gastronorm baking dish as well as another small dish or bowl. Put the ice cubes into the 4-inch/10-cm-deep dish. Place the sardine fillets in a single layer, skin side up, in the deeper dish and place it within the dish with the ice so it is completely surrounded. Light the charcoal in a perforated Gastronorm pan and once it burns down to embers, carefully put the embers into a heatproof bowl along with the mesquite chips. Put that bowl into the dish containing the sardine fillets (without letting it touch the fish); cover with a single layer of aluminum foil—enough to enclose all the dishes. Leave to smoke for 5 minutes, then remove the foil and transfer the smoked sardine fillets to a vacuum bag.

GREEN DRESSING
Blanch the parsley and cilantro (coriander) stems in salted boiling water for 3 minutes, then remove with a slotted spoon and cool in a bain-marie. Drain and put into a blender with the water. Blend on high speed for 2 minutes (no longer, to avoid oxidation). Reduce the speed and gradually drizzle in the oil as you continue to blend. Strain through a fine-mesh strainer (sifter) into a large measuring cup/jug and add the lime juice and salt. Transfer to a squeeze bottle.

SEARED TOMATOES
Cut each kidney tomato into 3 equal wedges and add salt to one of the sides.

Halve the cherry tomatoes and sprinkle salt over the cut surfaces.

Heat a skillet (frying pan) over high heat. Once very hot add several drops of vegetable oil to "varnish" the entire pan. When the oil is about to smoke, sear the tomatoes on the salted sides until a scorched crust appears.

TO SERVE
Place a tomato wedge and a halved cherry tomato on a plate with the salt crust face up. Place 2 smoked sardine fillets on the tomato; top with verdolaga leaves, fennel, purple onion, and 1 g fennel fronds.

Heat the dressing in a pan over very low heat (don't let it boil); season to taste and serve drizzled around the sardines.

1

Alice Waters

CHEZ PANISSE
Berkeley, California, USA

In 1971, aged just 27, Alice Waters opened her legendary restaurant in an Arts and Crafts house in the Californian university town of Berkeley. Inspired by time spent in Europe, she focused on provincial French cuisine, and went on to popularize the idea of plot-to-plate cooking in her native USA, using the very best local, organic, and sustainable produce, and celebrating the farmers who grew and farmed it. Although the restaurant's lettuce garden in her own backyard moved to a farm, her personal garden continues to delight Waters and informs and inspires initiatives such as The Edible Schoolyard.

I started my kitchen garden because I was longing for mesclun, that very particular French salad from Nice, made of distinctive sweet and bitter greens and herbs. It was the 1970s, and I had been daunted by the thought of growing food, but then, driven by the desire for that flavor from Nice, I brought lettuce seeds home with me from one of my trips to France, and I allowed my tiny backyard to become a salad garden for my restaurant, Chez Panisse. Our success surprised and delighted me. I was so excited to have my yard filled with the lettuces I loved, and the flavor they introduced into the restaurant was revelatory.

The lettuce garden in my backyard moved to a farm long ago, but my kitchen garden continues to grow. The grassy area of my little yard gets smaller every year. But I couldn't live without my beds of lettuces. My garden plot is quite small—a 20 x 20-foot (6 x 6-meter) patch of sun and dappled shade, anchored by a big hundred-year-old redwood tree—but every inch of it is put to work. And happily, we're blessed with a very mild climate year-round, which means that I almost always have something growing, even in winter. Herbs like thyme, parsley, lovage, lemon verbena, mint, and rosemary are planted throughout—they define my cooking, and I pick them daily. I let arugula (rocket) reseed itself all over the garden to eat young in salads, with its flowers sprinkled over, or wilted in pasta sauce when it matures and gets really spicy. In summer, I grow cherry tomatoes and beans. In the fall (autumn) and winter, I have plots of chicories, kales, and chard. I plant things in the garden that I cannot get at the farmers' market, or vegetables that I want on-hand to pick right as I'm cooking. And every year I like to make my own mix of salad from seed—I make my own mesclun, to my own taste.

There is plenty of fruit, too—a dwarf apple and a large "Gravenstein", a kumquat (*Citrus japonica*), a "Fuyu" persimmon (*Diospyros virginiana*). I'm gone frequently, so it's very important to have things that don't need a lot of care. That's why I like to have trees like my Meyer lemon—it takes care of itself, and I feel so grateful to have it. There's also a small thicket of raspberry canes, and on summer mornings I go out and eat the ripe berries right off the plant. Of course, some make it into the house, but I love that morning ritual. Fraises des bois (wild) strawberries (*Fragaria vesca*) plants are nestled in secret corners so that visiting small children can always discover a ripe wild strawberry on their wanderings through the garden. I tuck edible plants like purple basil and wild chervil in among the fragrant garden roses, and they are as beautiful as their neighboring flowers. (The rose petals are edible, too.) I have a couple of chairs and a small table, and a little grill is set up nearby so I can cook and eat right in the garden. I love to watch the ebb and flow of growth: tiny sprouts as they push up from the soil, blue borage flowers reaching out to bees and birds, the burgeoning harvest as it ripens. I feel connected to the whole cycle of life.

My own path to gardening has been through taste. I am forever falling in love with the fantastic range of varieties available for almost every food plant. Learning to discern these subtleties of texture and flavor—learning to distinguish an "Elberta" peach (*Prunus persica*) from a "Suncrest"—is a thrill for me. Using hand-selected produce that is still full of life and vitality is what makes cooking not just good, but irresistible.

I may not grow Chez Panisse's lettuces in my backyard any more—my tiny space couldn't keep up—but the lessons I've learned from it have never left me. Gardening has taught me empathy for farmers and farm workers, and respect for the hard work they do. It makes us all remember that food is precious, and we are dependent on the land for our survival. It is all about the land. At Chez Panisse, we source our food from over 85 different local sustainable farmers, ranchers, and purveyors.

In the beginning, we would tell the farmers what we would like them to grow; now, it's the farmers who give *us* the ideas for what we should cook. After the restaurant opened we were on the hunt for the best fruits in the area. We found this one guy who had a gigantic, ancient mulberry tree, and we started bringing the fruit to the restaurant from just that one tree. The mulberries are incredibly delicate, and the season is so short, and so we put them in our fruit bowl for the few weeks of the year that they're ripe. (We also make a syrup out of them that we keep for making ice cream.) A perfectly ripe mulberry is one of those mysterious flavors that isn't like anything else. Chez Panisse's daily changing menu is defined by the immediacy and aliveness of ingredients like this that are harvested at the peak of their season: tomatoes just plucked from the vine in the heat of summer, a tiny, sweet "Kishu" mandarin (*Citrus reticulata*) in winter. And indeed, our entire philosophy is shaped by the values that farmers bring into our restaurant. These purveyors are all dedicated to sustainable, regenerative agriculture—they know the land and the crops and the seasons better than anyone.

One of my most powerful gardening experiences has been watching the children at The Edible Schoolyard, a kitchen garden planted at Martin Luther King Jr. Middle School, a public school in Berkeley, California. Every time I see them measuring the vegetable beds for their math class, or harvesting ancient grains out in the garden for a history class, I am reminded that there is nothing more transformational than the experience of being in nature. In our current fast food culture, we have become divorced from nature, made to think that working the land is too difficult, or too slow. But as soon as we dig our hands into the soil and start watching things grow, we fall in love effortlessly—we realize we are a part of nature. I have seen this transformation happen in a school full of teenagers; I have seen it happen with inmates in a jail. This connection to and respect for nature can be awakened in all of us.

PLANTING HERBS

If you only plant one thing, plant some herbs. They are easy to grow and offer so much in return. Scatter them throughout your garden to take advantage of their fragrance and beauty. Given a reasonably comfortable environment—good soil, adequate water, plenty of sunlight—they will reseed themselves for years to come. They provide the freshness—aliveness, really—and the beauty, fragrance, and flavor that inspire and compel me in the kitchen. Branches and bouquets of herbs flavor my stocks, soups, roasts, and stews; the leaves of tender herbs are tossed into salads; chopped herbs are stirred into sauces and scattered over any number of dishes to

add a final burst of freshness. And finally, the way I end almost every meal is with a glass of tisane—fresh mint and maybe lemon verbena (*Aloysia citrodora*), snipped fresh from the garden and infused into boiling water. That might be my favorite recipe of all time.

GROWING LETTUCES

Spring and fall are easy times to grow salad greens. Many greens bolt in hot weather so use a plot or container that avoids full sun. A cold frame, tunnel, or greenhouse will keep cold-tolerant lettuces and other greens growing even in very cold weather. So in most climates, it is possible to grow lettuces and other greens year-round.

Once up, the young sprouts are quite susceptible to the creeping and crawling denizens of the garden. Patrol nightly with a flashlight to find and remove any slugs and snails, and plant in raised beds and containers to discourage marauders. Many lettuces may be harvested over an extended period of time: for a mesclun salad of young lettuces, harvest the leaves young, when they are just 3–4 inches/8–10 cm tall. Cut just enough lettuces for your salad, in the morning or in evening when the lettuce is cool and crisp. Keep harvesting the same bed until the lettuces become bitter and tough. For a constant supply of lettuce, plant successively in plots or containers every three to four weeks.

1. CANDIED ROSE PETALS

Roses are maybe my favorite flowers, particularly the old-fashioned fragrant ones like "Othello," "Monsieur Tillier," 'The Prince," and "William Shakespeare." It's such a gift to have roses that you can pick right at the moment when they open. I have them planted throughout my garden, and when a rose is at the height of its bloom I can't take my eyes off it—it makes me so in awe of nature. And the aroma is completely intoxicating. Candied rose petals look exquisite, but they also have a special and delicate flavor all their own. Serve them as an after-dinner candy with a cup of tea. They're also wonderful sprinkled on strawberry desserts or chocolate ice cream.

- several fragrant, organically grown roses, preferably a mix of colors
- 1 egg white at room temperature
- pinch of kosher salt
- organic cane sugar, for sprinkling

Before candying, refrigerate the roses so the petals stay firm and crisp. Pick the petals off the roses and select small- to medium-size petals for candying. Combine them in a small bowl.

Whisk the egg white and salt together in a bowl until frothy. Paint a very thin layer of the egg white onto both sides of each petal using a small pastry brush with fine bristles.

Sprinkle each petal all over with sugar. Shake off the excess sugar and place the sugared petals on a fine-mesh cooling rack to dry. Leave uncovered at room temperature for 1–2 days until the petals are crisp and completely dry. Use immediately or keep in an airtight container for up to 1 week.

VARIATION

To make candied mint leaves, use the large, fresh leaves of mint sprigs—no refrigeration in advance is necessary, as mint is hardier than roses. Serve sprinkled over ice cream, sorbet, or chilled melon.

2. LITTLE GEM SALAD WITH SUNGOLD TOMATOES, FINES HERBES, AND SHAVED RADISH

This salad brings together four of my favorite things from the garden: lettuce, herbs, tomatoes, and radishes. Little Gems are a wonderful variety of romaine lettuce. Fines herbes are a mix of tender tarragon, chervil, parsley, and chives, and are all in plentiful supply in my garden. These tender herbs are easy to pound into a flavorful paste and add loads of flavor to this creamy dressing. Little golden Sungold is my favorite cherry tomato of all; it is almost as sweet as candy. And shaving a radish over the top adds color, texture, and a nice spicy note. If your radishes need thinning, pull up the tiny plants and add them too. They're delicious.

SERVES 4
DRESSING
- 1 small green garlic stalk, trimmed and coarsely chopped
- ½ teaspoon salt
- 2 tablespoons chopped chervil, plus extra to serve (optional)
- 1 tablespoon chopped chives
- 1 tablespoon chopped tarragon
- 1 tablespoon chopped parsley
- 1 egg yolk
- ¼ teaspoon freshly ground black pepper
- 1 tablespoon lemon juice
- ½ teaspoon white wine vinegar
- 60 ml extra-virgin olive oil
- 60 ml buttermilk
SALAD
- 4 heads Little Gem lettuce, ends trimmed and any blemished outer leaves removed
- 150 g Sungold cherry tomatoes, washed, dried, and stems removed
- 4 small or 2 larger trimmed radishes (such as French Breakfast or Easter Egg), thinly sliced
- Parmesan cheese, to serve (optional)

DRESSING

Put the green garlic stalk and salt into a mortar. Pound the garlic to a smooth paste with the pestle, then add the chopped herbs. Continue pounding until you have a smooth puree. Stir in the egg yolk, pepper, lemon juice, and vinegar. Once everything is well mixed, slowly dribble in the oil, whisking constantly. Once all the oil is incorporated, whisk in the buttermilk. Taste and adjust the seasoning as needed.

SALAD

Separate the Little Gem lettuce leaves and wash them gently in cold water. Spin dry in a salad spinner. Slice the tomatoes in half.

Gently toss the Little Gem leaves with some of the dressing. Scatter the halved tomatoes, radishes, and a few additional sprigs of chervil over the top of the salad, or grate a little Parmesan cheese over the salad to finish.

3. ARUGULA PESTO

I eat a lot of arugula—or rocket, if you prefer. Nutty and spicy, with a hint of sweetness, it adds an exciting flavor to everything. Arugula is gratifyingly easy to grow and yields large rewards in the kitchen. It germinates quickly and is quite productive. It can be ready to harvest as early as three weeks after planting and it grows right back after cutting up to five times. Like lettuce, it prefers a richly amended (composted) soil and even moisture—I like to sow successive plots every three weeks for a constant supply.

Classic pesto is made with basil. In the winter at Chez Panisse Café, when basil is no longer available, we make pesto from arugula and walnuts. It is very spicy and full-flavored and it is delicious on wholegrain pasta and bean soups.

MAKES ABOUT 400 G
- 2 cloves garlic, peeled
- ¼ teaspoon salt
- 40 g walnuts, lightly toasted
- 20 g Parmesan or pecorino cheese, grated
- 25 g young arugula (rocket) leaves, washed and dried
- 120 ml extra-virgin olive oil
- salt

Put the garlic and salt into a mortar and pound to a paste with the pestle. Add the walnuts and continue to pound until the walnuts are finely ground, then add the grated cheese. Transfer this mixture to a bowl. Coarsely chop the arugula and put it into the mortar. Pound the leaves to a paste. Return the pounded walnut mixture to the mortar. Pound the leaves and the walnut mixture together, then continue pounding as you gradually pour in the oil. Taste and adjust the seasoning as needed.

1

Blaine Wetzel

THE WILLOWS INN
Lummi Island, Washington, USA

Blaine Wetzel arrived at the century-old Willows Inn in 2010, aged 24, after three years working alongside René Redzepi at Noma in Copenhagen. Describing his approach to food as "a story of the land," his hyper-local menu celebrates extraordinary produce that's foraged in the surrounding area or grown at nearby Loganita Farm, which employs two full-time farmers, growing heirloom and native produce solely for the restaurant using all biodynamic practices.

Perching on the northwestern tip of mainland America, Lummi Island covers just 11 square miles (28 square kilometers) of hills and meadows, forests, and farms, with gently lapping shores that are only accessible by ferry; the Willows Inn sits right on the shoreline facing west, giving us beautiful sunsets on our deck and into the dining room.

Our climate is relatively mild with temperatures between 40 and 80°F/5 and 27°C. Summers are fairly warm and dry with long daylight hours for prime growing conditions and we have rich, fertile soil. Here, you can pull vegetables out of the ground and the taste is just mind-blowing. So our aim is quite simple: to share the tastes of this place with everyone who comes and to share the experience of what we're lucky enough to get to grow and eat here.

We work directly with Loganita Farm, which is half a mile down the road from the Inn and grows solely for us. The farm is on a gentle, natural slope just 1,650 feet (500 meters) from the shore and gets full sun exposure. The acre of land is divided into four areas—4 hoop houses, a section of 18 raised beds, and 2 field-growing areas.

We grow 175–200 varieties of heritage or native plants each year including "Caraflex" cabbage (*Brassica oleracea,* Capitata group), "Sungold" tomatoes (*Solanum lycopersicum*), tomatillos, kale, Shishito peppers (*Capsicum annuum*), "Costata" zucchini (courgette, *Cucurbita pepo*), Cinderella pumpkins, lovage, fennel, snap peas, and cucumbers, as well as herbs, berries, fruit, and edible flowers. Many crops, including a "Natacha" escarole (*Cichorium endivia*) or "Spring Tower" celtuce (stem lettuce, *Lactuca sativa* var. *angustana*) are sown successively to provide the kitchen with a constant supply. Seeds are sourced from Uprising Organics, although we actively save seed too.

We describe our food as being a story about the land: the menu changes daily and it's a snapshot of what is caught, harvested, and foraged at that specific time. A toasted kale leaf with a puree of local black truffles and a sprinkling of crumbled rye bread is a really good example of a classic dish here. The crunchy texture and earthy flavor make the dish work well with the sweetness of the local cider before the meal begins. Many people come back for it.

We are always changing, developing, and exploring ingredients. Someone eating at the restaurant may have 20 new ingredients in a row that they'd previously never even heard of, or haven't eaten in

that way. At the beginning of spring, wild shoots, greens, and leaves will be the theme of the menu. We try to include some element to each dish that has that flavor in it, so we can showcase it through the whole menu. Our "Herbed tostada" is typical of this moment and brings all the flavorful first spring leaves and flowers together.

While the culinary garden isn't right next to the restaurant it inspires the menu every day. Crops are harvested and brought to the kitchen daily while they are at their peak flavor and we'll always try the earliest crops before the full harvest is ready, so that we can plan what to do with them. We can then provide clear and direct instructions. For example, we might want the nasturtium leaves harvested when they are 2–2¼ inches/5–6 cm wide. Guests from the Inn can take a guided farm tour the morning after dinner and try some produce fresh out of the ground or off the vine.

We grow a variety of flowers like anise hyssop (*Agastache foeniculum*), dahlias, and snapdragons that we use around the Inn for decoration, but also to attract bees and other pollinators, and we allow scissor-tail birds and others to graze the farm and eat pests.

The farm is low tech and labor intensive as we use only hand tools and hand-operated equipment. The bio-intensive farming in which there is a constant rotation of crops fosters healthy soils and conserves space while maximizing yields. Fertile soil is maintained by applications of rich compost that we make using trimmings and scraps of what we have harvested. We also use fish oil/meal fertilizers (blood fish and bone) that support healthy soil microbial populations. In the winter we cover crop to help protect and revitalize the soil ready for the following season.

The restaurant is closed from mid-December to mid-March. During this time we'll go through successes and struggles from the previous season and look through seed catalogues to brainstorm new varieties to grow. This year, for example, we are growing rat tail radish, which grows like peas in a pod and has a mildly peppery flavor. When we want to grow something new like this, we will start with three or four varieties in the first year before selecting the best variety to grow the following season.

In the winter we all travel as much as possible too—experiencing new restaurants, cuisines, and ingredients. This provides a fresh new outlook for the next season, with new techniques learned and a wealth of inspiration.

KEY VEGETABLE

Cucumbers (*Cucumus sativus*) are a key ingredient in the Willows Inn kitchen, whether they are used raw, pickled, or grilled, and we have grown several varieties but our favorites are:
- Lemon cucumbers, which taste best when harvested young and have a traditional cucumber flavor—the name comes from their size and color.
- "Dragon's Egg" cucumbers have beautiful pale skin and white flesh and a sweet flavor.
- The vine-grown "Sikkim" variety was originally from India and has a dark skin and can be used raw or cooked.
- "Hmong Red" cucumbers have a slightly sour but sweet taste while the large "Gagon," originally from Bhutan, can be pickled or eaten fresh.

1. HERBED TOSTADA

We serve this tasty bouquet in the spring when the herb garden is growing fast and all the new leaves are so tender and flavorful. We grow the specific arrangement of herbs for this recipe so each mouthful is different, with a curated mix of herbs and flowers in each bite. This "Herbed tostada" highlights the bounty of herbal plants growing at the farm and is a springtime staple.

SERVES 16
OYSTER CREAM
– 132 g oysters (raw, shucked, and dried on a paper towel)
– 28 g parsley leaves
– 140 g grapeseed oil, chilled
– verjus, to taste
– salt
MUSTARD LEAF BATTER
– 120 g all-purpose (plain) flour
– 120 g rice flour
– 8 g lovage-infused salt
– 8 g granulated sugar
– 120 g kale, chopped
– 160 ml water
– 80 ml sauerkraut brine
– 40 g beaten egg
HERB TOSTADA
– 64 small leaves from at least 12 types of herbs such as: anise hyssop, sorrel, sage, lovage, nasturtium, chamomile, mint, cilantro (coriander), tarragon, dill, shiso, watercress, oregano
– 16 small blossoms from at least 4 types of flower such as: calendula, nasturtium, parsley, violet, bee balm, sage
– 128 green seeds
DEEP-FRIED MUSTARD LEAVES
– 16 green mustard leaves
– grapeseed oil, for deep-frying

OYSTER CREAM
Put the oysters and parsley leaves in a blender and start to blend, slowly adding the oil until the mixture has emulsified to form a thick cream. Pass the cream through a fine-mesh strainer (sieve), chill and season to taste with salt and verjus when cold.

MUSTARD LEAF BATTER
Mix the dry ingredients together in a bowl.

Blend the kale with the water and sauerkraut brine in a blender, then strain the juice through a 100/200 micron Superbag.

Mix the kale liquid with the dry ingredients and beaten egg—the mixture should have the consistency of pancake batter.

HERB TOSTADA
Pick, rinse, and dry the small leaves of each type of herb growing in the garden and then arrange them in piles—16 piles of at least 4 types of herb.

Pick, rinse, and dry the blossoms and green seeds.

DEEP-FRIED MUSTARD LEAVES
Trim each mustard leaf to about 4 x 4 inches/ 10 x 10 cm and heat the oil in a deep pan to 350°F/180°C.

Dip each mustard leaf into the batter and shake off any excess. Deep-fry in batches—4 at a time. Carefully place in the hot oil and deep-fry for about 2 minutes until crispy. Remove with a slotted spoon and drain on a cooling rack for at least 3 minutes, so the crispy leaves can cool before the dish is assembled.

TO SERVE
Spread a thin layer of the oyster cream on top of a crispy mustard leaf and arrange the herbs and flowers in a layered pattern as a bouquet on top. Finish with 8 green seeds per serving.

2. SLOW-ROASTED RUTABAGA

Most root vegetables are best harvested before the first frost, then buried in sawdust and stored in the root cellar. Both horseradish and rutabagas (swede) improve greatly after a month or two of cellaring, which makes this is a favorite dish for the coldest times of the year. The aromas from slowly turning the rutabagas in browning butter and herbs fill the kitchen all afternoon. After the rutabagas are fully tender and the skin is crisp they are broken and dried. They are then glazed in the savory juices from caramelized squid and a few scrapes of fresh horseradish to make an exciting and unique entree. The final texture is that of a well-braised piece of meat.

SERVES 4
SQUID BROTH
– 30 small whole squid
– grapeseed oil, for frying
SLOW-ROASTED RUTABAGA
– 2 whole rutabaga (swede)
– 250 g unsalted butter
– 4 bay leaves
– 2 sprigs rosemary
– 4 sprigs oregano
– 4 sprigs marjoram
– 4 sprigs thyme
MUSHROOM BUTTER
– 200 g porcini mushrooms, finely chopped
– 200 g unsalted butter
TO SERVE
– 1 horseradish root
– leaves from 4 sprigs yarrow
– 16 ground elder leaves
– 8 woodruff leaves

SQUID BROTH
Put 1 teaspoon of grapeseed oil in a very hot large sauté pan and sear the squids in small batches until charred. Put the seared squid into a metal bowl and cover the bowl with plastic wrap (clingfilm). Let cool. The squid will release juices into the bowl. After 15 minutes strain the squid and juices through a fine-mesh strainer (sieve), pressing the squid to extract all the liquid. This concentrated juice is the broth.

SLOW-ROASTED RUTABAGA
Place the rutabaga and butter in a pan covered with a lid over medium heat, turning the rutabaga every 10 minutes for 1 hour.

Add the herbs to the pan and cook for another hour, turning the rutabaga regularly until they are well caramelized on all sides and completely cooked through. Remove from the heat and let cool.

Break each rutabaga using your hands into 2 rough chunks. Place the chunks in the dehydrator for 4 hours to dry slightly.

MUSHROOM BUTTER
Combine the chopped porcini with the butter in a pan. Heat until the butter has clarified and the mushroom flavor is infused into the butter. Strain the butter through a fine-mesh strainer (sieve) and discard the mushrooms.

TO SERVE
Peel and scrape the horseradish root into fine ribbons and tear the herbs into a small pile.

Reheat the rutabaga chunks in a warm oven for 10 minutes, then soak them in the squid broth briefly and roll them in the torn herbs and ribboned horseradish to coat.

Divide the coated rutabaga among 4 plates and drizzle each with a spoonful of the squid broth and the mushroom butter.

1

RECIPE NOTES

A number of the recipes require advanced techniques, specialist equipment, and professional experience to achieve good results.

Cooking times are for guidance only. If using a fan (convection) oven, follow the manufacturer's instructions concerning the oven temperatures.

Exercise a very high level of caution when following recipes involving any potentially hazardous activity, including the use of high temperatures, open flames, and when deep-frying. In particular, when deep frying add food carefully to avoid splashing, wear long sleeves, and never leave the pan unattended. Add a cube of day-old bread to see whether the oil for deep-frying is hot enough–it will brown in 30 seconds at 350°F/180°C.

Some recipes include lightly cooked eggs, meat, and fish. These should be avoided by the elderly, infants, pregnant women, convalescents, and anyone with an impaired immune system.

Butter is ussumed to be salted unless otherwise specified.

Individual fruits and vegetables are assumed to be medium size unless otherwise specified, and should be washed and/or peeled.

All herbs, shoots, flowers, berries, and seeds should be picked fresh. Herbs are fresh unless described as otherwise.

Exercise caution when foraging for ingredients. Any foraged ingredients should only be eaten if an expert has deemed them safe to eat.

All herbs, mosses, and lichens should be thoroughly washed before use.

Mushrooms should be wiped clean.

When no quantity is specified, particularly in serving instructions, quantities, for example, of herbs, shoots, flowers, berries, and seeds are discretionary and flexible, substituting more of one or the other if necessary. Unspecified amounts of oil are discretionary.

All spoon measurements are level. 1 teaspoon = 5 ml. 1 tablespoon = 15 ml. Australian standard tablespoons are 20 ml; Australian readers are advised to use 3 teaspoons in place of 1 tablespoon.

IMAGE CREDITS

All images are courtesy of the restaurants. Additional credits below:

Matt Austin: 64, 65; Simon Bajada: 243; Cris Barnett: 201, 196, 197; Sébastien Bras: 51; Charity Burggraaf: 244, 245, 247, 249; Fernando Gómez Carbajal: 232, 233, 235, 237; Luis Alejandro Delgado: 13, 15; Francesco Fioramonti: 202, 203; Suzan Gabrijan: 208, 209, 211, 213; ©2019 Galdones Photography: 94, 95, 97, 99; Chi George: 171; Adam Gibson: 100, 101, 103, 105; Toby Glanville: 142, 143, 145, 147; Alexandre Guirkinger: 124, 125, 127, 129; Mikkel Heriba: 184, 185, 187(tr,b), 189; Phil Huynh: 130, 131; Jason Ingram: 190; Gunnar Freyr: 28, 29, 31, 33; Rubens Kato: 57, 82, 83, 85, 87; Ryo Kawagoe: 220, 221, 223, 225; Ace Kvale: 63; Félix Ledru: 226, 227, 229, 231; Jennifer May: 160, 161, 163, 165; Tres Mitades: 10, 11; Marie Louise Munkergaard: 178, 179, 181, 183; Marie Pierre Morel: 106, 109, 111; Oscar Oliva: 17, 19; Erik Olsson: 172, 173, 175, 177; Colin Page: 124, 125, 127, 129; Iain and Matthew Pennington: 191, 193, 195; Courtesy The Restaurant at Meadowood, photography by Kelly Puleio: 154, 155, 157, 159; Benjamin Schmuck: 46; Laurent Seminel: 107; Brambilla Serrani: 207; Sara Stathas: 58, 59; Evan Sung: 34, 35, 27, 39; Jonathan Thompson: 12, 13, 15, 17; Nikki To: 118, 119, 121, 123; Rodrigo Torrezan: 52, 53; Lido Vannucchi: 88, 89, 91, 93; Rinze Vegelien: 136, 137, 139, 141; Eric Wolfinger: 76, 77, 79, 81, 148, 149, 151, 153; Photo courtesy Yanka Industries, Inc. d/b/a MasterClass from Alice Waters Teaches the Art of Home Cooking: 239; Jose Luis de Zubiria: 75, 16, 21.

Phaidon Press Limited
Regent's Wharf
All Saints Street
London N1 9PA

Phaidon Press Inc.
65 Bleecker Street
New York, NY 10012

phaidon.com

First published in 2019
© 2019 Phaidon Press Limited

ISBN 978 0 7148 7822 5

A CIP catalog record for this book is available from the Library of Congress and the British Library.

Commissioning Editor: Victoria Clarke
Project Editor: Sophie Hodgkin
Production Controller: Sarah Kramer

Designed by Apartamento Studios

The publisher would like to thank all the participating chefs and their teams for their generosity and time; chefs Jeremy Fox, Will Goldfarb, and Kamal Mouzawak for their contributions to the book; Leanne Clancey, Clare Coulson, Mark Diacono, Nikki Duffy, Charlotte Fauve, Eve O'Sullivan, Rebecca Roke, Kendra Wilson, and Yuta Yagishita for their work on the texts; Gerard Elias Hernández, Claudia Mandelli, and Mariana Martín Zumárraga for their work on the design; and Vanessa Bird, Jamie Compton, Anne Heining, Joanne Murray, Laura Nickoll, Ellie Smith, Emily Takoudes, and William Winning for their editorial work on the book.

Printed in China